CALIFORNIA MIDDLE SCHOOL

Mathematics

Concepts and Skills

COURSE 2

Larson   Boswell   Kanold   Stiff

California Standards Key Concepts Book

This book contains a review of pre-course skills, key standards support including teaching and practice, and special topics.

McDougal Littell
A HOUGHTON MIFFLIN COMPANY
Evanston, Illinois • Boston • Dallas

Acknowledgement

We acknowledge with special thanks the contributions to the planning, writing, and reviewing of the Special Topics section on pages T1–T21 by:

Special Contributor

Richard Askey
Professor of Mathematics
University of Wisconsin
Madison, Wisconsin

ISBN: 0-618-07846-0

56789-DIW-06 05 04 03 02 01

Contents

Contents continued

Part 3 Special Topics

Part 1 Pre-Course Review

Diagnostic Tests

Topic 1: *Working With Decimals*

Lesson 1

In Exercises 1 and 2, compare the numbers. Write $<$, $>$, or $=$.

1. 5.4 ___?___ 5.35

2. 3.2 ___?___ 3.20

3. Order the decimals 56.417, 57.4, and 56.14 from least to greatest.

Lesson 2

Find each sum or difference.

4. $42.95 + 6.1$

5. $1.5 - 0.34$

Lesson 3

Estimate each product. Then find the actual product.

6. 21.8×4

7. 0.41×0.88

Lesson 4

Estimate each quotient, then divide. Compare your estimate with the actual quotient to check for reasonableness.

8. $49.52 \div 8$

9. $124.74 \div 54$

Topic 2: *Working with Fractions*

Lesson 1

Write each fraction in simplest form. If it is already in simplest form, write *simplest form*.

10. $\dfrac{20}{64}$

11. $\dfrac{27}{45}$

Lesson 2

Write each mixed number as an improper fraction.

12. $5\dfrac{3}{5}$

13. $1\dfrac{24}{25}$

Write each improper fraction as a mixed number.

14. $\dfrac{20}{11}$

15. $\dfrac{82}{7}$

Lesson 3

Find each sum or difference. Write each answer as a fraction or mixed number in simplest form.

16. $\dfrac{15}{16} + \dfrac{1}{4}$ **17.** $1\dfrac{3}{7} + 2\dfrac{1}{2}$ **18.** $\dfrac{2}{3} - \dfrac{5}{12}$

Topic 3: *Relating Decimals, Fractions, and Percents*

Lesson 1

Write each fraction or mixed number as a decimal.

19. $\dfrac{7}{20}$ **20.** $2\dfrac{11}{30}$

Lesson 2

What percent of each design is shaded? What percent is unshaded?

21. 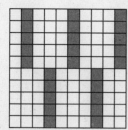   **22.**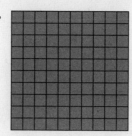

Write each ratio as a percent.

23. $\dfrac{18}{100}$ **24.** $\dfrac{75}{100}$

Lesson 3

Write each decimal as a percent.

25. 0.3   **26.** 0.97

Write each percent as a decimal.

27. 36%   **28.** 4%

Lesson 4

Write each percent as a fraction in simplest form.

29. 45%   **30.** 8%

Write each fraction as a percent.

31. $\dfrac{4}{5}$ **32.** $\dfrac{41}{100}$

Topic 4: *Angles and Polygons*

Lesson 1

Use a protractor to find the measure of each angle to the nearest 5°.

33.
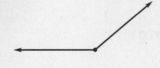

34.

Use a protractor to draw an angle of the given measure.

35. 55°   **36.** 118°

Lesson 2

Estimate to classify each angle as *acute, right, obtuse,* or *straight.*

37.
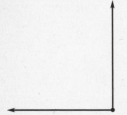

38.

39. Suppose the measure of ∠R is 50°. Find the measures of angles that are congruent to ∠R, complementary to ∠R, and supplementary to ∠R.

40. Find the measures of two angles that are congruent and complementary.

Lesson 3

In Exercises 41 and 42, sketch each figure.

41. an isosceles right triangle   **42.** a rhombus

43. Is a rhombus *always, sometimes,* or *never* a parallelogram?

44. Is a rectangle *always, sometimes,* or *never* a square?

Lesson 4

45. A photograph is 5 in. long and 3 in. wide. Write the dimensions of the photograph when it is enlarged by the scale factor 1.2.

46. If the figures are similar, give the ratio of a side of the smaller figure to the corresponding side of the larger figure. If they are not similar, explain why not.

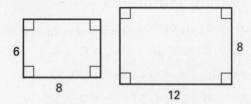

47. The figures shown are similar. Find the missing angle value.

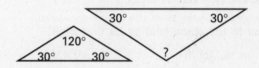

Topic 5: *Measurement*

Lesson 1

Complete.

48. 1.25 mi = _?_ yd   **49.** 6 in. = _?_ ft   **50.** 8 lb = _?_ oz

Lesson 2

Complete.

51. 400 mL = _?_ L   **52.** 100 kg = _?_ g   **53.** 2 m = _?_ cm

Lesson 3

54. Find the perimeter of a rectangle with a length of 25 cm and a width of 20 cm.

55. Find the circumference of a circle with diameter 48 mm. Use 3.14 for π.

Lesson 4

56. A square with sides of length 10 m is cut in half along one of the diagonals. Find the area of one of the triangles formed.

57. Find the area of a rectangle with a length of 2 ft and a width of 0.5 ft.

58. Use the formula $A = \frac{1}{2}(b_1 + b_2) \cdot h$ to find the area of the trapezoid shown.

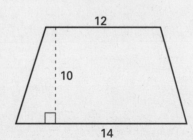

Topic 1 · LESSON 1 · *Warm-ups*

Standardized Testing Warm-Ups

1. Which of the following statements is true?

   A $16 < 16$ **B** $10 > 14$ **C** $8 < 7$ **D** $18 > 17$

2. Order the numbers from least to greatest: 4, 0, 12, 3, 7.

   A 0, 4, 3, 7, 12   **B** 12, 7, 4, 3 0   **C** 0, 3, 4, 7, 12   **D** 4, 0, 12, 3, 7

Homework Review Warm-Ups

Round each number to the place held by its first digit.

3. 638   **4.** 2175   **5.** 49,825   **6.** 625,190

Topic 1

Reading, Comparing, and Ordering Decimals

GOAL

Read and write decimals.
Compare and order
decimals.

The Dewey decimal system is a numbering system that libraries use to arrange books. A media specialist is shelving books numbered 512.23 and 512.196. She must know how to read and compare the decimals to shelve the books properly.

Terms to Know	Example / Illustration
Decimal a number with one or more digits to the right of the decimal point	0.2 0.19 3.465 These numbers are decimals.
Decimal Point a dot, or point, in a decimal that separates the whole number from the decimal part	512.196 The decimal point divides the whole number 512 from the decimal part, 196.
Greater than, Less than inequalities between two numbers; Inequalities let you compare and order numbers.	$512.23 > 512.196$ The ">" sign means "is greater than." The decimal 512.23 is greater than the decimal 512.196. $512.196 < 512.23$ The "<" sign means "is less than." The decimal 512.196 is less than the decimal 512.23.

UNDERSTANDING THE MAIN IDEAS

Read a decimal from left to right, reading the whole number first, then the decimal part. You can read the decimal point as "*and.*"

Example 1

In 1968, Bobby Unser won the Indianapolis 500 by driving 500 miles at an average speed of 152.882 miles per hour. Write out Unser's speed as you would read it.

■ Solution ■

Step 1: Write out the whole number part of the decimal.

1 5 2

The whole number is one hundred fifty-two.

Step 2: Write "and" to show the placement of the decimal point.

Step 3: Write out the decimal part as the fraction that it represents.

- Read the decimal part beginning from the tenths' place as you would read a whole number.

- Name the last place where there is a decimal value.

152. 8 8 2

The decimal part is eight hundred eighty-two thousandths.

Bobby Unser averaged one hundred fifty-two and eight hundred eighty-two thousandths miles per hour.

Write out each decimal as you would read it.

1. 27.15   **2.** 41.352   **3.** 4.8267   **4.** 958.004

Write each decimal in numerical form.

5. eight and ninety-nine hundredths

6. six hundred twelve and seventeen ten-thousandths

7. one thousand two hundred eight and fifty-seven thousandths

You can compare decimals just as you do whole numbers, from the largest place value to the smallest place value.

Example 2

Compare 214.36 and 214.359. Write an inequality describing their relationship.

■ Solution ■

Step 1: Line up the decimal points.

    214.36

    214.359

Step 2: Work from left to right, comparing digits at each place value. The digits are alike at each place value until the hundredths' place.

    214.36

    214.359

The 6 in the hundredths' place of 214.36 is greater than the 5 in the hundredths' place of 214.359. So, 214.36 is greater than 214.359.

An inequality is 214.36 > 214.359. Saying "214.36 is greater than 214.359" means the same as saying "214.359 is less than 214.36," so you can also write the inequality 214.359 < 214.36.

Compare the numbers. Write <, >, or =.

8. 9.01 _?_ 9.04   **9.** 0.039 _?_ 0.390   **10.** 0.052 _?_ 0.0520

11. 4.96 _?_ 5.02   **12.** 0.01 _?_ 0.008   **13.** 1.6849 _?_ 1.685

14. 1.336 _?_ 1.431   **15.** 0.902 _?_ 0.899   **16.** 4.707 _?_ 4.770

Order the decimals from least to greatest.

17. 0.951   1.0   0.98   **18.** 312.56   313.1   312.80

19. 3.54   3.5   3.4   3.49   **20.** 2.325   2.4   2.099

Spiral Review

21. In what place is the 7 in 3,279,425?

22. A film starts at 7:45 and lasts $1\frac{1}{2}$ hours. At what time does the film end?

Topic 1 Practice

Write out each decimal as you would read it.

1. 1.01   **2.** 12.33   **3.** 495.67   **4.** 18.048

5. 21.009   **6.** 4836.7   **7.** 476.101   **8.** 706.3849

Write each decimal in numerical form.

9. four hundred and fifteen hundredths

10. five and two hundred sixty-three thousandths

11. seventeen and seventy-six thousandths

12. sixty-eight and three hundred ninety-seven ten-thousandths

13. twelve and nine thousand, four hundred two ten-thousandths

14. nine hundred and nine thousand nine ten-thousandths

Compare the numbers. Write $<$, $>$, or $=$.

15. 0.93 _?_ 0.94   **16.** 0.864 _?_ 8.60   **17.** 9.02 _?_ 9.20

18. 6.18 _?_ 6.180   **19.** 0.998 _?_ 0.9980   **20.** 6.032 _?_ 6.03

21. 20.6 _?_ 20.66   **22.** 8.062 _?_ 8.026   **23.** 0.777 _?_ 0.0777

Order the decimals from least to greatest.

24. 3.426   3.246   3.624   **25.** 0.894   0.9   1.01   0.89

26. 618.26   61.926   617.26   **27.** 42.98   43.1   42.89   42.9

28. 31.4   31.827   32   31.8   **29.** 830.7   837   83.7   88.37

Topic 1 LESSON 2 *Warm-ups*

Standardized Testing Warm-Ups

1. Which of the following inequalities is *not* true?

A $47.208 > 47.199$

B $47.199 < 47.208$

C $501.123 < 501.097$

D $0.0744 > 0.00988$

2. What is the correct ordering from least to greatest of the decimals 3.4, 3.001, 2.979, 3.38, and 3.3099?

A 2.979, 3.001, 3.4, 3.38, 3.3099

B 2.979, 3.001, 3.3099, 3.38, 3.4

C 2.979, 3.001, 3.3099, 3.4, 3.38

D 3.001, 2.979, 3.3099, 3.38, 3.4

Homework Review Warm-Ups

3. Write thirty-five and forty-seven thousandths in numerical form.

4. Compare 6.908 and 6.89. Use $<$ or $>$.

5. Order 4.358, 4.038, 4.38, and 4.385 from least to greatest.

Topic 1 *Adding and Subtracting Decimals*

GOAL

Add and subtract decimals. Use estimation to check the reasonableness of an answer.

You can use what you know about whole number addition and subtraction, combined with place value concepts, to add and subtract decimals. Using estimation and number sense will help you decide if an answer is reasonable.

Terms to Know

Example / Illustration

Terms to Know	Example / Illustration
Estimate in a calculation, using a number close to an exact value instead of the exact value	$27.87 - 9.33 = ?$ Round 27.87 to 28. Round 9.33 to 9. $28 - 9 = 19$ An estimate for $27.87 - 9.33$ is 19.
Number sense the ability you develop to see what kind of answer might make sense for a given problem or situation	$27.87 - 9.33 = ?$ Using your number sense, you can expect the following to be true. • You are subtracting from 27.87, so the answer is smaller than 27.87. • Because $9.33 > 7.87$, the answer is less than 20. Remember to line up the decimal points.
Reasonableness a comparison of an actual result with an estimated answer	$27.87 - 9.33 = 18.54$ Recall that an estimate for $27.87 - 9.33$ is 19. The answer of 18.54 is close to 19, so it is reasonable.

UNDERSTANDING THE MAIN IDEAS

When adding decimals, always pay careful attention to the position of the decimal point.

Example 1

Find the sum $24.26 + 3.8 + 7.62$.

■ **Solution** ■

Step 1: Line up the numbers by place value. The easiest way to do this is to align the decimal points.

$$\begin{array}{r} 24.26 \\ 3.8 \\ +\ \ 7.62 \\ \hline \end{array}$$

Step 2: Place the decimal point for the answer directly below the other decimal points. Add the digits as you would for whole numbers. You may want to insert a zero in the hundredths' place of 3.8 for clarity.

$$\begin{array}{r} ^{1\ 1} \\ 24.26 \\ 3.80 \\ +\ \ 7.62 \\ \hline 35.68 \end{array}$$

Step 3: Use estimation to see if your answer is reasonable. Round each decimal to the nearest whole number. Since 36 is close to 35.68, the sum is reasonable.

$$24 + 4 + 8 = 36$$

The sum is $24.26 + 3.8 + 7.62 = 35.68$.

Find each sum.

1. $14.75 + 72.88$ **2.** $42.69 + 9.89$ **3.** $5.9 + 7.057$

4. $67.85 + 34.9$ **5.** $0.92 + 0.836$ **6.** $0.057 + 12.143$

7. $4.7 + 8.8 + 0.45$ **8.** $2.36 + 3.78 + 2.67$ **9.** $0.381 + 0.2 + 0.377$

When subtracting decimals, it often helps to write equivalent decimals. (In Example 1, 3.80 and 3.8 are equivalent decimals.) To do this, insert zeros as place holders at the end of the decimal.

Example 2

The mass of a substance is 8.3 kilograms. After the water evaporates from it, its mass decreases to 3.617 kilograms. How much of the substance's mass is water?

■ Solution ■

The mass of the water is the mass that "disappears." This is the difference in the mass before and after the water evaporates, or $8.3 - 3.617$.

Step 1: Use the decimal points to align the numbers. Insert zeros to write an equivalent decimal.

$$
\begin{array}{r}
8.300 \\
- 3.617 \\
\end{array}
$$

Step 2: Place the decimal point for the answer directly below the other decimal points. Subtract as you would for whole numbers.

$$
\begin{array}{r}
7\;\;12\;9 \\
8.3\cancel{0}0 \\
- 3.617 \\
\hline
4.683 \\
\end{array}
$$

Step 3: Use estimation to decide if your answer is reasonable. Since 4 is close to 4.683, the difference is reasonable.

$$8 - 4 = 4$$

The mass of the water in the substance is 4.683 kilograms.

Find each difference.

10. $265.3 - 121.44$ **11.** $703.02 - 98.86$ **12.** $8.004 - 2.572$

13. $0.6 - 0.17$ **14.** $1.04 - 0.999$ **15.** $12.1 - 8.879$

16. Lawanda places a dish on a scale. Its mass is 12.998 grams. When she adds a chemical to the dish, its mass increases to 13.2 grams. What is the mass of the chemical?

. . . .
Spiral Review

17. Write out the decimal 812.376 as you would read it.

18. Order the decimals from least to greatest: 7.843   7.483   7.348   7.384

Topic 1 — Practice

Find each sum or difference.

1. $6.8 + 7.9$ **2.** $8.74 + 9.327$ **3.** $14.8 - 7.9$

4. $37.52 - 16.7$ **5.** $7.9 + 116.32$ **6.** $6.5 - 0.0032$

7. $8.4 + 7.007$ **8.** $10 - 1.02$ **9.** $1.25 + 0.025$

10. $50.1 - 35.43$ **11.** $6.2 + 1.73$ **12.** $30.29 - 19.5$

13. $10 - 5.98$ **14.** $77.9 - 2.836$ **15.** $3.68 + 9.753$

16. $72.6 + 123.12 + 2.4$ **17.** $42.83 + 36.356 + 75.6$

18. $238.72 + 65.3 + 7.84$ **19.** $0.47 + 0.463 + 3.27$

20. $439.6 + 7.049 + 12.32 + 0.0009$

Choose numbers from the number box to answer each question.

21. Find two numbers whose sum is about 20.

22. Find three numbers whose sum is about 70.

23. Find two numbers whose difference is about 10.

24. Which two numbers have a sum of exactly 28.289?

25. The difference between which two numbers is exactly 52.43?

Number Box

2.657
26.57
4.625
46.25
7.9
79
1.719
17.19

Solve.

26. A pipe is 4.8629 cm in diameter. It needs to pass through a hole that measures 4.8634 cm in diameter. Will it fit? If so, by what margin?

27. Mauro thinks that the sum of two decimals less than 1 is always less than 1. Is he correct? Give an example to support your answer.

Standardized Testing Warm-Ups

1. What is the difference between 24.034 and 19.098?

   A 5.064   **B** 4.936   **C** 4.964   **D** 5.936

2. Using estimation, which sum is most reasonable for $100.89 + 11.009 + 288.997$?

   A 390   **B** 300.977   **C** 401   **D** 40.1

Homework Review Warm-Ups

3. Consuela is 153.95 cm tall. Marcus is 160.2 cm tall. Who is taller? By how much?

4. Crystal bought three gifts for $8.98, $9.26, and $13.47. How much did she spend for gifts all together?

Topic 1 · Lesson 3 · *Multiplying Decimals*

GOAL

Estimate and calculate decimal products.

A warehouse store sells beverages in cases of 24 bottles. Each bottle holds 0.75 liters. To find the total amount of beverage sold in each case, multiply 0.75 liters by 24.

Terms to Know	Example / Illustration
Product the result of multiplying two or more numbers	In 24 × 0.75 = 18.00, the product is 18.00.
Factors the numbers multiplied to give a product	In 24 × 0.75 = 18.00, the factors are 24 and 0.75.

UNDERSTANDING THE MAIN IDEAS

When multiplying a whole number and a decimal or two decimals, first estimate the product. This will help you decide if your answer is reasonable.

Example 1

Jerry fills his truck up with 17 gallons of gasoline. The gas costs $1.39 per gallon. How much will Jerry pay for the fill-up?

▪ Solution ▪

The amount Jerry pays is the product of 17 and $1.39.

Step 1: Estimate the product. Round 17 up to 20 and round $1.39 down to $1. The product of 20 and $1 is $20. Jerry will spend about $20 on gasoline.

Step 2: Multiply to find the actual product.
Add the decimal places in the factors.
There are two decimal places in the factors.
The product has that many decimal places.

$$\begin{array}{r} 1.39 \\ \times\ \ 17 \\ \hline 973 \\ +\ 1390 \\ \hline 23.63 \end{array}$$

Step 3: The estimate is 20. The product 23.63 is reasonable.

Jerry will spend $23.63 on gasoline.

Estimate each product. Then find the actual product.

1. 6.22×11 **2.** 4.38×25 **3.** 5.3×5

4. 5.07×21 **5.** 6.11×47 **6.** 1.75×12

7. Sandy has $20. She wants to buy 18 souvenir pencils that cost $1.15 each. Does she have enough money? Explain.

Example 2

A sweatshirt with the new school logo costs $22.50, plus tax. The tax is 0.06 for every dollar spent. What is the tax on the sweatshirt?

■ Solution ■

The tax is the product of $22.50 and 0.06.

Step 1: Estimate the product. Round $22.50 down to $20 and round 0.06 up to 0.1. The product of $20 and 0.1 is $2.00 because one tenth of 20 is 2. The tax should be about $2.00.

Step 2: Multiply to find the actual product. Add the decimal places in the factors. There are four decimal places in the factors. The product has that many decimal places.

$$\begin{array}{r} 22.50 \\ \times\ \ 0.06 \\ \hline 1.3500 \end{array}$$

Step 3: The estimate is 2.00. The product 1.35 is reasonable.

The tax on the sweatshirt is $1.35.

Estimate, then calculate the product. Use the estimate to check the reasonableness of your answer.

8. 5.7×3.4 **9.** 5.765×7.2 **10.** 2.41×6.8

11. 3.45×2.4 **12.** 9.56×0.15 **13.** 0.82×0.55

14. Will the product of 15.25 and 0.3 be greater than or less than 10? Explain.

. . . .

Spiral Review

15. In the number 89.7241, the value of the 4 is _____.

16. Find the difference of 3.590 and 2.186.

PRE-COURSE REVIEW

LESSON

3

Practice

Find the product. Then estimate the product to check the reasonableness of your answer.

1. 32.6 × 5

2. 4.38 × 7

3. 7.39 × 0.6

4. 53.7 × 0.9

5. 64.2 × 0.7

6. 79.65 × 0.3

7. 6.38 × 0.9

8. 5.96 × 6

9. 8.35 × 6

10. 47.6 × 0.7

11. 0.73 × 42

12. 0.37 × 68

13. 5.6 × 8.3

14. 0.85 × 2.8

15. 0.69 × 0.54

16. 0.47 × 5.8

17. 8.4 × 3.9

18. 6.5 × 0.72

19. 0.58 × 0.43

20. 0.75 × 0.82

21. 8.42 × 73

22. 7.58 × 48

23. 53.7 × 6.9

24. 4.86 × 3.7

25. 110 × 0.02

26. 0.55 × 0.05

27. 12.03 × 0.015

Use the graph showing gasoline prices at a highway station.

28. How much will it cost to purchase 8 gallons of regular gas?

29. How much will it cost to purchase 12 gallons of plus gas?

30. How much will it cost to purchase 15.3 gallons of premium gas?

31. How much will you save by buying 12.5 gallons of regular gas instead of premium gas?

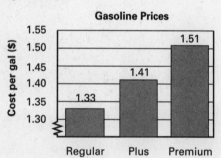

Gasoline Prices

Use number sense to indicate whether each product will be closer to 0.3, 3, 30, or 300.

32. 1.5 × 2.1

33. 0.15 × 21

34. 0.15 × 2.1

35. 18 × 0.18

36. 0.18 × 1.8

37. 180 × 1.8

Topic 1 LESSON 4 *Warm-ups*

Standardized Testing Warm-Ups

1. Which is the best estimate for 23.65×0.82?

   A 2000 **B** 200 **C** 20 **D** 2

2. Jason spends $8.95 each month for club dues. How much will he spend for dues in a year?

   A $1074.00 **B** $108.00 **C** $107.40 **D** $107.90

Homework Review Warm-Ups

Find the product. Use an estimate to check the reasonableness of your answer.

3. 21.7×12

4. 10.5×2.4

5. 101.1×0.012

Topic 1 · 4 · *Dividing with Decimals*

GOAL
Estimate and calculate decimal quotients.

Myra and three friends go to a restaurant. The bill including tax and tip is $35.12. Myra estimates that each person's share is $9.00. She divides to find the actual amount owed by each person.

Terms to Know

Example / Illustration

Dividend the number that is divided in a division problem	$\$35.12 \div 4 = \$8.78$ The dividend is $35.12.
Divisor the number by which you divide the dividend in a division problem	$\$35.12 \div 4 = \$8.78$ The divisor is 4.
Quotient the answer to a division problem	$\$35.12 \div 4 = \$8.78$ The quotient is $8.78.
Compatible numbers numbers that are easy to work with mentally; You use them in place of actual numbers to make an estimate, especially when dividing.	The divisor, 4, does not divide 35 evenly, but it does divide 36 with a remainder of 0. The numbers 36 and 4 are compatible. $\$36 \div 4 = \$9$ Because $36 is close to $35.12, $36 \div 4$ is a good estimate for $35.12 \div 4$.

UNDERSTANDING THE MAIN IDEAS

Because you can divide compatible numbers using mental math, they make easy work of estimating quotients when you need to determine if an exact quotient is reasonable.

Example 1

Andrea is carving a totem pole out of a piece of wood 47.4 in. high. She wants to carve 6 faces, using the same amount of wood for each face. Estimate and then calculate the height of each face.

■ Solution ■

To find the height of each face, divide the total height of the totem pole, 47.4 in., by the number of faces, 6.

Step 1: Use compatible numbers to estimate the quotient. Because 48 and 6 are compatible, and 48 is close to 47.4, use 48 to estimate 47.4.

$$48 \div 6 = 8$$

Each face should be about 8 in. high.

Step 2: Find the actual quotient. Remember to place the decimal point in the answer directly above the one in the dividend.

$$
\begin{array}{r}
7.9 \\
6{\overline{\smash{\big)}\,47.4}} \\
\underline{-\ 42} \\
54 \\
\underline{-\ 54} \\
0
\end{array}
$$

Step 3: Compare your estimate to the actual quotient to check for reasonableness.

Because 7.9 is close to 8, the quotient makes sense.

Each totem pole face should be 7.9 inches high.

Use compatible numbers to estimate each quotient. Then divide. Compare your estimate with the actual quotient to check for reasonableness.

1. $8.76 \div 3$ **2.** $72.24 \div 2$ **3.** $32.670 \div 4$ **4.** $17.82 \div 3$

5. $61.38 \div 9$ **6.** $9.506 \div 7$ **7.** $480.64 \div 32$ **8.** $158.34 \div 78$

To divide a decimal by another decimal, you will need to recall what you know about place value and multiplying by powers of ten.

Example 2

Find the quotient 44.28 ÷ 5.4.

■ Solution ■

Step 1: Use compatible numbers to estimate the quotient. First round 5.4 to 5. Because 45 is divisible by 5 and is close to 44.28, use 45 to estimate 44.28.

$$45 \div 5 = 9$$

The estimated quotient is 9.

Step 2: It is easier to divide with a whole number divisor. Multiply the divisor and the dividend by 10. This gives you an equivalent division problem. Equivalent problems have the same answer.

To multiply by 10, move the decimal point one place to the right.

$$5.4 \overline{)44.28} \longrightarrow 54 \overline{)442.8}$$

Step 3: Divide.

$$
\begin{array}{r}
8.2 \\
54\overline{)442.8} \\
-432 \\
\hline
108 \\
-108 \\
\hline
0
\end{array}
$$

Step 4: Compare your estimate to the actual quotient to check for reasonableness. Because 8.2 is close to 9, the quotient makes sense. You can also check by multiplying 8.2 × 5.4. The product should be the dividend, 44.28.

The quotient of 44.28 and 5.4 is 8.2.

Use compatible numbers to estimate each quotient. Then divide. Compare your estimate with the actual quotient to check for reasonableness.

9. 12.92 ÷ 3.4   **10.** 26.08 ÷ 0.8   **11.** 3.618 ÷ 0.67   **12.** 1.44 ÷ 0.45

. . . .
Spiral Review

13. Find the product of 234.5 and 4.7.

14. Order the decimals 63.3, 63.34, 62.99, 63.09, and 63.401 from least to greatest.

Topic 1 · LESSON 4 · *Practice*

Use compatible numbers to estimate each quotient. Then divide. Compare your estimate with the actual quotient to check for reasonableness.

1. $16.30 \div 5$ **2.** $30.66 \div 7$ **3.** $44.34 \div 6$

4. $44.94 \div 6$ **5.** $23.895 \div 3$ **6.** $57.42 \div 9$

7. $35.76 \div 6$ **8.** $33.32 \div 7$ **9.** $306.6 \div 42$

10. $251.6 \div 37$ **11.** $464.8 \div 56$ **12.** $238.0 \div 28$

13. $372.6 \div 69$ **14.** $614.66 \div 73$ **15.** $363.84 \div 48$

16. $370.53 \div 69$ **17.** $179.82 \div 37$ **18.** $490.20 \div 76$

19. $461.13 \div 57$ **20.** $389.12 \div 76$ **21.** $27.26 \div 5.8$

22. $32.37 \div 8.3$ **23.** $23.45 \div 3.5$ **24.** $46.113 \div 5.7$

25. $73.72 \div 7.6$ **26.** $43.095 \div 6.5$ **27.** $20.64 \div 2.4$

28. $54.32 \div 5.6$ **29.** $3.15 \div 0.15$ **30.** $41.75 \div 0.25$

In Exercises 31–34, use number sense to decide which is the correct answer.

31. $19.68 \div 6$ **A** 0.328 **B** 3.28 **C** 32.8

32. $25.8 \div 120$ **A** 0.215 **B** 2.15 **C** 21.5

33. $660.3 \div 6.2$ **A** 1.065 **B** 10.65 **C** 106.5

34. $39.82 \div 1.1$ **A** 36.2 **B** 362 **C** 3620

35. To find the time a trip takes, divide the distance traveled by the average speed. If your family drove 611.1 mi today at an average speed of 58.2 mi/h, how long were you driving?

Topic 2 — *Warm-ups*

Standardized Testing Warm-Ups

1. Which pair of numbers is *not* compatible for estimating quotients?

   A 115 and 5   **B** 110 and 4   **C** 270 and 30   **D** 96 and 12

2. What is the quotient $9.66 \div 0.12$?

   A 805   **B** 80.5   **C** 8.05   **D** 0.805

Homework Review Warm-Ups

Use compatible numbers to estimate the quotient. Then find the actual quotient.

3. $61.38 \div 9$ 4. $9.72 \div 9$ 5. $80.46 \div 18$ 6. $17.528 \div 2.8$

Topic 2 | *Fractions in Simplest Form*

GOAL

Determine when a fraction is in simplest form. Write fractions in simplest form.

One day during the winter cold and flu season, 56 of the 336 students in Grant's grade were out sick. You can write this as the fraction $\frac{56}{336}$. But the fraction would probably mean a lot more to you if you saw it in its simpler equivalent form of $\frac{1}{6}$.

Terms to Know

Example / Illustration

Terms to Know	Example / Illustration
Equivalent fractions fractions that represent the same number	 $$\frac{4}{8} = \frac{1}{2}$$ The fractions $\frac{4}{8}$ and $\frac{1}{2}$ name the same portion of the circle. They are equivalent fractions.
Simplest form of a fraction a fraction whose numerator and denominator have no common factors other than 1	 Of the 12 characters, 8 are Os. Of each 3 characters, 2 are Os. The simplest form of $\frac{8}{12}$ is $\frac{2}{3}$.
Greatest common factor (GCF) the largest common factor of two or more numbers	The common factors of 8 and 12 are 1, 2, and 4. The greatest common factor of 8 and 12 is 4.

UNDERSTANDING THE MAIN IDEAS

As long as you can divide the numerator and denominator of a fraction by common factors, you can simplify the fraction.

Example 1

Nicole has 24 games on her computer. She already knows how to play 18 of them. What is the simplest form of the fraction that describes the portion of computer games that Nicole knows how to play?

■ Solution ■

Step 1: Write the fraction that represents the situation.

The fraction is $\frac{18}{24}$.

Step 2: Divide the numerator and the denominator by any common factor. Because 2 is a common factor, divide 18 and 24 by 2.

$$\frac{18 \div 2}{24 \div 2} = \frac{9}{12}$$

The new fraction is $\frac{9}{12}$.

Step 3: Keep dividing the numerator and denominator by common factors until the resulting numerator and denominator have no common factors other than 1. Because 3 is a common factor of 9 and 12, divide 9 and 12 by 3.

$$\frac{9 \div 3}{12 \div 3} = \frac{3}{4}$$

3 and 4 have no common factors other than 1. Therefore, $\frac{3}{4}$ is in simplest form.

Nicole knows how to play $\frac{3}{4}$ of the games on her computer.

Indicate whether or not the fraction is in simplest form by writing *yes* or *no*. If the answer is *no*, give the simplest form of the fraction.

1. $\frac{3}{6}$ 2. $\frac{6}{8}$ 3. $\frac{12}{20}$ 4. $\frac{17}{25}$

5. $\frac{8}{12}$ 6. $\frac{4}{10}$ 7. $\frac{5}{12}$ 8. $\frac{50}{100}$

Another way to find the simplest form of a fraction is first to find the greatest common factor of the numerator and the denominator. Then you can divide the numerator and denominator by the greatest common factor.

Example 2

Neeti made a patchwork quilt out of fabric scraps. She had 30 fabric scraps. Of these, 18 were prints or stripes. What is the simplest form of the fraction that describes the portion of the scraps that were prints or stripes?

■ Solution ■

Step 1: Write the fraction that represents the situation.

The fraction is $\dfrac{18}{30}$.

Step 2: Find the greatest common factor of the numerator and denominator of the fraction.

Factors of 18: 1, 2, 3, 6, 9, 18

Factors of 30: 1, 2, 3, 5, 6, 10, 15, 30

Common factors of 18 and 30: 1, 2, 3, 6

The GCF of 18 and 30 is 6.

Step 3: Divide the numerator and denominator by the greatest common factor.

$$\frac{18 \div 6}{30 \div 6} = \frac{3}{5}$$

The portion of Neeti's fabric scraps that were prints or stripes is $\dfrac{3}{5}$.

Use the greatest common factor to write each fraction in simplest form. If it is already in simplest form, write *simplest form*.

9. $\dfrac{12}{28}$ 10. $\dfrac{14}{42}$ 11. $\dfrac{21}{35}$ 12. $\dfrac{15}{45}$

13. $\dfrac{24}{36}$ 14. $\dfrac{18}{48}$ 15. $\dfrac{35}{40}$ 16. $\dfrac{23}{34}$

....
Spiral Review

17. You buy two T-shirts for $12.69 each. How much money do you need to pay?

18. You give the sales clerk $30 to pay for the two T-shirts in Exercise 17. How much change will you get back?

Indicate whether or not the fraction is in simplest form. Write *yes* or *no*.

1. $\dfrac{5}{15}$ 2. $\dfrac{2}{7}$ 3. $\dfrac{9}{16}$ 4. $\dfrac{8}{32}$

5. $\dfrac{25}{35}$ 6. $\dfrac{10}{13}$ 7. $\dfrac{4}{12}$ 8. $\dfrac{16}{21}$

9. $\dfrac{6}{27}$ 10. $\dfrac{18}{27}$ 11. $\dfrac{19}{20}$ 12. $\dfrac{23}{46}$

Write each fraction in simplest form. Use any method you wish. If the fraction is already in simplest form, write *simplest form*.

13. $\dfrac{16}{27}$ 14. $\dfrac{6}{35}$ 15. $\dfrac{9}{30}$ 16. $\dfrac{4}{16}$

17. $\dfrac{7}{28}$ 18. $\dfrac{40}{70}$ 19. $\dfrac{3}{18}$ 20. $\dfrac{8}{21}$

21. $\dfrac{34}{50}$ 22. $\dfrac{9}{12}$ 23. $\dfrac{21}{35}$ 24. $\dfrac{16}{40}$

25. $\dfrac{12}{25}$ 26. $\dfrac{9}{24}$ 27. $\dfrac{13}{20}$ 28. $\dfrac{6}{16}$

29. $\dfrac{16}{30}$ 30. $\dfrac{50}{75}$ 31. $\dfrac{18}{27}$ 32. $\dfrac{40}{100}$

33. $\dfrac{24}{42}$ 34. $\dfrac{12}{36}$ 35. $\dfrac{18}{73}$ 36. $\dfrac{4}{15}$

Use the table below for Exercises 37–40. Give your answers in simplest form.

The scoreboard shows the wins, losses and ties of the Cougars baseball team.

37. What part of its games did the team win?

38. What part of its games did the team lose?

39. What part of its games did the team tie?

40. What part of its games did the team win or tie?

Cougars team record

Wins	Losses	Ties
16	12	8

Standardized Testing Warm-Ups

1. Which of the following fractions is in simplest form?

   A $\dfrac{17}{51}$ **B** $\dfrac{14}{52}$ **C** $\dfrac{23}{26}$ **D** $\dfrac{12}{27}$

2. Which one of the following fractions is not equivalent to the others?

   A $\dfrac{5}{6}$ **B** $\dfrac{21}{24}$ **C** $\dfrac{15}{18}$ **D** $\dfrac{35}{42}$

Homework Review Warm-Ups

Match each fraction with an equivalent fraction in simplest form.

   A $\dfrac{1}{6}$ **B** $\dfrac{1}{4}$ **C** $\dfrac{1}{3}$ **D** $\dfrac{2}{3}$ **E** $\dfrac{3}{4}$

3. $\dfrac{3}{12}$ **4.** $\dfrac{9}{12}$ **5.** $\dfrac{4}{12}$ **6.** $\dfrac{8}{12}$ **7.** $\dfrac{2}{12}$

Topic 2

Improper Fractions and Mixed Numbers

GOAL

Write improper fractions as mixed numbers. Write mixed numbers as improper fractions.

You have $2\frac{1}{3}$ loaves of bread. How many pieces will you have if you slice the loaves into thirds?

Terms to Know

Example / Illustration

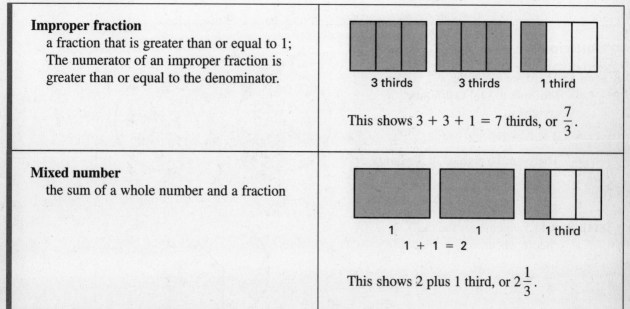

Terms to Know	Example / Illustration
Improper fraction a fraction that is greater than or equal to 1; The numerator of an improper fraction is greater than or equal to the denominator.	3 thirds 3 thirds 1 third This shows $3 + 3 + 1 = 7$ thirds, or $\frac{7}{3}$.
Mixed number the sum of a whole number and a fraction	1 1 1 third $1 + 1 = 2$ This shows 2 plus 1 third, or $2\frac{1}{3}$.

UNDERSTANDING THE MAIN IDEAS

You can see above that the mixed number $2\frac{1}{3}$ and the improper fraction $\frac{7}{3}$ show

the same quantity. You can rewrite a mixed number as an equivalent improper fraction. To do this, first write the whole number as an improper fraction.

Example 1

Mr. Katz has 2 whole wheels and $\frac{5}{8}$ of a wheel of swiss cheese in the deli display case. He divides the whole amount into eighths of a wheel for packaging. Rewrite $2\frac{5}{8}$ as an improper fraction. How many packages of cheese will Mr. Katz have if each package contains $\frac{1}{8}$ of a wheel?

■ Solution ■

Step 1: There are 8 eighths in 1 whole. Multiply to find the number of eighths in 2 wholes.

$2 \times 8 = 16$

There are 16 eighths in 2 wholes.

$$2 = \frac{16}{8}$$

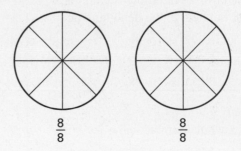

$\frac{8}{8}$ $\frac{8}{8}$

Step 2: Add 5 eighths for the third cheese wheel.

$$\frac{16}{8} + \frac{5}{8} = \frac{21}{8}$$

So, $2\frac{5}{8} = \frac{21}{8}$.

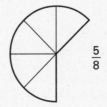

$\frac{5}{8}$

Mr. Katz will have 21 packages of swiss cheese.

In Exercises 1–5, write each mixed number as an improper fraction.

1. $2\frac{2}{3}$ **2.** $1\frac{4}{5}$ **3.** $3\frac{1}{8}$ **4.** $5\frac{3}{4}$ **5.** $8\frac{1}{2}$

6. Trudy has $3\frac{1}{4}$ muffins. How many pieces can Trudy make if she cuts the muffins into fourths?

It is often easier to picture an improper fraction as a mixed number. To change an improper fraction to a mixed number, think about how many wholes the improper fraction contains.

Example 2

The PTA is sending out a newsletter. Each page of the newsletter will require one half of a ream of paper. This month's newsletter is 7 pages long. So, the PTA needs $\frac{7}{2}$ reams of paper. Written as a mixed number, how many reams will they use?

■ Solution ■

It takes 2 halves to make each whole. Divide to find the number of wholes in seven halves.

$7 \div 2 = 3 \text{ R1} \leftarrow$ There are 3 whole reams, with 1 half ream left over.

The PTA will use $3\frac{1}{2}$ reams of paper for its newsletter.

In Exercises 7–11, write each improper fraction as a mixed number.

7. $\frac{9}{2}$ **8.** $\frac{22}{5}$ **9.** $\frac{15}{7}$ **10.** $\frac{17}{4}$ **11.** $\frac{11}{3}$

12. There were $\frac{17}{8}$ pizzas left after the party. Mr. Davies decided to keep whole pizzas only. How many whole pizzas did Mr. Davies save? What part did he throw away?

. . . .
Spiral Review

13. Find the quotient $391.22 \div 6.2$.

14. Write $\frac{45}{105}$ in simplest form.

Topic 2   LESSON 2   *Practice*

Write each mixed number as an improper fraction.

1. $3\dfrac{1}{3}$ **2.** $3\dfrac{1}{2}$ **3.** $3\dfrac{3}{4}$ **4.** $7\dfrac{5}{6}$

5. $3\dfrac{2}{5}$ **6.** $6\dfrac{3}{10}$ **7.** $2\dfrac{2}{5}$ **8.** $4\dfrac{5}{7}$

Write each improper fraction as a mixed number.

9. $\dfrac{25}{8}$ **10.** $\dfrac{28}{6}$ **11.** $\dfrac{17}{3}$ **12.** $\dfrac{24}{5}$

13. $\dfrac{15}{4}$ **14.** $\dfrac{13}{10}$ **15.** $\dfrac{4}{3}$ **16.** $\dfrac{46}{10}$

17. Each number below corresponds to a point on the number line shown. Give the letters in the order that they match the points from left to right.

A $1\dfrac{2}{5}$ **B** $2\dfrac{1}{2}$ **C** 2.75   **D** $\dfrac{5}{4}$ **E** $\dfrac{10}{3}$ **F** 3.05

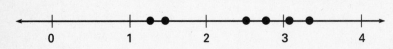

18. You have $2\dfrac{1}{4}$ pounds of turkey. How many sandwiches can you make if each sandwich contains $\dfrac{1}{4}$ pound of turkey?

19. Each batch of cookies calls for $\dfrac{1}{2}$ cup of brown sugar. You decide to make three batches. So, you use $\dfrac{3}{2}$ cups of brown sugar. Written as a mixed number, how many cups will you use?

Topic 2 *Warm-ups*

Standardized Testing Warm-Ups

1. Which improper fraction is equivalent to the mixed number $7\frac{5}{8}$?

   A $\frac{75}{8}$ B $\frac{61}{8}$ C $\frac{56}{5}$ D $\frac{56}{8}$

2. Which one of the following numbers is not equivalent to the other three?

   A $\frac{56}{100}$ B 5.6 C $5\frac{3}{5}$ D $\frac{28}{5}$

Homework Review Warm-Ups

Write each improper fraction as a mixed number.

3. $\frac{5}{4}$ 4. $\frac{11}{10}$ 5. $\frac{27}{20}$ 6. $\frac{76}{25}$

Topic 2 LESSON 3 *Adding and Subtracting Fractions*

GOAL

Add and subtract fractions that have like and unlike denominators.

Ruby is helping at a bake sale. There are parts of two pies left. How can she tell if there is more than a whole pie left to sell?

UNDERSTANDING THE MAIN IDEAS

You can add and subtract fractions. To add two fractions with the same, or like, denominators, add the numerators. Write your answer in simplest form.

Example 1

Find each sum.

a. $\dfrac{1}{9} + \dfrac{5}{9}$

b. $\dfrac{6}{10} + \dfrac{9}{10}$

■ Solution ■

a.

$$\dfrac{1}{9} \quad + \quad \dfrac{5}{9} \quad = \quad \dfrac{6}{9} \quad = \quad \dfrac{2}{3}$$

b.

$$\dfrac{6}{10} \quad + \quad \dfrac{9}{10} \quad = \quad \dfrac{15}{10} \quad = \quad 1\dfrac{1}{2}$$

To add fractions with different, or unlike, denominators, you need to write equivalent fractions that have a common denominator, which means the fractions are in the same size pieces. After you add, write your answer in simplest form.

Example 2

Find each sum.

a. $\dfrac{7}{10} + \dfrac{1}{2}$ 　　　　　　　　**b.** $\dfrac{2}{3} + \dfrac{1}{4}$

■ Solution ■

a. Since $\dfrac{1}{2} = \dfrac{1 \cdot 5}{2 \cdot 5} = \dfrac{5}{10}$, use 10 as the common denominator.

$$\dfrac{7}{10} \;+\; \dfrac{1}{2} \;=\; \dfrac{7}{10} \;+\; \dfrac{5}{10} \;=\; \dfrac{12}{10} = 1\dfrac{2}{10} \;=\; 1\dfrac{1}{5}$$

b. Because 3 and 4 have no common factor, write equivalent fractions using the common denominator 3 • 4 or 12.

$$\dfrac{2}{3} \;+\; \dfrac{1}{4} \;=\; \dfrac{2 \cdot 4}{3 \cdot 4} \;+\; \dfrac{1 \cdot 3}{4 \cdot 3} \;=\; \dfrac{8}{12} + \dfrac{3}{12} = \dfrac{11}{12}$$

Find each sum. Write each answer as a fraction or mixed number in simplest form.

1. $\dfrac{9}{20} + \dfrac{7}{20}$ 　　　　**2.** $\dfrac{5}{6} + \dfrac{5}{6}$ 　　　　**3.** $\dfrac{1}{10} + \dfrac{7}{20}$

4. $\dfrac{3}{4} + \dfrac{7}{12}$ 　　　　**5.** $\dfrac{1}{3} + \dfrac{1}{4}$ 　　　　**6.** $\dfrac{1}{2} + \dfrac{2}{3}$

To subtract fractions, you also need to write equivalent fractions that have a common denominator. Remember to write your answer in simplest form. When dealing with mixed numbers, it is often helpful to convert to an improper fraction first.

Example 3

Find each difference.

a. $1\dfrac{2}{5} - \dfrac{4}{5}$

b. $1\dfrac{1}{5} - \dfrac{7}{10}$

■ Solution ■

a.

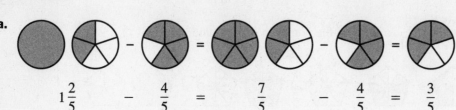

$$1\dfrac{2}{5} \quad - \quad \dfrac{4}{5} \quad = \quad \dfrac{7}{5} \quad - \quad \dfrac{4}{5} \quad = \quad \dfrac{3}{5}$$

b. Since $1\dfrac{1}{5} = \dfrac{6}{5} = \dfrac{6 \cdot 2}{5 \cdot 2} = \dfrac{12}{10}$, use 10 as the common denominator.

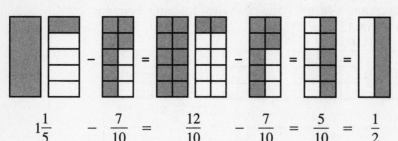

$$1\dfrac{1}{5} \quad - \quad \dfrac{7}{10} \quad = \quad \dfrac{12}{10} \quad - \quad \dfrac{7}{10} \quad = \quad \dfrac{5}{10} \quad = \quad \dfrac{1}{2}$$

Find each difference. Write each answer as a fraction or mixed number in simplest form.

7. $\dfrac{7}{9} - \dfrac{4}{9}$

8. $1\dfrac{5}{12} - \dfrac{7}{12}$

9. $1\dfrac{1}{8} - \dfrac{7}{8}$

10. $\dfrac{11}{15} - \dfrac{2}{3}$

11. $1\dfrac{2}{3} - \dfrac{8}{9}$

12. $1\dfrac{1}{8} - \dfrac{7}{16}$

· · · · · · · · · · · · · · · · · · ·
Spiral Review

13. Write $9\dfrac{3}{7}$ as an improper fraction.

14. Write $\dfrac{90}{165}$ in simplest form.

Topic 2 LESSON 3 Practice

Find each sum or difference. Write each answer as a fraction or mixed number in simplest form.

1. $\dfrac{2}{15} + \dfrac{11}{15}$

2. $\dfrac{8}{15} + \dfrac{13}{15}$

3. $\dfrac{1}{2} + \dfrac{1}{4}$

4. $\dfrac{5}{9} - \dfrac{4}{9}$

5. $\dfrac{5}{6} - \dfrac{1}{6}$

6. $\dfrac{3}{4} - \dfrac{5}{8}$

7. $\dfrac{1}{3} + \dfrac{4}{9}$

8. $\dfrac{3}{10} + \dfrac{3}{5}$

9. $\dfrac{1}{4} + \dfrac{4}{5}$

10. $\dfrac{2}{3} - \dfrac{1}{6}$

11. $\dfrac{5}{9} - \dfrac{2}{5}$

12. $\dfrac{7}{12} - \dfrac{1}{4}$

13. $1\dfrac{3}{7} + \dfrac{1}{14}$

14. $2\dfrac{1}{2} + \dfrac{7}{10}$

15. $2\dfrac{1}{2} + 3\dfrac{1}{3}$

16. $3\dfrac{1}{25} - \dfrac{3}{100}$

17. $5\dfrac{9}{20} - 2\dfrac{1}{2}$

18. $\dfrac{4}{7} + \dfrac{1}{3}$

19. $3\dfrac{3}{8} - 2$

20. $5\dfrac{1}{5} + 1\dfrac{3}{10}$

21. $\dfrac{2}{7} - \dfrac{1}{4}$

22. $5 - \dfrac{3}{5}$

23. $\dfrac{23}{100} + \dfrac{1}{2}$

24. $\dfrac{17}{30} - \dfrac{1}{6}$

25. One batch of trail mix requires $\dfrac{2}{3}$ cups of raisins and $1\dfrac{1}{3}$ cups of peanuts. If the trail mix contains only raisins and peanuts, how many cups of trail mix are in one batch?

26. Mrs. Quant buys a beef roast that weighs $5\dfrac{1}{4}$ pounds and a ham that weighs $8\dfrac{1}{2}$ pounds. How many pounds of meat did she buy?

27. Angela is making costumes for a play. She needs $1\dfrac{1}{3}$ yards of ribbon for one costume, $2\dfrac{1}{8}$ yards of ribbon for another costume, and $2\dfrac{1}{4}$ yards of ribbon for a third costume. What is the total amount of ribbon she needs?

28. If Angela buys 6 yards of ribbon for the three costumes in Exercise 27, how many yards of ribbon will be left over?

Standardized Testing Warm-ups

1. What is the simplest form of the sum $\dfrac{5}{18} + \dfrac{7}{18}$?

   A $\dfrac{2}{3}$ **B** $\dfrac{1}{3}$ **C** $\dfrac{6}{9}$ **D** $\dfrac{12}{18}$

2. What is the simplest form of the difference $\dfrac{1}{2} - \dfrac{1}{8}$?

   A $\dfrac{1}{6}$ **B** $\dfrac{3}{8}$ **C** $\dfrac{5}{8}$ **D** $\dfrac{7}{8}$

Homework Review Warm-ups

Find the sum or difference. Write each answer as a fraction or mixed number in simplest form.

3. $\dfrac{5}{9} + \dfrac{1}{3}$ **4.** $\dfrac{9}{10} - \dfrac{4}{10}$ **5.** $\dfrac{2}{5} + \dfrac{4}{5}$

Topic 3 LESSON 1   *Converting Fractions to Decimals*

GOAL

Write fractions and mixed numbers as terminating or repeating decimals.

The fraction $\frac{1}{2}$ and the decimal 0.5 are equivalent. This is because $\frac{1}{2}$ and $\frac{5}{10}$ are two ways to express the same amount, and 0.5 is another way to write $\frac{5}{10}$. You can change, or convert, any fraction or mixed number to an equivalent decimal.

Terms to Know   Example / Illustration

Terms to Know	Example / Illustration
Terminating decimal a decimal that has a limited number of decimal places and naturally ends	0.325 0.5 0.6767 0.3333 2.0 35.701
Repeating decimal a decimal with one or more digits repeating without end; A bar over the digits indicates the digits that repeat.	0.333... is written as $0.\overline{3}$. 0.48777... is written as $0.48\overline{7}$. 2.676767... is written as $2.\overline{67}$. 5.123123123... is written as $5.\overline{123}$.

UNDERSTANDING THE MAIN IDEAS

To write a fraction as a decimal, you can always divide the numerator by the denominator. You will need to add zeros to the end of the numerator in order to complete the division. If the decimal terminates, you will eventually get a remainder of 0.

Example 1

Write $\dfrac{5}{8}$ as a decimal.

Solution

Step 1: Rewrite the fraction as division. Use the denominator as the divisor. Use the numerator as the dividend. Add one zero.

$$8\overline{)5.0}$$

Step 2: Divide. Add additional zeros until there is a remainder of zero and the decimal ends.

$$\begin{array}{r} 0.625 \\ 8\overline{)5.000} \\ -\,4\,8 \\ \hline 20 \\ -\,16 \\ \hline 40 \\ -\,40 \\ \hline 0 \end{array}$$

$\dfrac{5}{8}$ can be written as 0.625.

If you notice that the denominator of a fraction is a factor of a power of ten, it is often easier to write an equivalent fraction with a denominator of a power of ten, and then convert the resulting fraction to a decimal.

Example 2

Write $\dfrac{2}{5}$ as a decimal.

Solution

Step 1: Because the denominator is a factor of 10, rewrite the fraction with a denominator of ten by multiplying the numerator and denominator by 2.

$$\frac{2}{5} \cdot \frac{2}{2} = \frac{4}{10}$$

Step 2: Convert the resulting fraction to a decimal.

$$\frac{4}{10} = 0.4$$

$\dfrac{2}{5}$ can be written as 0.4. Check by using long division to divide 2 by 5.

Write each fraction as a decimal.

1. $\dfrac{1}{5}$ 2. $\dfrac{3}{4}$ 3. $\dfrac{3}{8}$ 4. $\dfrac{3}{10}$ 5. $\dfrac{13}{20}$

6. $\dfrac{4}{5}$ 7. $\dfrac{7}{8}$ 8. $\dfrac{19}{20}$ 9. $\dfrac{7}{10}$ 10. $\dfrac{11}{16}$

11. You have learned how to convert a fraction to a decimal. Describe how you would convert the decimal 0.6 to a fraction.

Sometimes when you divide the numerator of a fraction by its denominator, you never get a zero remainder. This results in a decimal that never ends. Part of such a decimal may form a repeating pattern. The repeating portion may be one or more digits, depending on the fraction.

Example 3

Write $\dfrac{5}{11}$ as a decimal.

■ Solution ■

Step 1: Rewrite the fraction as division.

Step 2: Divide. Add additional zeros until a pattern is evident.

$$
\begin{array}{r}
0.4545\ldots \\
11\overline{)5.0000} \\
-4\,4 \\
\hline
60 \\
-55 \\
\hline
50 \\
-44 \\
\hline
60 \\
-55 \\
\hline
5
\end{array}
$$

Notice that the remainder is 6 (60) after the first division, 5 (50) after the second division, then 6 (60), then 5.

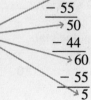

You can see a pattern in the remainders that will continue.

$\dfrac{5}{11}$ can be written as the repeating decimal $0.\overline{45}$.

Write each fraction as a decimal.

12. $\dfrac{1}{3}$ 13. $\dfrac{1}{6}$ 14. $\dfrac{1}{9}$ 15. $\dfrac{4}{33}$ 16. $\dfrac{6}{11}$

17. Explain the difference between the decimals 0.53333 and $0.5\overline{3}$.

Improper fractions and mixed numbers also can be written as decimals.

Example 4

Write each improper fraction or mixed number as a decimal.

a. $\dfrac{14}{3}$ **b.** $3\dfrac{6}{25}$

■ Solution ■

a. Step 1: Rewrite the fraction as division.

$$3\overline{)14}$$

Step 2: Divide. Add additional zeros. until the decimal ends or a pattern is evident.

$$
\begin{array}{r}
4.66... \\
3\overline{)14.00} \\
-12 \\
\hline
2\,0 \\
-1\,8 \\
\hline
2\,0 \\
-1\,8 \\
\hline
2
\end{array}
$$

$\dfrac{14}{3}$ can be written as $4.\overline{6}$.

b. Step 1: Since 25 is a factor of 100 rewrite $\dfrac{6}{25}$ with a denominator of 100 by multiplying the numerator and denominator by 4.

$$3\dfrac{6}{25} = 3\dfrac{6 \cdot 4}{25 \cdot 4} = 3\dfrac{24}{100}$$

Step 2: Convert the resulting fraction to a decimal.

$$3\dfrac{24}{100} = 3.24$$

$3\dfrac{6}{25}$ can be written as 3.24.

Write each improper fraction as a decimal.

18. $\dfrac{19}{5}$ **19.** $\dfrac{11}{8}$ **20.** $\dfrac{5}{3}$ **21.** $\dfrac{46}{11}$

Write each mixed number as a decimal.

22. $2\dfrac{4}{5}$ **23.** $5\dfrac{3}{8}$ **24.** $1\dfrac{4}{9}$ **25.** $9\dfrac{10}{11}$

. . . .

Spiral Review

26. Write $\dfrac{16}{36}$ in simplest form. **27.** Estimate the quotient $102 \div 21$.

Topic 3 **1** *Practice*

Write each fraction as a decimal.

1. $\dfrac{2}{5}$
2. $\dfrac{3}{5}$
3. $\dfrac{1}{4}$
4. $\dfrac{3}{8}$
5. $\dfrac{5}{8}$

6. $\dfrac{1}{10}$
7. $\dfrac{3}{10}$
8. $\dfrac{1}{20}$
9. $\dfrac{7}{20}$
10. $\dfrac{17}{20}$

11. $\dfrac{3}{16}$
12. $\dfrac{5}{16}$
13. $\dfrac{7}{16}$
14. $\dfrac{9}{16}$
15. $\dfrac{4}{25}$

16. $\dfrac{11}{25}$
17. $\dfrac{14}{25}$
18. $\dfrac{21}{25}$
19. $\dfrac{8}{30}$
20. $\dfrac{17}{30}$

21. $\dfrac{1}{3}$
22. $\dfrac{1}{6}$
23. $\dfrac{5}{6}$
24. $\dfrac{1}{9}$
25. $\dfrac{4}{9}$

26. $\dfrac{4}{15}$
27. $\dfrac{7}{15}$
28. $\dfrac{11}{15}$
29. $\dfrac{1}{12}$
30. $\dfrac{5}{12}$

Write each improper fraction or mixed number as a decimal.

31. $\dfrac{8}{5}$
32. $\dfrac{29}{3}$
33. $\dfrac{26}{8}$
34. $\dfrac{100}{3}$
35. $\dfrac{80}{11}$

36. $7\dfrac{2}{5}$
37. $1\dfrac{1}{11}$
38. $2\dfrac{2}{33}$
39. $3\dfrac{3}{4}$
40. $2\dfrac{2}{3}$

In Exercises 41–45, match each decimal with its fraction equivalent.

A $0.\overline{23}$ **B** $0.\overline{98}$ **C** $0.7\overline{12}$ **D** $0.\overline{78}$ **E** $0.\overline{57}$

41. $\dfrac{23}{99}$
42. $\dfrac{26}{33}$
43. $\dfrac{19}{33}$
44. $\dfrac{98}{99}$
45. $\dfrac{47}{66}$

46. List five fractions of your own that can be written as repeating decimals, and give the equivalent decimals.

47. List five fractions of your own that can be written as terminating decimals, and give the equivalent decimals.

Standardized Testing Warm-Ups

1. What is the decimal equivalent of the fraction $\frac{5}{8}$?

A 0.625   **B** 0.58   **C** 0.62   **D** 0.6

2. Which one of the following fractions has a decimal equivalent that does *not* repeat?

A $\frac{1}{3}$ **B** $\frac{2}{9}$ **C** $\frac{3}{4}$ **D** $\frac{2}{11}$

Homework Review Warm-Ups

Write each fraction as a decimal.

3. $\frac{4}{5}$ **4.** $\frac{11}{12}$ **5.** $\frac{3}{10}$ **6.** $\frac{4}{11}$

Topic 3 *Understanding Percent*

GOAL

Interpret percents as part of a hundred. Write ratios with denominators of 100 as percents.

A recent poll claims that 30 out of every 100 pet owners leave the television set on for their animals to watch. In other words, the ratio of pet owners with TV-watching pets to all pet owners is 30 to 100. A third way to say this is that 30% of the pet owners surveyed have TV-watching animals.

Terms to Know

Example / Illustration

Terms to Know	Example / Illustration
Ratio a quotient of two numbers that have the same unit of measure	The ratio of owners of TV-watching pets to all pet owners is $\dfrac{30}{100}$. The fraction bar represents division. The numerator and denominator are both numbers of pet owners, so the units are the same.
Percent a special ratio comparing a number to 100; "Percent" means "per hundred." The symbol % is used to show percent.	The poll also claims that 24 out of 100 pet owners celebrate their pets' birthdays. As a ratio, this is $\dfrac{24}{100}$. As a percent, this is 24%.

UNDERSTANDING THE MAIN IDEAS

Percents are all around you. Your tests, assessments, or report card grades may be measured with percents. Businesses measure growth and profits in percents. Sale prices at the store are expressed in "percent off" the regular price. Just remember that for any ratio with a denominator of 100, the percent is the numerator followed by the percent sign.

Example 1

What percent of the tile design below is shaded?

Solution

Step 1: Write a ratio comparing the number of shaded tiles to the total number of tiles.

$$\dfrac{28}{100} \begin{array}{l} \leftarrow \text{shaded tiles} \\ \leftarrow \text{tiles in all} \end{array}$$

Step 2: Use the ratio to write a percent.

$$\dfrac{28}{100} = 28\%$$

Of the 100 tiles, 28% are shaded.

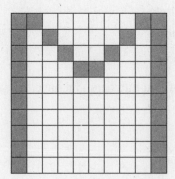

What percent of each design is shaded? What percent is unshaded?

1.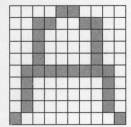

2.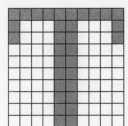

3.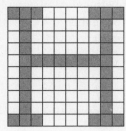

4. In Exercises 1–3, what did you find out about the percent that is shaded and the percent that is unshaded?

Write each ratio as a percent.

5. $\dfrac{56}{100}$ **6.** $\dfrac{87}{100}$ **7.** $\dfrac{19}{100}$ **8.** $\dfrac{8}{100}$

....
Spiral Review

9. Patti uses 3.75 yards of fabric for a cape. She has enough fabric for 2.5 capes. How much fabric does Patti have?

10. Estimate and calculate the quotient $34.89 \div 3$.

What percent of each design is shaded? What percent is unshaded?

1.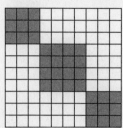

2.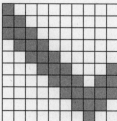

3.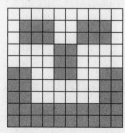

4.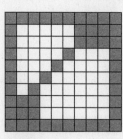

5.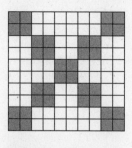

6.

Write each ratio as a percent.

7. $\dfrac{34}{100}$

8. $\dfrac{41}{100}$

9. $\dfrac{12}{100}$

10. $\dfrac{1}{100}$

11. $\dfrac{15}{100}$

12. $\dfrac{83}{100}$

13. $\dfrac{90}{100}$

14. $\dfrac{42}{100}$

Write each percent as a ratio with a denominator of 100.

15. 92%

16. 79%

17. 5%

18. 100%

For Exercises 19–21, use the bar graph. It shows survey results about how 100 people prefer to wash their pets.

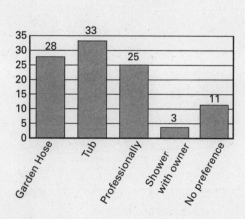

19. Write a ratio for each method of washing pets.

20. Write a percent for each method of washing pets.

21. Add the amounts shown in the table. Express the total as a percent. How can you explain your results?

Topic 3 **Warm-ups**

Standardized Testing Warm-Ups

1. Which of the following can *not* be expressed as a ratio?

   A 9 doctors out of 10 doctors

   B 275 calories from fat compared to a total intake of 1000 calories

   C 2 cups of flour for every 40 cookies

   D one person out of one million people

2. Express 85 points out of 100 points as a percent.

   A 0.85%   **B** 85%   **C** 8.5%   **D** $\frac{85}{100}$

Homework Review Warm-Ups

What percent of each design is shaded? What percent is unshaded?

3.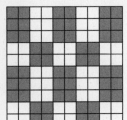
4.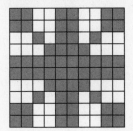
5.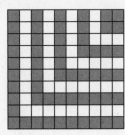

Topic 3

PRE-COURSE REVIEW LESSON 3

Converting between Decimals and Percents

GOAL

Write decimals as percents. Write percents as decimals.

Recall from the previous lesson the poll that revealed that 30 out of 100 pet owners leave the television set on for their animals. The ratio $\frac{30}{100}$ is 30%, and is also 0.30. So, 30% and 0.30 name the same quantity.

UNDERSTANDING THE MAIN IDEAS

To write a decimal as a percent, all you need to do is move the decimal point two places to the right and add a percent sign.

Example 1

One survey showed that about 2 out of 10 people know whose face is on the $10 bill. What percent of the people is this?

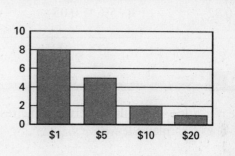

Solution

Step 1: Write the ratio as a decimal.

The ratio 2 out of 10 is $\frac{2}{10}$, or 0.2.   0.2

Step 2: Move the decimal point two places to the right. Add zeros as placeholders if necessary.   020.

Step 3: Add a percent sign.   20%

About 20% of the people know which person's face is on the $10 bill.

Use the bar graph in Example 1 to write a decimal and a percent showing how many people know whose face appears on each U.S. bill.

1. $1 bill   2. $5 bill   3. $20 bill

4. Suppose that only 0.08 of the people surveyed know whose face is on a $100 bill (Benjamin Franklin). Write the decimal 0.08 as a percent.

To write a percent as a decimal, take away the percent sign and move the decimal point two places to the left.

Example 2

Write each percent as a decimal.

  a. 32%   **b.** 5%   **c.** 170%

Solution

Step 1: Write the number without the percent sign.   **a.** 32   **b.** 5   **c.** 170

Step 2: Move the decimal point two places to the left.   .32   .05   1.70
         Add zeros as placeholders if necessary.

  a. 32% = 0.32   **b.** 5% = 0.05   **c.** 170% = 1.7

Example 3

Charmaine leaves a 15% tip with her server at the restaurant. For every dollar, how much money does Charmaine leave?

Solution

Step 1: Write 15% as a decimal.   15% = 0.15

Step 2: Convert the decimal to cents.   0.15 = $.15

Charmaine leaves $.15 for every dollar she spends at the restaurant.

Write each percent as a decimal.

  5. 95%   **6.** 87%   **7.** 71%   **8.** 50%   **9.** 125% **10.** 7%

Spiral Review

Write each ratio as a percent.

  11. $\dfrac{15}{100}$ **12.** $\dfrac{23}{100}$ **13.** $\dfrac{70}{100}$ **14.** $\dfrac{7}{100}$

Topic 3 **3** *Practice*

Write each decimal as a percent.

1. 0.85   **2.** 0.43   **3.** 0.17   **4.** 0.25   **5.** 0.79

6. 0.4   **7.** 0.06   **8.** 1.75   **9.** 1.01   **10.** 3.1

What percent of one dollar is each amount?

11. $.05   **12.** $.49   **13.** $.31   **14.** $.20   **15.** $1.80

Write each percent as a decimal.

16. 70%   **17.** 10%   **18.** 2%   **19.** 98%   **20.** 30%

21. 45%   **22.** 15%   **23.** 6%   **24.** 219%   **25.** 128%

Write a money amount for each percent of a dollar.

26. 50%   **27.** 4%   **28.** 98%   **29.** 30%   **30.** 100%

For Exercises 31–34, use the bar graph. It shows the music preferences of 100 preteens and teens between 9 and 13 years old.

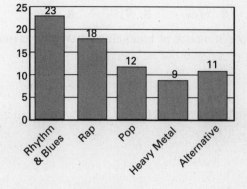

31. Write a decimal and a percent equivalent for each music type.

32. Which types of music received a popularity vote of more than 15%?

33. What percent of preteens and teens voted for one of the music choices shown?

34. What percent of preteens and teens did not have a preference shown in this survey?

Standardized Testing Warm-Ups

1. In which set of numbers are all the values *not* equivalent?

A $\frac{40}{100}$, 0.4, 40%

B $\frac{7}{10}$, 0.7, 70%

C $\frac{3}{10}$, 0.03, 3%

D $\frac{86}{100}$, 0.86, 86%

2. You have a quarter, two dimes, 3 nickels, and 4 pennies. What percent of a dollar is their value?

A 0.59%　　　B 0.64%　　　C 59%　　　D 64%

Homework Review Warm-Ups

Write each percent as a decimal.

3. 45%　　**4.** 80%　　**5.** 91%　　**6.** 19%　　**7.** 9%　　**8.** 115%

9. Evan bought a pack of baseball cards with two quarters and a dime. What percent of a dollar did he spend?

Topic 3

Converting between Fractions and Percents

GOAL

Write fractions as percents. Write percents as fractions.

If you toss a penny 100 times, you can expect it to land on "heads" about half of those times. Therefore, about $\frac{1}{2}$, or 50% of the time, the penny will land heads up.

UNDERSTANDING THE MAIN IDEAS

When you write a percent as a fraction with a denominator of 100, the numerator and denominator may share factors other than 1. To write an equivalent fraction in simplest form, divide the numerator and denominator by their greatest common factor (GCF).

Example 1

More than half of the Americans who eat fast food use the drive-through window. The circle graph shows that 20% of the women surveyed say they use the drive-through window "occasionally." What fractional part of the women is this?

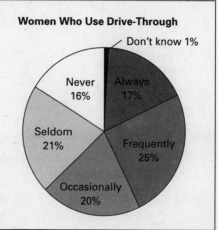

Women Who Use Drive-Through

Don't know 1%
Always 17%
Never 16%
Frequently 25%
Seldom 21%
Occasionally 20%

■ Solution ■

Step 1: Write the percent as a fraction with a denominator of 100.

$$20\% = \frac{20}{100}$$

Step 2: Divide the numerator and the denominator by their greatest common factor to find an equivalent fraction in simplest form.

$$\frac{20 \div 20}{100 \div 20} = \frac{1}{5} \quad \leftarrow \text{ The GCF of 20 and 100 is 20.}$$

One fifth of the women surveyed use the drive-through window occasionally.

Use the circle graph in Example 1 to write a fraction in simplest form for each answer category.

1. Always

2. Frequently

3. Seldom

4. Never

5. Don't know

6. Sum of all percents

To write a fraction with a denominator of 100 as a percent you need only to write the numerator followed by a percent sign. Sometimes, when the denominator is not 100, you can rewrite a fraction as an equivalent fraction with a denominator of 100.

Example 2

A store is having a $\frac{1}{4}$-off sale. By what percent will they reduce the cost of each item?

■ Solution ■

Step 1: Find a fraction with a denominator of 100 that is equivalent to $\frac{1}{4}$.

Because $100 \div 4 = 25$, multiply the numerator and denominator by 25.

$$\frac{1}{4} = \frac{1 \cdot 25}{4 \cdot 25} = \frac{25}{100}$$

Step 2: Express the fraction as a percent.
The cost of each item will be reduced by 25%.

$$\frac{25}{100} = 25\%$$

Write each fraction as a percent.

7. $\frac{3}{4}$

8. $\frac{1}{5}$

9. $\frac{3}{10}$

10. $\frac{13}{20}$

11. $\frac{8}{25}$

12. Two shirts are on sale: one shirt is $\frac{1}{4}$ off, and the other shirt is 30% off. If they have the same regular price, which shirt has the greater savings? Explain.

· · · · · · · · · · · · · · · · · · · ·
Spiral Review

Write each fraction as a decimal.

13. $\frac{1}{4}$

14. $\frac{5}{8}$

15. $\frac{5}{6}$

16. $\frac{19}{20}$

17. $\frac{7}{9}$

Topic 3 **4** *Practice*

Write each percent as a fraction in simplest form.

1. 50%   **2.** 35%   **3.** 15%   **4.** 20%   **5.** 6%

6. 18%   **7.** 90%   **8.** 40%   **9.** 12%   **10.** 45%

11. 13%   **12.** 80%   **13.** 75%   **14.** 64%   **15.** 1%

16. 2%   **17.** 21%   **18.** 68%   **19.** 65%   **20.** 44%

Write each fraction as a percent.

21. $\dfrac{1}{50}$ **22.** $\dfrac{1}{25}$ **23.** $\dfrac{1}{20}$ **24.** $\dfrac{3}{50}$ **25.** $\dfrac{1}{10}$

26. $\dfrac{3}{20}$ **27.** $\dfrac{7}{20}$ **28.** $\dfrac{1}{5}$ **29.** $\dfrac{1}{4}$ **30.** $\dfrac{7}{25}$

31. $\dfrac{17}{20}$ **32.** $\dfrac{12}{25}$ **33.** $\dfrac{9}{20}$ **34.** $\dfrac{23}{50}$ **35.** $\dfrac{51}{100}$

36. $\dfrac{3}{5}$ **37.** $\dfrac{3}{4}$ **38.** $\dfrac{81}{100}$ **39.** $\dfrac{43}{50}$ **40.** $\dfrac{9}{10}$

For Exercise 41–43, use the graph. It shows how Francesca uses her time each day.

41. Write a percent for each activity that is shown in Francesca's graph.

42. Does Francesca spend a greater amount of time visiting with friends or doing homework?

43. On which activity does Francesca spend less than 10% of her time?

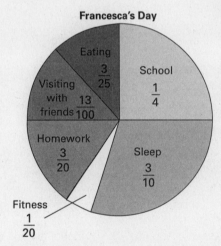

Francesca's Day

Eating $\dfrac{3}{25}$

School $\dfrac{1}{4}$

Visiting with friends $\dfrac{13}{100}$

Homework $\dfrac{3}{20}$

Sleep $\dfrac{3}{10}$

Fitness $\dfrac{1}{20}$

Topic 4   *Warm-ups*

Standardized Testing Warm-Ups

1. In which set of numbers are all the values *not* equivalent?

   A $0.6, \dfrac{3}{5}, \dfrac{60}{100}, 60\%$ **B** $0.7, \dfrac{7}{20}, \dfrac{70}{100}, 70\%$

   C $0.78, \dfrac{39}{50}, \dfrac{78}{100}, 78\%$ **D** $0.65, \dfrac{13}{20}, \dfrac{65}{100}, 65\%$

2. If 17 of the 25 students in your class prefer hot chocolate over hot cider, what percent prefer hot cider?

   A 68%   **B** 17%   **C** 0.68%   **D** 32%

Homework Review Warm-Ups

3. Write a fraction in simplest form equivalent to 85%.

4. Hua buys a shirt marked $\dfrac{1}{4}$ off. By what percent will the price be reduced?

Topic 4 LESSON 1 *Drawing and Measuring Angles*

GOAL

Measure angles using a protractor. Draw angles of a given measure.

Architects, builders, carpenters, and engineers all need to understand angles in order to do their work. Because they have tools to draw and measure angles, they can accurately communicate the angles among each other.

Terms to Know   *Example / Illustration*

Ray a part of a line that has one endpoint and extends in one direction without ending	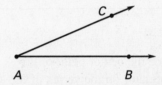 This is ray $\overrightarrow{AB}$. Its endpoint is A.
Angle a figure formed by two rays that have a common endpoint; The rays form the *sides* of the angle. The symbol for angle is $\angle$.	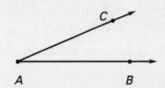 This is angle *CAB*, or $\angle CAB$. Other names are $\angle BAC$ and $\angle A$. Rays $\overrightarrow{AB}$ and $\overrightarrow{AC}$ form the sides of the angle.
Vertex the shared endpoint of the two rays of an angle	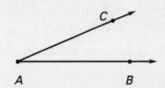 The vertex of $\angle CAB$ is point A.
Protractor a tool that you use to measure angles; Protractors measure angles in units called *degrees* (°).	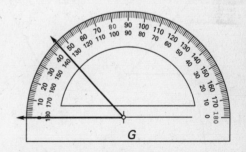 The protractor shows that the measure of $\angle G$ is 45 degrees, or 45°.

Understanding The Main Ideas

Most protractors have two scales. The scale starting at the left edge is read clockwise from 0° to 180°. The scale starting at the right edge is read counterclockwise from 0° to 180°.

Example 1

Find the measure of the angle shown by the hands of the clock.

■ Solution ■

Step 1: Place the center point of the protractor on the vertex of the angle.

Step 2: Line up the protractor's 0° line with one ray of the angle.

Step 3: Read the measure on the protractor where the other ray crosses it. Because you are using the 0° measure on the right, read the counterclockwise scale.

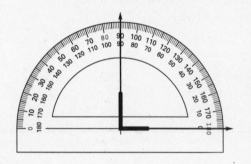

The measure of the angle formed by the clock hands is 90°.

Find the measure of each angle to the nearest 5°.

1.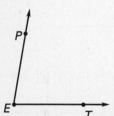

2.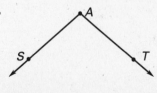

3.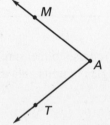

4.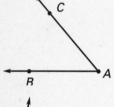

5.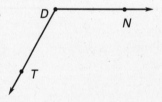

6.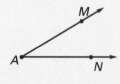

You can also use a protractor to draw an angle of a given measure.

Example 2

An architect designs a 5° wheelchair ramp at the entrance of a building. Draw a 5° angle, as might appear on her blueprint.

■ Solution ■

Step 1: Use the straight side of the protractor to draw a horizontal ray.

Step 2: Place the center point of the protractor on the endpoint of the ray, with the 0° mark along the ray. Mark a point at the edge of the protractor at a measure of 5°.

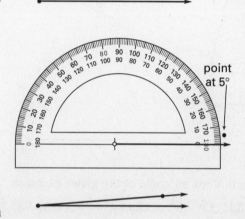

point at 5°

Step 3: Use the straight side of the protractor to draw a ray from the vertex through the new point.

Use a protractor to draw an angle of the given measure.

7. 50°   **8.** 105°   **9.** 145°   **10.** 35°   **11.** 90°

∙∙∙∙∙∙∙∙∙∙∙∙∙∙∙∙∙∙∙∙∙∙
Spiral Review

12. Estimate the product of 4.2 and 7.9. Then find the actual product.

13. Write $\frac{79}{3}$ as a mixed number.

Find the measure of each angle to the nearest 5°.

1.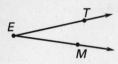

2.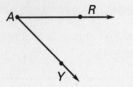

3.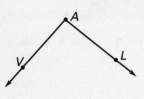

4.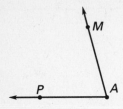

5.

6.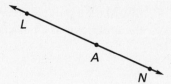

7.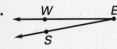

8.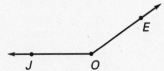

9.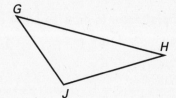

Use a protractor to draw an angle of the given measure.

10. 40°   **11.** 52°   **12.** 73°   **13.** 98°   **14.** 123°

Measure the angles in each triangle shown. Then find the sum of the measures of the angles of each triangle.

15.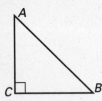

16.

17.

18. What can you conclude about the sum of the measures of the angles in a triangle?

19. Pat thinks the measure of the angle shown is 70°.
Chris thinks its measure is 110°. Who is right?
Tell why you think so.

Standardized Testing Warm-Ups

1. Which one of the following statements about the angle shown is true?

   A The sides of the angle are rays $\overrightarrow{BA}$ and $\overrightarrow{DC}$.

   B The vertices of the angle are A and C.

   C A name for the angle is $\angle CDB$.

   D The sides of the angle are segments $\overline{DA}$ and $\overline{DC}$.

2. Which one of the following statements is *not* true?

   A The point where the sides of an angle meet is called the vertex.

   B Rays form the two sides of an angle.

   C A ray has only one endpoint.

   D An angle always has only one name.

Homework Review Warm-Ups

Use a protractor to find the measure of each angle to the nearest 5°.

3.

4.
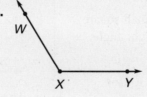

5.
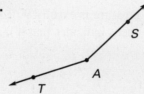

Topic 4   *Classifying Angles*

GOAL

Classify angles as acute, right, obtuse, or straight. Classify pairs of angles as complementary or supplementary. Identify congruent angles.

Angles are all around you—in the design of your classroom, in the way the parts of your chair or desk meet, in the bend of your elbow. You can classify these angles by their measures.

Terms to Know

Example / Illustration

Terms to Know	Example / Illustration
Acute angle an angle whose measure is between 0° and 90°	 70° 35° These are acute angles.
Right angle an angle whose measure is exactly 90°; A small square where an angle opens indicates that it is a right angle.	 These are right angles.
Obtuse angle an angle whose measure is greater than 90° and less than 180°	 105° 140° These are obtuse angles.
Straight angle an angle whose measure is exactly 180°	 180° This is a straight angle.

Terms to Know	Example / Illustration
Complementary angles two angles whose measures have a sum of exactly 90°	 $\angle ABC$ and $\angle CBD$ are complementary angles.
Supplementary angles two angles whose measures have a sum of exactly 180°	 $\angle EFG$ and $\angle GFH$ are supplementary angles.
Congruent angles angles with the same measure	 These angles are congruent.

UNDERSTANDING THE MAIN IDEAS

As you classify angles, you will learn to relate the appearance of an angle to its measure. Then you will become better able to estimate the measures of angles.

Example 1

Classify the angles shown
into the following categories:

Acute
Right
Obtuse
Straight

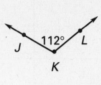

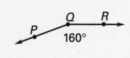

Solution

Use the definitions for each class of angle to sort the angles into appropriate
categories.

Acute	**Right**	**Obtuse**	**Straight**
(between 0° and 90°)	(exactly 90°)	(between 90° and 180°)	(exactly 180°)
∠ABC (54°)	∠GHI	∠DEF (94°)	∠VWX
∠MNO (27°)	∠STU	∠JKL (112°)	
		∠PQR (160°)	

**Estimate to classify each angle as acute, right, obtuse, or straight. Then use a
protractor to find the measurement to the nearest 5° and check your predictions.**

1.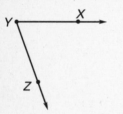

2.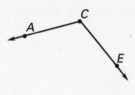

3.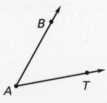

4.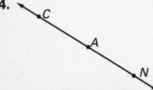

5.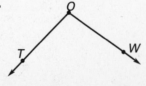

6.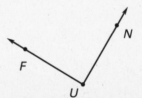

7. Use a straightedge to draw (a) an acute angle and (b) an obtuse angle. Then use a protractor to find the actual measure of each angle.

You can combine angles to form right angles or straight angles. Angle pairs whose combined measures equal 90° are *complementary*. Angle pairs whose combined measures equal 180° are *supplementary*.

Example 2

∠MAT and ∠HAT are complementary. Find the measure of ∠MAT.

∠DOT and ∠GOT are supplementary. Find the measure of ∠DOT.

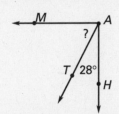

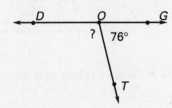

▪ Solution ▪

Step 1: The measures of complementary angles have a sum of 90°. To find the unknown angle measure, subtract the known angle measure from 90°.

The measures of supplementary angles have a sum of 180°. To find the unknown angle measure, subtract the known angle measure from 180°.

Step 2: 90° − 28° = 62°.

The measure of ∠MAT is 62°.

180° − 76° = 104°.

The measure of ∠DOT is 104°.

Each pair of angles is complementary or supplementary. Find the unknown angle measure.

8.
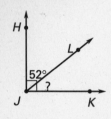

9.
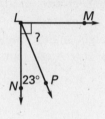

10.
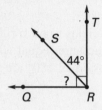

11.
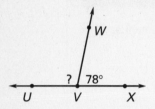

12.
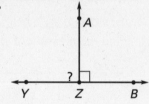

13.
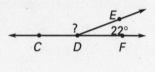

Classify each statement as *true* or *false*. Explain your answer.

14. All acute angles are congruent.

15. All right angles are congruent.

16. All obtuse angles are congruent.

17. All straight angles are congruent.

······················
Spiral Review

Use compatible numbers to estimate each quotient. Then divide.

18. $39.52 \div 8$ **19.** $821.4 \div 9.25$ **20.** $7.777 \div 2.02$

21. Write $\dfrac{1}{9}$ as a decimal.

Use estimation to classify each angle as acute, right, obtuse, or straight.
Then use a protractor to find the measurement to the nearest 5°.

1.

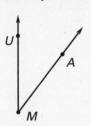

2.

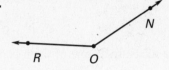

3.

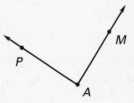

4.

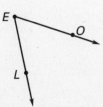

5.

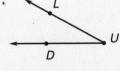

6.

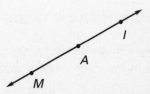

7. List a pair of supplementary angles from the angles shown.

8. List a pair of complementary angles from the angles shown.

Give the measure of an angle that is (a) congruent, (b) complementary,
and (c) supplementary to each given angle.

9.

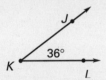

10.

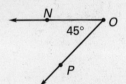

11.

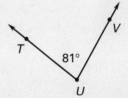

Use the figure at the right. List the following angles or pairs of angles.

12. seven acute angles

13. five obtuse angles

14. four right angles

15. two straight angles

16. three pairs of complementary angles

17. three pairs of supplementary angles

18. three pairs of congruent angles

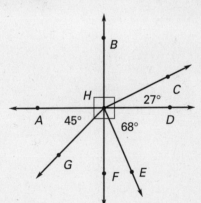

Standardized Testing Warm-Ups

1. The measure of an angle equals one fourth of a straight angle. What is its measure?

   A 90° **B** 60° **C** 45° **D** 22.5°

2. Two angles are complementary. If the measure of one of them is 33°, what is the measure of the other?

   A 33° **B** 57° **C** 66° **D** 147°

Homework Review Warm-Ups

Classify each angle as acute, right, or obtuse. Then find the measure of the angle that is the given angle's supplement.

3.

56°

4.

90°

5.

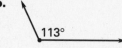

113°

Topic 4 LESSON 3 *Identifying Polygons*

GOAL

Identify the special features of polygons. Identify and sketch polygons by description.

Tennis courts, soccer fields, and baseball diamonds are just a few of the four-sided sports playing areas. Quadrilaterals may all have four sides, but they are not all alike. Triangles also are not all alike. In this lesson, you'll learn about some of the special polygons and their characteristics.

Terms to Know	Example / Illustration
Polygon a closed figure, in a plane, formed by line segments joined only at their endpoints	
Quadrilateral a polygon with four sides	
Triangle a polygon with three sides	

Parallel lines
    lines in the same plane that never meet.
    The arrowheads (▸) show that the lines are parallel.
	Pairs of parallel lines

UNDERSTANDING THE MAIN IDEAS

Triangles can be identified using angles or side lengths. An **acute triangle** has three acute angles. A **right triangle** has one right angle. An **obtuse triangle** has one obtuse angle. An **equilateral triangle** has all three sides the same length. An **isosceles triangle** has at least two sides of the same length. A **scalene triangle** has no sides of the same length.

Example 1

Give the most specific name for each triangle.

a.   b.  c.

■ Solution ■

a. All three sides have the same length, and all three angles are acute. This is an acute equilateral triangle.

b. All three sides have different lengths. One angle is a right angle. This is a scalene right triangle.

c. Two sides are equal and one angle is obtuse. This is an obtuse isosceles triangle.

Give the most specific name for each triangle.

1.   2. 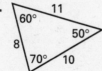 3.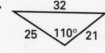

Decide if there can be a triangle that matches the description. Explain.

4. equilateral and all equal angles

5. a right acute triangle

6. an isosceles equilateral triangle

One way to identify quadrilaterals is to look for parallel sides. A **parallelogram** is a quadrilateral that has two pairs of parallel sides. A **trapezoid** has exactly one pair of parallel sides.

Example 2

Which of the quadrilaterals below are parallelograms? Which are trapezoids?

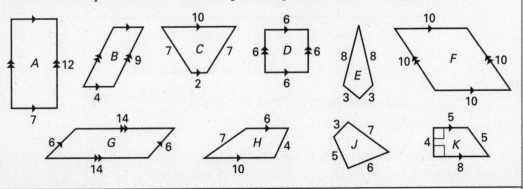

■ Solution ■

Look for parallel sides.

Quadrilaterals *A*, *B*, *D*, *F*, and *G* have two pairs of parallel sides, so quadrilaterals *A*, *B*, *D*, *F*, and *G* are parallelograms.

Quadrilaterals *C*, *H*, and *K* have one pair of parallel sides, so quadrilaterals *C*, *H*, and *K* are trapezoids.

Parallelograms *A* and *D* from Example 2 are shown again at the right. *Rectangles* and *squares* are both special types of parallelograms. A **rectangle** is a parallelogram with four right angles. A **square** is a special rectangle, one with all of its sides the same length.

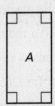

Tell whether or not each quadrilateral is a special quadrilateral. If it is not, tell why not. If it is a special quadrilateral, identify it. Be as specific as possible.

7.   8.   9.   10.

Another type of special parallelogram is called a *rhombus*. A **rhombus** is a parallelogram whose four sides are all the same length.

Example 3

Which of the quadrilaterals in Example 2 are rhombuses?

■ Solution ■

In Example 2, you found that quadrilaterals A, B, D, F, and G are parallelograms. To be a rhombus, all four sides must also be the same length. All four sides of parallelograms D and F are the same length, so D and F are rhombuses.

You saw in Example 2 that a square is a special kind of parallelogram. In Example 3, you see that a square is also a special type of rhombus. A square is a rhombus with four right angles.

Tell whether or not each quadrilateral is a rhombus. If it is not, tell why not. If it is a special rhombus, identify it.

11.

12.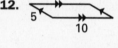

13.

14.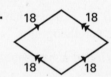

Answer each question.

15. How are a square and a rectangle different?

16. How are a parallelogram and a rhombus different?

17. How are a square and a rhombus alike?

18. How is a trapezoid different from the other special quadrilaterals?

19. Write as many different quadrilateral names as you can for each figure.

a.

b.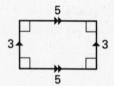

c.

·····················
Spiral Review

Write each percent as a fraction or mixed number in simplest form.

20. 35%   **21.** 2%   **22.** 98%   **23.** 250%

Topic 4   3   *Practice*

Classify each statement as *true* or *false*.

1. Every rectangle is a parallelogram.

2. Every parallelogram is a square.

3. Every square is a rhombus.

4. Every rhombus is a parallelogram.

5. Every trapezoid is a rectangle.

6. Some trapezoids are rectangles.

7. Some rhombuses are squares.

8. Some parallelograms are trapezoids.

9. Some rectangles are rhombuses.

Solve each riddle.

10. I am a triangle with two sides of the same length and one right angle. What am I?

11. I am a triangle with three 60° angles and all sides the same length. What am I?

12. I am a quadrilateral with exactly one pair of parallel sides. What am I?

13. I am any quadrilateral with two pairs of parallel sides. What am I?

Sketch each figure.

14. obtuse scalene triangle

15. acute isosceles triangle

Sketch each figure. Make your figure fit as few other special quadrilateral names as possible.

16. rectangle

17. parallelogram

18. trapezoid

19. rhombus

20. Evan said, "Every rectangle is a square." Joan said, "No, you're wrong. Every square is a rectangle." Who is right? Explain your answer.

21. What is the fewest number of figures you would have to draw to display a square, a rhombus, a rectangle, a parallelogram, and a trapezoid? What are the figures?

Standardized Testing Warm-Ups

1. Which of the following can *never* be a rhombus?

   A parallelogram   **B** square   **C** rectangle   **D** trapezoid

2. Which of the following is *not* a polygon?

   A trapezoid   **B** triangle   **C** circle   **D** rhombus

Homework Review Warm-Ups

3. How are a rhombus and a square alike? How are they different?

4. What is the name for a quadrilateral that has one and only one pair of parallel sides? Do any of the sides of this quadrilateral have to have the same length?

Topic 4 LESSON 4 *Similarity in Polygons*

PRE-COURSE REVIEW

GOAL

Decide if polygons are similar. Use scale factors to find the dimensions of similar figures.

The geoboard shows two triangles of different sizes. Each triangle has a right angle at one corner of the geoboard. Each triangle has two congruent sides. The triangles are *similar* figures.

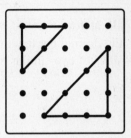

Terms to Know	Example / Illustration
Similar figures geometric figures that have the same shape; Similar figures always have the same angles, but may not be the same size.	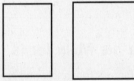 These figures are similar. They have the same shape, although they are oriented differently.
Corresponding sides or angles matched sides or angles of two similar polygons (Remember that a *polygon* is a closed plane figure made of line segments connected only at their endpoints.)	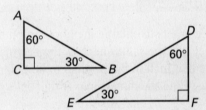 Corresponding sides of triangles *ABC* and *DEF* are $\overline{AB}$ and $\overline{DE}$; $\overline{BC}$ and $\overline{EF}$; and $\overline{AC}$ and $\overline{DF}$. Corresponding angles are $\angle A$ and $\angle D$; $\angle B$ and $\angle E$; and $\angle C$ and $\angle F$.
Proportional having the same ratio; The corresponding sides of similar figures are *proportional* because they have the same ratio.	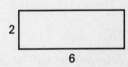 The ratio of the heights of the rectangles is 1 to 2, or $\frac{1}{2}$. The ratio of the widths is $\frac{3}{6}$, which is also equivalent to $\frac{1}{2}$.

Terms to Know	**Example / Illustration**
Scale factor the ratio of the lengths of corresponding sides of two similar figures	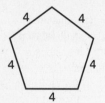 The ratio of a side of the larger pentagon to a side of the smaller one is 4 to 2. The scale factor is $\frac{4}{2}$, or 2.

UNDERSTANDING THE MAIN IDEAS

You can use scale factors to sketch one figure so that it is similar to another. For example, engineers and architects use scale factors to make models or blueprints. You also use scale factors when you need to reduce or enlarge anything.

Example 1

Aimee wants to enlarge the photograph at the right so that it is the same shape as the original. She wants one inch in the original to be enlarged to four inches. Find the dimensions of the enlargement.

3 in.

5 in.

■ Solution ■

The ratio of a side of the enlargement to the corresponding side of the original is 4 to 1, or $\frac{4}{1}$. The scale factor is 4. Multiply the height and width of the original by the scale factor.

New width: 5 in. × 4 = 20 in.   New height: 3 in. × 4 = 12 in.

The enlargement will be 20 inches wide and 12 inches high.

Write the dimensions of the enlargement if the photo at the right is enlarged by the given scale factor.

1. 2   **2.** 2.5   **3.** 6   **4.** 7.5   **5.** 10

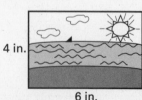

4 in.

6 in.

To check figures for similarity, see if corresponding angles have equal measures and the ratios of the lengths of corresponding sides are all equivalent.

Example 2

A company makes pocket-size and display-size calendars. For the pictures to fit properly, the calendars must be similar rectangles. If the small calendar is 2 in. by 3 in. and the large calendar is 12 in. by 18 in., check that the calendars are similar.

■ Solution ■

Step 1: The angles of the rectangles are all right angles, with measures of 90°.

Step 2: Write ratios comparing the lengths and widths of the calendars.

Pocket-size: $\dfrac{length}{width} = \dfrac{3 \text{ in.}}{2 \text{ in.}} = \dfrac{3}{2}$ Display-size: $\dfrac{length}{width} = \dfrac{18 \text{ in.}}{12 \text{ in.}} = \dfrac{18 \div 6}{12 \div 6} = \dfrac{3}{2}$

Because the corresponding angles have equal measures and the ratios of corresponding sides are equivalent, the calendars are similar.

If the figures are similar, give the ratio of a side of the smaller figure to the corresponding side of the larger figure. If they are not, explain why.

6.

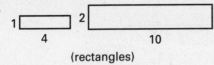

(rectangles)

7.

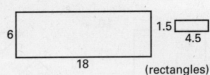

(rectangles)

8.

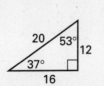 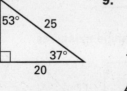

9.

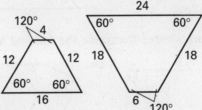

10. Are all squares similar to each other? Give a reason for your answer.

⋯⋯⋯⋯⋯⋯⋯
Spiral Review

Find each sum or difference.

11. $\dfrac{5}{6} + \dfrac{2}{3}$ **12.** $\dfrac{3}{5} + \dfrac{3}{10}$ **13.** $1\dfrac{2}{7} - \dfrac{4}{7}$ **14.** $\dfrac{5}{16} - \dfrac{1}{4}$

An art print measures 1.5 ft by 2 ft. Give the dimensions of the print if it is enlarged by the given scale factor.

1. 1.5   **2.** 2   **3.** 2.5   **4.** 4   **5.** 5   **6.** 7.5

You scan a 12 in. by 16 in. photograph into your computer. Give the dimensions of the computer image if the photograph is reduced by the given scale factor.

7. 0.75   **8.** 0.6   **9.** $\frac{1}{2}$ **10.** 0.35   **11.** $\frac{1}{4}$ **12.** 0.2

If the figures are similar, give the ratio of a side of the smaller figure to the corresponding side of the larger figure. If they are not, explain why.

13.

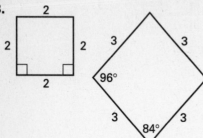

14.

 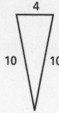

15.

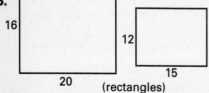

16.

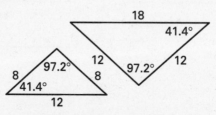

The figures in each pair are similar. Complete the missing angle measures.

17.

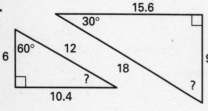

18.

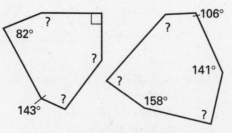

Topic 5   *Warm-ups*

Standardized Testing Warm-Ups

1. Which statement about similar polygons is false?

   A Corresponding angles of similar polygons always have the same measure.

   B Corresponding sides of similar polygons are always proportional.

   C Corresponding sides are never equal.

   D Similar polygons always have the same shape.

2. The scale factor of an actual car to a model you are building is $\frac{25}{2}$. If the width of the model is 0.15 m, what is the width of the actual car?

   A 3.75 m   **B** 2.0 m   **C** 1.875 m   **D** not enough information

Homework Review Warm-Ups

Triangles *ABC* and *DEF* are similar.

3. Give the measure of each angle in Triangle *DEF*.

4. What must be true about the sides of these triangles?

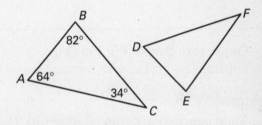

Topic 5 — LESSON 1 — *Conversions in the Customary System*

PRE-COURSE REVIEW
LESSON
1

GOAL

Convert customary system units for length, distance, weight, and capacity.

A soup recipe calls for 2 pounds of tomatoes. Tomatoes are sold in 8-ounce cans. To know how many cans of tomatoes to buy, you need to know how to convert between ounces and pounds.

Terms to Know	Example / Illustration
Inch (in.), Foot (ft), Yard (yd), Mile (mi) customary system units for measuring length or distance	12 in. = 1 ft 3 ft = 1 yd 1760 yd = 1 mi Also, 36 in. = 1 yd 5280 ft = 1 mi
Ounce (oz), Pound (lb), Ton (T) customary system units for measuring weight	16 oz = 1 lb 2000 lb = 1 T
Fluid ounce (fl oz), Cup (c), Pint (pt), Quart (qt), Gallon (gal) customary system units for measuring capacity	8 fl oz = 1 c 2 c = 1 pt 2 pt = 1 qt 4 qt = 1 gal

UNDERSTANDING THE MAIN IDEAS

Using your number sense will help you convert between customary system units. To convert from a smaller unit, like inches, to a larger unit, like feet, divide. This makes sense because it takes fewer larger units than smaller units to describe a quantity. For example, it might take 60 *inches* to describe Laeticia's height, but it takes only 5 *feet*.

Example 1

The drama club is making 16 costumes for a school play. Each costume takes $2\frac{1}{2}$ feet of ribbon. The ribbon is sold in yards. At least how many yards of ribbon does the drama club need to buy?

■ Solution ■

Step 1: To find the total amount of ribbon needed in feet for all the costumes, multiply.

$$16 \times 2\frac{1}{2} \text{ ft} = 40 \text{ ft}$$

Step 2: You are converting from a smaller unit, feet, to a larger unit, yards, so *divide*.

$3 \text{ ft} = 1 \text{ yd}$ Divide by 3 to convert from feet to yards.

$$40 \text{ ft} \rightarrow 40 \div 3 = 13\frac{1}{3} \rightarrow 13\frac{1}{3} \text{ yd}$$

The drama club needs to buy at least $13\frac{1}{3}$ yards of ribbon.

Complete.

1. 18 ft = __?__ yd   **2.** 18 in. = __?__ ft   **3.** 108 in. = __?__ yd

4. 16 fl oz = __?__ c   **5.** 10 c = __?__ pt   **6.** 6 pt = __?__ qt

7. 20 qt = __?__ gal   **8.** 32 oz = __?__ lb   **9.** 4000 lb = __?__ T

To convert from a larger unit, like tons, to a smaller unit, like pounds, multiply. This makes sense because it takes more smaller units than larger units to describe a quantity. For example, a bull might weigh 1 *ton*, but it weighs 2000 *pounds*.

You may need to multiply or divide more than once to convert between customary system measurements.

Example 2

Kahlil bought four gallons of lemonade to serve at the business club meeting. How many one-cup servings can he serve if all of the lemonade is used?

■ Solution ■

You aren't given an equivalence between cups and gallons. You will have to perform more than one conversion.

Step 1: Find the number of cups in each gallon. Since you are converting from a larger unit, gallons, to a smaller unit, cups, you will need to *multiply*.

$$1 \text{ gallon} = 4 \text{ quarts}$$

$$4 \text{ quarts} \rightarrow 4 \times 2 = 8 \rightarrow 8 \text{ pints}$$

$$8 \text{ pints} \rightarrow 8 \times 2 = 16 \rightarrow 16 \text{ cups}$$

So, 1 gallon = 16 cups.

Step 2: To find the number of cups of lemonade in 4 gallons, multiply the number of cups in 1 gallon by 4.

$$4 \text{ gallons} \rightarrow 4 \times 16 = 64 \rightarrow 64 \text{ cups}$$

Four gallons of lemonade will make 64 one-cup servings.

Determine whether there will be more or fewer of the new units after the conversion. Then find the equivalent measure.

10. $2 \text{ c} = \underline{\ ?\ } \text{ fl oz}$

11. $3 \text{ pt} = \underline{\ ?\ } \text{ c}$

12. $3 \text{ T} = \underline{\ ?\ } \text{ lb}$

13. $10 \text{ lb} = \underline{\ ?\ } \text{ oz}$

14. $12 \text{ oz} = \underline{\ ?\ } \text{ lb}$

15. $1000 \text{ lb} = \underline{\ ?\ } \text{ T}$

16. $1 \text{ gal} = \underline{\ ?\ } \text{ pt}$

17. $8 \text{ qt} = \underline{\ ?\ } \text{ gal}$

18. $2 \text{ qt} = \underline{\ ?\ } \text{ pt}$

19. Hannah ran a 440-yard dash in $1\frac{1}{2}$ minutes.

 a. What fractional part of a mile did Hannah run?

 b. If Hannah could run a mile at the same speed she ran the dash, how long would it take her to run the mile?

20. Paulo needs 3 pounds of mushrooms for a sauce recipe. Mushrooms are sold in 4-ounce cans. What does Paul need to know in order to buy the mushrooms? How many cans of mushrooms does Paul need to make the recipe?

· · · · · · · · · · · · · · · · · · · ·
Spiral Review

Write each percent as a decimal.

21. 20% **22.** 101% **23.** 2% **24.** 257%

Complete.

1. 6 yd = __?__ ft

2. 2 yd = __?__ in.

3. 10 mi = __?__ yd

4. 24 ft = __?__ yd

5. 15,840 ft = __?__ mi

6. 100 yd = __?__ ft

7. 24 yd = __?__ ft

8. 27 ft = __?__ yd

9. 8 yd = __?__ in.

10. $\frac{1}{2}$ gal = __?__ c

11. 3 qt = __?__ c

12. 16 fl oz = __?__ pt

13. 32 c = __?__ qt

14. $\frac{1}{2}$ pt = __?__ fl oz

15. 16 fl oz = __?__ c

16. 10 c = __?__ pt

17. 8 pt = __?__ qt

18. 1 qt = __?__ gal

19. 3 lb = __?__ oz

20. 2.5 T = __?__ lb

21. 1.5 lb = __?__ oz

22. $\frac{1}{2}$ lb = __?__ oz

23. $\frac{1}{2}$ T = __?__ lb

24. 160 oz = __?__ lb

25. 1 mi = __?__ in.

26. 1 T = __?__ oz

27. 1344 oz = __?__ gal

Solve.

28. Amber and Jason have put 6 qt of water into their fish tank. It holds 4 gal. How many more quarts of water do they need to put into the tank to fill it?

29. Rita had a piece of wood $3\frac{1}{2}$ feet long. She sawed off a piece 9 in. long to make a sign. How long was the piece of wood that was left?

30. Francis combined 24 oz of dry cereal, 8 oz of nuts, $\frac{3}{4}$ lb of pretzels, and $\frac{1}{4}$ lb of sesame sticks to make a trail mix. What was the total weight of the mix?

31. Grace ran $\frac{3}{4}$ mile, Hank ran 1000 yd, and Shawna ran 2640 ft. Order their distances from least to greatest.

Standardized Testing Warm-Ups

1. Which quantity is the greatest?

   A 5 pt   **B** 75 fl oz   **C** 2 qt   **D** 7 c

2. How many yards are equivalent to $4\frac{1}{2}$ miles?

   A 7040 yd   **B** 4500 yd   **C** 23,760 yd   **D** 7920 yd

Homework Review Warm-Ups

3. Jerome is 72 inches tall. How tall is Jerome in feet?

4. A 3-gallon jug is filled with 5 quarts of liquid. Is the jug full? If not, how many more quarts will it take to fill it?

5. A fruit fizz recipe calls for 3 pints of orange juice, 3 cups of pineapple juice, 6 ounces of lemon juice, and a quart of seltzer water. Order the amounts of the ingredients from least to greatest.

Topic 5

Conversions in the Metric System

GOAL

Convert metric system units for length, distance, mass, and capacity

You fill a glass from a full 1 liter bottle of water. The bottle now contains 750 milliliters of water. How much water is in the glass? To find out, you'll need to know how to convert metric system units.

Terms to Know	*Example / Illustration*
Millimeter (mm), Centimeter (cm), Meter (m), Kilometer (km) metric system units for measuring length or distance	10 mm = 1 cm 100 cm = 1 m 1000 m = 1 km Also, 1000 mm = 1 m
Milligram (mg), Gram (g), Kilogram (kg) metric system units for measuring mass (For most purposes, you can think of weight and mass as the same thing.)	1000 mg = 1 g 1000 g = 1 kg
Milliliter (mL), Liter (L), Kiloliter (kL) metric system units for measuring capacity	1000 ml = 1 L 1000 L = 1 kL

UNDERSTANDING THE MAIN IDEAS

Like our place value system, the metric measurement system is based on powers of 10. Just as in the customary system, multiply to convert from a larger unit to a smaller unit. Since the metric system is based on powers of 10, your multiplication will be by numbers like 10, 100, or 1000.

Example 1

Nicole is training to try out for the track team. She runs 1.2 km on Monday, 3.5 km on Wednesday, and 2.8 km on Friday. Her coach suggests that she run 7000 meters per week. Has Nicole run enough this week?

■ Solution ■

Step 1: Find the total distance that Nicole has run in kilometers.

$$1.2 \text{ km} + 3.5 \text{ km} + 2.8 \text{ km} = 7.5 \text{ km}$$

Step 2: You are converting from a larger unit, kilometers, to a smaller unit, meters, so multiply.

$$1 \text{ km} = 1000 \text{ m} \qquad \text{Multiply by 1000 to convert from kilometers to meters.}$$

$$7.5 \text{ km} \rightarrow 7.5 \times 1000 = 7500 \rightarrow 7500 \text{ m}$$

$$7500 \text{ m} > 7000 \text{ m}$$

Nicole has run more than 7000 m this week.

Complete.

1. $3 \text{ km} = \underline{\ ?\ } \text{ m}$

2. $6 \text{ m} = \underline{\ ?\ } \text{ mm}$

3. $2 \text{ g} = \underline{\ ?\ } \text{ mg}$

4. $4 \text{ L} = \underline{\ ?\ } \text{ mL}$

5. $2.4 \text{ km} = \underline{\ ?\ } \text{ m}$

6. $9.1 \text{ m} = \underline{\ ?\ } \text{ mm}$

7. $1.2 \text{ kg} = \underline{\ ?\ } \text{ g}$

8. $8.97 \text{ m} = \underline{\ ?\ } \text{ cm}$

9. $4.26 \text{ g} = \underline{\ ?\ } \text{ mg}$

10. $6.752 \text{ L} = \underline{\ ?\ } \text{ mL}$

11. $0.342 \text{ m} = \underline{\ ?\ } \text{ cm}$

12. $0.9 \text{ kg} = \underline{\ ?\ } \text{ g}$

Divide to convert from a smaller unit to a larger unit. Since the metric system is based on powers of 10, your division will be by numbers like 10, 100, or 1000.

Example 2

Martha's punch mix recipe contains 750 mL of lime sherbet, 750 mL of orange sherbet, and 1500 mL of lemonade. How many liters of punch does Martha's recipe make?

■ Solution ■

Step 1: Find the total amount of ingredients in milliliters.

750 mL + 750 mL + 1500 mL = 3000 mL

Step 2: You are converting from a smaller unit, milliliters, to a larger unit, liters, so divide.

1000 mL = 1 L   Divide by 1000 to convert from milliliters to liters.

3000 mL → 3000 ÷ 1000 = 3 → 3 L

The punch mix recipe makes 3 liters of punch.

Determine whether there will be more or fewer of the new units after the conversion. Then find the equivalent measure.

13. 3000 mg = __?__ g   **14.** 1400 g = __?__ kg   **15.** 1000 L = __?__ kL

16. 2.3 m = __?__ mm   **17.** 1.89 mL = __?__ L   **18.** 890 cm = __?__ m

19. 78 g = __?__ mg   **20.** 90.3 m = __?__ km   **21.** 6.7 m = __?__ cm

....
Spiral Review

Solve each riddle.

22. I am a quadrilateral with two pairs of parallel sides and four sides of the same length. All of my angles are the same measure, too. What am I?

23. I am a quadrilateral with two pairs of parallel sides. All of my angles are the same measure, but my sides are not all the same length. What am I?

Topic 5 2 *Practice*

Complete.

1. 4 m = ? km   **2.** 1 g = ? mg   **3.** 2 g = ? kg

4. 4000 mL = ? L   **5.** 2.8 km = ? cm   **6.** 9 L = ? kL

7. 37 kg = ? g   **8.** 480 cm = ? mm   **9.** 674 cm = ? m

10. 6.589 g = ? mg   **11.** 5.726 m = ? mm   **12.** 0.432 m = ? cm

13. 842 g = ? kg   **14.** 93 mL = ? L   **15.** 873 kL = ? L

16. 2374 mL = ? L   **17.** 375 mL = ? L   **18.** 1435 L = ? kL

19. 0.5 g = ? mg   **20.** 8346 g = ? kg   **21.** 1756 mg = ? g

22. 0.25 kL = ? L   **23.** 476 L = ? kL   **24.** 4100 mm = ? cm

Complete.

25. To convert from liters to milliliters, —————————————.

26. To convert from liters to kiloliters, —————————————.

27. Multiply when you are converting from meters to —————————————.

28. Divide when you are converting from meters to —————————————.

Solve.

29. A bolt of fabric is 2 m long. Charles cuts a 25 cm length from the bolt of fabric. How many centimeters of fabric are left on the bolt?

30. You pour 6 cans of juice containing 200 mL each and 3 cans of juice containing 750 mL each into a punchbowl. How many liters of juice are in the bowl?

Topic 5 **Warm-ups**

Standardized Testing Warm-Ups

1. Which distance is the smallest?

   A 100,000 mm   **B** 60,000 cm   **C** 700 m   **D** 0.56 km

2. How many kiloliters are equivalent to 345,000 milliliters?

   A 345   **B** 345,000,000   **C** 34.5   **D** 0.345

Homework Review Warm-Ups

3. Mario has 379 mL of water left in his 1-liter container. How much has he already had to drink?

Express each measurement in terms of meters.

4. 453 cm   5. 9562 mm   6. 0.345 km   7. 4 km

Topic 5

Using Formulas to Find Perimeter and Circumference

GOAL

Find the perimeters of polygons. Find the circumference of a circle.

Marianne is putting a border around the outside of her vegetable garden. To determine the total length of border she needs, Marianne can measure the perimeter of the garden.

Terms to Know

Example / Illustration

Terms to Know	Example / Illustration
Perimeter the distance around a polygon	3.5 yd 3.25 yd 3.25 yd — Garden 1.75 yd 6.25 yd The perimeter of the garden is 3.25 + 3.5 + 3.25 + 1.75 + 6.25 = 18 yd.
Radius (r) the length of any segment that has one endpoint at the center of a circle and the other endpoint on the circle	$C \approx 31.4$ cm $r = 5$ cm $d = 10$ cm
Diameter (d) the distance across a circle through its center	The radius of the circle is 5 cm. The diameter of the circle is 10 cm.
Circumference (C) the distance around a circle	The circumference of the circle is about 31.4 cm.
Pi (π) the number that is the ratio of the circumference of any circle to its diameter	$\pi \approx 3.14159265\ldots$ For most purposes, you can use the approximation $\pi \approx 3.14$.
Regular a polygon with all sides the same length and all angle measures equal	(square)

UNDERSTANDING THE MAIN IDEAS

To find the perimeter of any polygon, find the sum of the lengths of its sides. If a polygon is regular, then you can multiply the measure of one side by the number of sides.

Example 1

Find the perimeter of each polygon.

a.
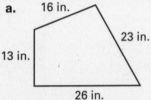
16 in.

13 in.

23 in.

26 in.

b.
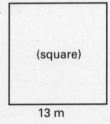
(square)

13 m

c.
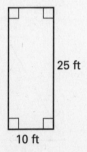
25 ft

10 ft

■ Solution ■

a. The quadrilateral is not a regular polygon. The sides are different lengths. Add the length of each side to find the perimeter.

    $$13 + 16 + 23 + 26 = 78$$

The perimeter is 78 in.

b. A square is a regular quadrilateral. All sides are the same length. To find the perimeter, multiply the length of one side by the number of sides.

    $$4 \cdot 13 = 52$$

The perimeter is 52 m.

c. The polygon is a quadrilateral with four right angles, so it is a rectangle. This rectangle is not a regular polygon, but its opposite sides have the same lengths. The perimeter is twice the length plus twice the width.

   Perimeter of a rectangle = $2\ell + 2w$

For the rectangle shown,

    $$P = 2\ell + 2w = (2 \cdot 25) + (2 \cdot 10) = 50 + 20 = 70$$

The perimeter of the rectangle is 70 ft.

Find the perimeter of each polygon. If only one side length is given, assume that the polygon is regular.

1.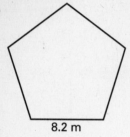

8.2 m

2.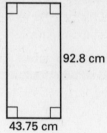

92.8 cm

43.75 cm

3.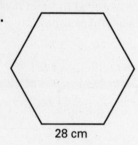

28 cm

4.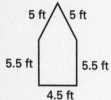

5 ft   5 ft

5.5 ft   5.5 ft

4.5 ft

5.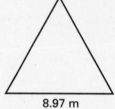

8.97 m

6.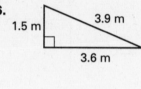

1.5 m   3.9 m

3.6 m

7. The Pentagon is one of the largest office buildings in the United States. It has the shape of a regular pentagon with a side length of about 281 m. Find its perimeter.

If you know a circle's diameter, there is a simple formula for its circumference.

Circumference of a circle = πd

Because the diameter of a circle is twice the radius, you can also write the formula in the following form.

Circumference of a circle = $2\pi r$

Example 2

Find the circumference of each circle.

a.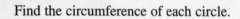

4 in.

b.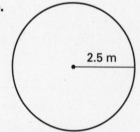

2.5 m

■ Solution ■

Step 1: **a.** The diameter is given.
Use the formula $C = \pi d$.

b. The radius is given.
Use the formula $C = 2\pi r$.

Step 2: **a.** Substitute numbers for the letters in the formula. Then solve. (Use 3.14 for π.)

$$C = \pi d$$
$$= 3.14 \cdot 4$$
$$= 12.56$$

The circumference of the circle is about 12.56 in.

b. Substitute numbers for the letters in the formula. Then solve. (Use 3.14 for π.)

$$C = 2\pi r$$
$$= 2 \cdot 3.14 \cdot 2.5$$
$$= 15.7$$

The circumference of the circle is about 15.7 m.

Find the circumference of each circle. Use 3.14 for π.

8.
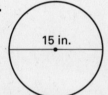
15 in.

9.
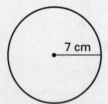
7 cm

10.
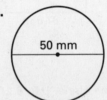
50 mm

11.
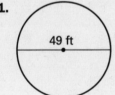
49 ft

12.
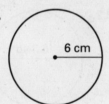
6 cm

13.
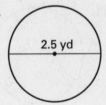
2.5 yd

Estimate whether the circumference is greater than or less than 100 ft.

14. $d = 35$ ft

15. $d = 25$ ft

16. $d = 30$ ft

....
Spiral Review

Complete.

17. 378 in. = ___?___ yd

18. 214.5 lb. = ___?___ oz

19. 6 qt = ___?___ fl oz

20. Write the fraction $\dfrac{4}{25}$ as a decimal and as a percent.

Find the perimeter of each polygon. If only one side length is given, assume that the polygon is regular.

1.
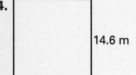
17 cm 19 cm
22 cm

2.
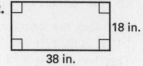
18 in.
38 in.

3.
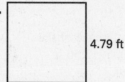
15 ft

4.
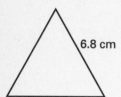
14.6 m

5.
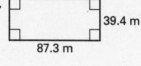
8 yd
5.6 yd   5.6 yd

6.

4.79 ft

7.
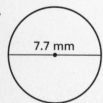
6.8 cm

8.
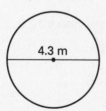
39.4 m
87.3 m

9.
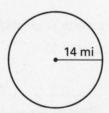
9.23 ft

Find the circumference of each circle. Use 3.14 for π. Round answers to the nearest hundredth.

10.
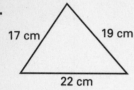
2 cm

11.
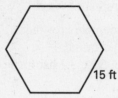
7.1 m

12.
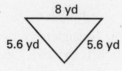
6.3 yd

13.
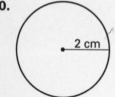
7.7 mm

14.
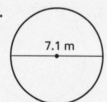
4.3 m

15.
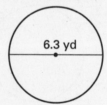
14 mi

Solve.

16. Suzanne is making a frame for an 8-inch by 10-inch photo. She has a yard of wood. Is that enough to make the frame? Explain.

17. The diameter of a quarter is 24 mm. What is the quarter's circumference?

Topic 5   *Warm-ups*

Standardized Testing Warm-Ups

1. A regular *nonagon* has nine sides. If one of the sides has a length of 12 mm, what is the perimeter?

   A 42 mm   **B** 108π mm   **C** 98 mm   **D** 108 mm

2. A circle has a radius of 30 m. What is the best estimate for its circumference?

   A 90 m   **B** 94 m   **C** 180 m   **D** 188 m

Homework Review Warm-Ups

3. Which has a greater perimeter, a square with sides measuring 1.2 m or a rectangle measuring 2.2 m long and 1.1 m wide?

4. Each side of a regular octagon is 4.65 m long. What is its perimeter?

5. A flying disk has a diameter of 9 in. What is its circumference? Use 3.14 for π.

Topic 5 LESSON 4 *Using Formulas to Find Area*

GOAL

Use formulas to find the areas of rectangles, squares, parallelograms, trapezoids, and triangles.

Joseph is redecorating his kitchen. He is laying new tiles on the rectangular floor, which measures 6 feet by 10 feet. The perimeter of the kitchen is $2 \cdot 6 + 2 \cdot 10 = 32$ feet. But to know how much tile to buy, Joseph instead needs to know the *area* of the floor.

Terms to Know

	Example / Illustration
Square unit a measurement unit that is exactly one unit long and one unit wide; A square unit may be a square inch, a square centimeter, a square mile, and so on.	1 ft 1 ft ▢ Each tile measures 1 square foot.
Area the number of square units needed to cover a figure in a plane	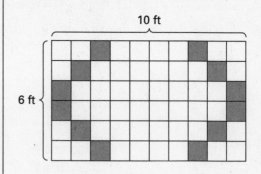 10 ft 6 ft It takes 60 tiles to cover the floor. The area is 60 square feet.

UNDERSTANDING THE MAIN IDEAS

There are formulas for finding the areas of many different polygons. For the kitchen floor, notice that the area is 60 square feet, and the length times the width is $6 \times 10 = 60$. You can also think of the length and width in terms of a *base* and a *height*.

Area of a rectangle: Area = base $\times$ height, or $A = b \cdot h$

Area of a parallelogram: Area = base $\times$ height, or $A = b \cdot h$

A square is just a rectangle with an equal base and height, or four equal sides (*s*).

Area of a square: Area = side $\times$ side, or $A = s \cdot s = s^2$

Remember that you always give an area in square units, or units^2.

Example 1

Find the area of each figure.

a.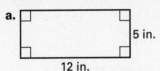
5 in.
12 in.

b.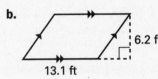
6.2 ft
13.1 ft

c.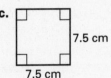
7.5 cm
7.5 cm

■ Solution ■

a. The figure is a rectangle with a base of 12 in. and a height of 5 in. Use these numbers in the formula. The answer will have units of square inches.

$$A = b \cdot h = 12 \cdot 5 = 60$$

The area of the rectangle is 60 in.^{2}.

b. The figure is a parallelogram with a base of 13.1 ft and a height of 6.2 ft. Use these numbers in the formula. The height is the shortest distance from the base to the top; it is not actually a side of this parallelogram. The answer will have units of square feet.

$$A = b \cdot h = 13.1 \cdot 6.2 = 81.22$$

The area of the parallelogram is 81.22 ft^2.

c. The figure is a square with a side length of 7.5 cm. Use this number in the formula. The answer will have units of square centimeters.

$$A = s^2 = 7.5^2 = 7.5 \cdot 7.5 = 56.25$$

The area of the square is 56.25 cm^2.

Find the area of each rectangle, square, or parallelogram. Remember to express your answer in square units.

1.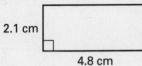
2.1 cm
4.8 cm

2.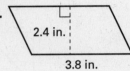
2.4 in.
3.8 in.

3.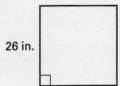
26 in.

4.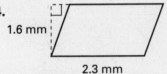
1.6 mm
2.3 mm

5.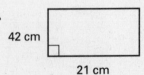
42 cm
21 cm

6.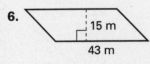
15 m
43 m

Imagine cutting a parallelogram in half between opposite corners. The result is two congruent triangles. The area of each triangle is just half the area of the parallelogram.

Area of a triangle: Area $= \frac{1}{2} \times$ base $\times$ height, or $A = \frac{1}{2} \cdot b \cdot h$

Example 2

Find the area of each triangle.

a.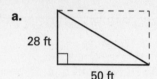

28 ft

50 ft

b.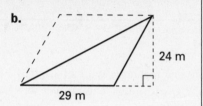

24 m

29 m

Solution

a. You can see that the area of the triangle is one half the area of the rectangle with the same base and height. The triangle has a base of 50 ft and a height of 28 ft. Use these numbers in the formula.

$$A = \frac{1}{2} \cdot b \cdot h = \frac{1}{2} \cdot 50 \cdot 28 = 700$$

The area of the triangle is 700 ft².

b. You can see that the area of the triangle is one half the area of the parallelogram with the same base and height. The triangle has a base of 29 m and a height of 24 m. Use these numbers in the formula.

$$A = \frac{1}{2} \cdot b \cdot h = \frac{1}{2} \cdot 29 \cdot 24 = 348$$

The area of the triangle is 348 m².

Calculate the area of each triangle. Use the formula $A = \frac{1}{2} \cdot b \cdot h$.

7.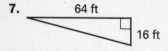
64 ft
16 ft

8.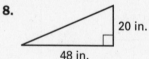
20 in.
48 in.

9.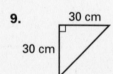
30 cm
30 cm

10.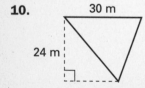
30 m
24 m

11.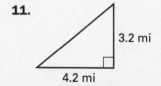
3.2 mi
4.2 mi

12.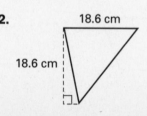
18.6 cm
18.6 cm

Recall that a *trapezoid* is a quadrilateral with exactly one pair of parallel sides. Both of the parallel sides of a trapezoid are called *bases*. You write them as b_1 and b_2. The area of a trapezoid is just the average length of the bases, $\frac{1}{2}(b_1 + b_2)$, times the height of the trapezoid.

Area of a trapezoid: Area $= \frac{1}{2} \times$ sum of bases $\times$ height, or $A = \frac{1}{2}(b_1 + b_2) \cdot h$

Example 3

Find the area of the polygon.

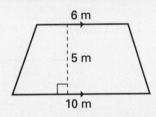

6 m

5 m

10 m

Solution

The figure is a trapezoid with a height of 5 m. Its two bases have lengths of 6 m and 10 m. Use these numbers in the formula. It doesn't really matter which base length you use for b_1 and which you use for b_2. The answer will have units of square meters.

$$A = \frac{1}{2}(b_1 + b_2) \cdot h = \frac{1}{2}(6 + 10) \cdot 5 = 8 \cdot 5 = 40$$

The area of the trapezoid is 40 m².

Find the area of each trapezoid. Use the formula $A = \frac{1}{2}(b_1 + b_2) \cdot h$.

13.

53 in.

24 in.

23 in.

14.

2.4 ft

3.7 ft

5 ft

15.

37 m

21 m

18 m

. . . .

Spiral Review

16. Order the quantities 4.5 pt, 75 fl oz, 2 qt, and 9.5 c from greatest to least.

17. Give the measures of the angles that are complementary and supplementary to an angle of 41°.

PRE-COURSE REVIEW
LESSON 4

Find the area of each polygon.

1.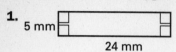
5 mm
24 mm

2.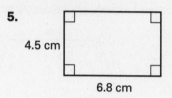
4 ft
8 ft

3.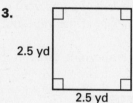
2.5 yd
2.5 yd

4.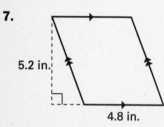
24 m
12 m
10 m

5.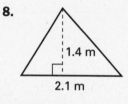
4.5 cm
6.8 cm

6.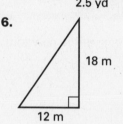
18 m
12 m

7.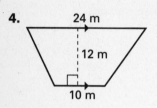
5.2 in.
4.8 in.

8.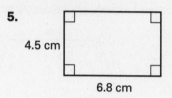
1.4 m
2.1 m

9.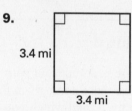
3.4 mi
3.4 mi

10.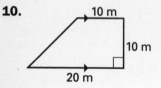
10 m
10 m
20 m

11.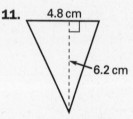
4.8 cm
6.2 cm

12.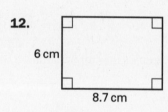
6 cm
8.7 cm

13.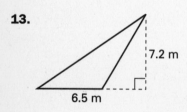
7.2 m
6.5 m

14.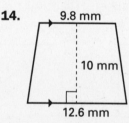
9.8 mm
10 mm
12.6 mm

15.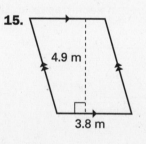
4.9 m
3.8 m

Solve.

16. The height of a rectangular wall is 8 m less than its base. The base is 17 m. What is the height of the wall? What is its area?

17. A triangle and a rectangle have the same base and the same height. What do you know about their areas?

18. Francis has 36 inches of string. What are the dimensions of the rectangle of greatest area that he can outline with the string? What is its area?

Part 2　Key Standards

Add, subtract, multiply, and divide rational numbers (integers, fractions, and terminating decimals) and take positive rational numbers to whole-number powers.

TEXTBOOK REFERENCES
Lessons 3.2, 3.3, 3.4
Extra Practice, p. 694

KEY WORDS
• number line
• integer
• positive number
• negative number
• sum

Integer Operations

ADDING INTEGERS

You can add two integers by using a number line. When you add a positive number, move right in the positive direction. When you add a negative number, move left in the negative direction.

To add a positive number, move right.

To add a negative number, move left.

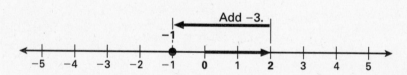

Example 1

Find the sum 2 + (−3).

▶ **Solution**

❶ **Start** at 0.

❷ **Add** +2 by moving 2 units to the right.

❸ **Add** −3 by moving 3 units to the left.

Add −3.

▶ You end at −1, so the sum of 2 and −3 is −1. So, 2 + (−3) = −1.

Checkpoint ✓ **Sum of Positive and Negative Integers**

Find the sum.

1. −3 + 1

2. 4 + (−5)

3. 3 + (−1)

My Notes

KEY WORDS

• difference
• inverse operation
• opposite of a number

SUBTRACTING INTEGERS

Addition and subtraction are inverse operations.

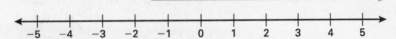

To subtract a positive number, move left.

To subtract a negative number, move right.

Example 2

Find the difference 2 − 5.

▶ **Solution**

Start at 0. Add 2 by moving 2 units to the right. Then subtract 5 by moving 5 units to the left.

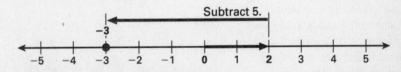

▶ **STUDY TIP**
Check the result of a subtraction by using addition. For example, to check that
$3 − 6 = −3$, note that
$−3 + 6 = 3$.

▶ You end at −3. The difference of 2 and 5 is −3. So, $2 − 5 = −3$.

Example 3

Find the difference 2 − (−5).

▶ **Solution**

Start at 0. Move 2 units to the right. Then move 5 units to the right.

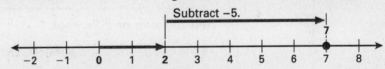

▶ You end at 7. The difference of 2 and −5 is 7. So, $2 − (−5) = 7$.

Checkpoint ✓   *Difference of Positive and Negative Integers*

Find the difference.

4. $3 − 6$ **5.** $5 − (−2)$ **6.** $−2 − (6)$

Addition and subtraction are inverse operations which means that they undo each other. Look at how each pair of subtraction and addition sentences are related.

$5 - 2 = 3$	$2 - 5 = -3$	$2 - (-5) = 7$
$5 + (-2) = 3$	$2 + (-5) = -3$	$2 + 5 = 7$

Subtracting 2 is the same as adding −2.

Subtracting 5 is the same as adding −5.

Subtracting −5 is the same as adding 5.

Subtracting an integer is the same as adding its opposite.

SUMMARIZING KEY IDEAS

Addition and subtraction are opposite operations. When you add a negative number, the result is less than the original number. When you subtract a negative number, the result is greater than the original number.

Exercises   *Adding and Subtracting Integers*

Find the sum.

1. $-5 + 8$ **2.** $7 + (-19)$ **3.** $12 + (-13)$

4. $-15 + 16$ **5.** $11 + (-9)$ **6.** $9 + (-12)$

7. $-21 + 31$ **8.** $32 + (-16)$ **9.** $22 + (-19)$

Find the difference.

10. $-12 - 9$ **11.** $7 - (-8)$ **12.** $14 - (-11)$

13. $-16 - 8$ **14.** $24 - (-31)$ **15.** $10 - (-3)$

16. $-11 - (-4)$ **17.** $-3 - (-2)$ **18.** $3 - 9$

Find the sum or difference.

19. $5 - (-12)$ **20.** $6 + (-4)$ **21.** $-7 - 2$

22. $-8 + (-12)$ **23.** $7 - (-2)$ **24.** $-2 + 19$

25. $16 - (-6)$ **26.** $18 + (-12)$ **27.** $8 - (-9)$

Answer the question. Give examples to explain your reasoning.

28. When you subtract a positive number, is the difference greater or less than the original number?

29. When you subtract a negative number, is the difference greater or less than the original number?

TEXTBOOK LINK

On pages S2–S4, you used a number line to help you add and subtract integers. You will learn rules for adding and subtracting integers in Lessons 3.3 and 3.4 of your textbook.

KEY STANDARD

NS1.2   *continued*

TEXTBOOK REFERENCES

Lessons 3.5, 3.6

KEY WORDS

- factor
- product
- absolute value
- quotient

My Notes

▶**STUDY TIP**

Notice in part (b) of Example 1 that the product of two negative numbers is positive.

MULTIPLYING AND DIVIDING INTEGERS

You can find the product of two whole numbers using repeated addition. You can also use repeated addition to find the product of a positive integer and -1.

$$7(-1) = (-1) + (-1) + (-1) + (-1) + (-1) + (-1) + (-1)$$
$$= -7$$

Notice that the product of 7 and -1 is the opposite of 7, or -7.

The product of any number and -1 is the opposite of the number. You can use this fact and properties of multiplication to find the product of any two integers.

Example 1

Find the product.

   a. $3(-8)$ **b.** $(-9)(-4)$

▶ **Solution**

a. $3(-8) = 3(8)(-1)$ The product of -1 and a number is the opposite of the number.

$= (24)(-1)$ Left-to-right rule

$= -24$ The product of -1 and a number is the opposite of the number.

b. $(-9)(-4) = (-1)(9)(-1)(4)$ The product of -1 and a number is the opposite of the number.

$= (9)(4)(-1)(-1)$ Commutative property of multiplication

$= (36)(-1)(-1)$ Left-to-right rule

$= (-36)(-1)$ Left-to-right rule

$= 36$ The product of -1 and a number is the opposite of the number.

Checkpoint ✓ **Products of Positive and Negative Integers**

Find the product.

   1. $6 \times (-1)$ **2.** -11×5 **3.** $-13 \times (-4)$

When you divide integers, thinking about the related multiplication problem can help you determine the sign of the quotient.

Example 2

Find the quotient.

a. $6 \div 3$ **b.** $(-12) \div 4$ **c.** $24 \div (-6)$ **d.** $(-35) \div (-7)$

▶ *Solution*

a. Think about the related multiplication problem.

$$6 \div 3 = \boxed{?} \longrightarrow 3 \cdot \boxed{?} = 6$$

$$3 \cdot 2 = 6, \text{ so } 6 \div 3 = 2.$$

b. Think about the related multiplication problem.

$$(-12) \div 4 \longrightarrow 4 \cdot \boxed{?} = -12 \quad \text{The second factor must be negative.}$$

$$4 \cdot (-3) = -12, \text{ so } (-12) \div 4 = -3.$$

c. Think about the related multiplication problem.

$$24 \div (-6) \longrightarrow (-6) \cdot \boxed{?} = 24 \quad \text{The second factor must be negative.}$$

$$(-6) \cdot (-4) = 24, \text{ so } 24 \div (-6) = -4.$$

d. Think about the related multiplication problem.

$$(-35) \div (-7) \longrightarrow -7 \cdot \boxed{?} = -35 \quad \text{The second factor must be positive.}$$

$$(-7) \cdot 5 = -35, \text{ so } (-35) \div (-7) = 5.$$

· · · · · · · · · · · · · · · · · · ·

The quotient of two integers with the same sign is positive, as you can see in parts (a) and (d) of Example 2. The quotient of two integers with different signs is negative, as you can see in parts (b) and (c) of Example 2.

When multiplying and dividing integers, you can multiply or divide the absolute values of the numbers and then attach the correct sign.

Checkpoint ✓ **Quotients of Positive and Negative Integers**

Find the quotient.

4. $56 \div (-8)$ **5.** $-88 \div (-22)$ **6.** $-120 \div 6$

▶**STUDY TIP**
Check the result of a division by using multiplication. For example, to check that $6 \div (-3) = -2$, note that $(-3) \times (-2) = 6$.

Remember that multiplication and division are inverse operations.

Follow these rules for multiplying integers.

positive $\times$ positive = positive

positive $\times$ negative = negative

negative $\times$ positive = negative

negative $\times$ negative = positive

Follow these rules for dividing integers.

positive $\div$ positive = positive

positive $\div$ negative = negative

negative $\div$ positive = negative

negative $\div$ negative = positive

SUMMARIZING KEY IDEAS

For multiplication and division, if both integers have the same sign, then the result of the operation is positive. If the integers have different signs, the result of the operation is negative. Remember that this is not true for addition and subtraction.

Exercises   *Multiplying and Dividing Integers*

Find the product.

1. $5 \times (-7)$

2. $(-6) \times 4$

3. $(-8) \times (-2)$

4. $3 \times (-24)$

5. $9 \times (-18)$

6. $(-50) \times (-4)$

7. $(-90) \times (-4)$

8. $(-7) \times (-27)$

9. $(-7) \times 45$

Find the quotient.

10. $(-8) \div 2$

11. $14 \div (-7)$

12. $(-24) \div 8$

13. $30 \div (-5)$

14. $42 \div (-6)$

15. $(-81) \div (-3)$

16. $(-54) \div (-9)$

17. $(-260) \div 5$

18. $(-432) \div (-12)$

Find the product or quotient.

19. $12 \times (-3)$

20. $(-9) \times (-9)$

21. $(-50) \div 5$

22. $(-72) \div 9$

23. $(-16) \times 7$

24. $(-31) \times (-9)$

25. $(-112) \div (-8)$

26. $(-132) \div 12$

27. $368 \div (-4)$

28. $(-51) \times 8$

29. $216 \div (-8)$

30. $8 \times (-53)$

Answer the question.

31. What do you know about the signs of two integers if their product is positive?

32. What do you know about the signs of two integers if their quotient is negative?

TEXTBOOK LINK

On pages S5–S7, you used properties of multiplication to help you multiply and divide integers. You will use these properties and rules in Lessons 3.5 and 3.6 in your textbook.

Topic Review *Integer Operations*

These exercises will help you check that you can add, subtract, multiply, and divide integers. If you have any questions about integer operations, be sure to get them answered before going on to the next section.

Find the sum or difference.

1. $4 + (-3)$ **2.** $(-3) + (-5)$ **3.** $(-11) - (-11)$

4. $(-99) - 10$ **5.** $(-5) + 3$ **6.** $0 - (-7)$

7. $6 + (-6)$ **8.** $23 - 10$ **9.** $(-13) - (-6)$

10. $25 + 9$ **11.** $10 + (-29)$ **12.** $(-23) - 43$

Find the product or quotient.

13. 6×9 **14.** $42 \div 7$ **15.** $(-1) \div (-1)$

16. $(-20) \times (-2)$ **17.** $(-4) \times (-16)$ **18.** $12 \div (-3)$

19. $(-22) \div 11$ **20.** $(-148) \div (-2)$ **21.** $34 \times (-11)$

22. $12 \times (-12)$ **23.** $250 \div (-25)$ **24.** $14 \times (-30)$

Evaluate.

My Review Questions

25. $(-12) - 5$ **26.** $(-11) + 22$ **27.** $(-93) \times (-8)$

28. $(-32) \div 8$ **29.** $(-28) + 21$ **30.** $25 \times (-22)$

31. $34 - 54$ **32.** $(-279) \div (-9)$ **33.** $(-33) + 47$

34. $(-19) - (-25)$ **35.** $(-53) \times 19$ **36.** $(-144) \div (-12)$

Complete the sentence using *sometimes*, *always*, or *never*.

37. The sum of a positive number and a negative number is __?__ negative.

38. The quotient of two negative numbers is __?__ negative.

39. The product of a negative number and a positive number is __?__ negative.

40. When you subtract a negative number from a positive number, the difference is __?__ positive.

41. When you divide a negative number by a positive number, the quotient is __?__ positive.

TEXTBOOK REFERENCES

Skills Review, pp. 677, 678

Lessons 6.1, 6.2

KEY WORDS

- like fractions
- common denominator
- sum
- difference

Fraction Operations

ADDING AND SUBTRACTING LIKE FRACTIONS

To add or subtract fractions with the same denominator, add or subtract the numerators and write the result over the common denominator.

Example 1

Find the sum $\dfrac{5}{12} + \dfrac{11}{12}$.

▶ **Solution**

$$\frac{5}{12} + \frac{11}{12} = \frac{5 + 11}{12} \qquad \text{Add numerators.}$$

$$= \frac{16}{12} \qquad \text{Simplify numerator.}$$

$$= \frac{4}{3}, \text{ or } 1\frac{1}{3} \qquad \text{Simplify fraction.}$$

Example 2

Find the difference $\dfrac{7}{10} - \dfrac{9}{10}$.

▶ **Solution**

$$\frac{7}{10} - \frac{9}{10} = \frac{7 - 9}{10} \qquad \text{Subtract numerators.}$$

$$= \frac{-2}{10} \qquad \text{Simplify numerator.}$$

$$= -\frac{1}{5} \qquad \text{Simplify fraction.}$$

Checkpoint ✓ *Adding and Subtracting Like Fractions*

Find the sum or difference. Write the answer in simplest form.

1. $\dfrac{2}{7} + \dfrac{3}{7}$ **2.** $\dfrac{7}{12} - \dfrac{5}{12}$ **3.** $-\dfrac{5}{8} + \dfrac{25}{8}$ **4.** $3\dfrac{4}{9} - 1\dfrac{7}{9}$

My Notes

KEY WORDS
- unlike fractions
- least common denominator
- improper fraction

ADDING AND SUBTRACTING UNLIKE FRACTIONS

To add or subtract fractions with different denominators, rewrite the fractions with a common denominator before you find the sum or difference. It is convenient to use the least common denominator (LCD).

Example 3

Find the sum $-\dfrac{3}{7} + \dfrac{1}{4}$.

▶ **Solution**

$$-\frac{3}{7} + \frac{1}{4} = \frac{-3 \cdot 4}{7 \cdot 4} + \frac{1 \cdot 7}{4 \cdot 7}$$ Rewrite fractions using the LCD, 28.

$$= \frac{-12 + 7}{28}$$ Add numerators.

$$= -\frac{5}{28}$$ Simplify.

Example 4

My Notes

Find the difference $3\dfrac{7}{9} - 1\dfrac{5}{6}$.

▶ **Solution**

$$3\frac{7}{9} - 1\frac{5}{6} = \frac{34}{9} - \frac{11}{6}$$ Rewrite as improper fractions.

$$= \frac{34 \cdot 2}{9 \cdot 2} - \frac{11 \cdot 3}{6 \cdot 3}$$ Rewrite fractions using the LCD, 18.

$$= \frac{68 - 33}{18}$$ Subtract numerators.

$$= \frac{35}{18}, \text{ or } 1\frac{17}{18}$$ Simplify.

Checkpoint ✓ *Adding and Subtracting Unlike Fractions*

Find the sum or difference. Write the answer in simplest form.

5. $\dfrac{2}{3} + \dfrac{3}{4}$ **6.** $\dfrac{7}{6} - \dfrac{7}{18}$ **7.** $-\dfrac{4}{5} + 2\dfrac{3}{10}$ **8.** $1\dfrac{5}{8} - 4\dfrac{1}{6}$

You can use these rules to add or subtract fractions with the same denominator:

Adding fractions

$$\frac{a}{c} + \frac{b}{c} = \frac{a+b}{c}$$

Subtracting fractions

$$\frac{a}{c} - \frac{b}{c} = \frac{a-b}{c}$$

To add or subtract fractions with different denominators, first rewrite the fractions with a common denominator and then use the appropriate rule.

Exercises *Adding and Subtracting Fractions*

Find the sum or difference. Write the answer in simplest form.

1. $\dfrac{3}{11} + \dfrac{4}{11}$

2. $\dfrac{7}{8} + \dfrac{5}{8}$

3. $\left(-\dfrac{1}{6}\right) + \dfrac{5}{6}$

4. $\dfrac{17}{45} + \dfrac{8}{45}$

5. $\left(-\dfrac{19}{22}\right) + \dfrac{41}{22}$

6. $\left(-\dfrac{3}{5}\right) + 4\dfrac{2}{5}$

7. $\dfrac{12}{13} - \dfrac{9}{13}$

8. $\dfrac{8}{9} - \dfrac{2}{9}$

9. $\dfrac{7}{12} - \dfrac{11}{12}$

10. $\dfrac{3}{10} - \left(-\dfrac{9}{10}\right)$

11. $\dfrac{23}{32} - \dfrac{15}{32}$

12. $2\dfrac{1}{7} - \dfrac{6}{7}$

Find the sum or difference. Write the answer in simplest form.

13. $\dfrac{1}{2} + \dfrac{1}{4}$

14. $\dfrac{2}{5} + \dfrac{1}{6}$

15. $\left(-\dfrac{11}{12}\right) + \dfrac{3}{8}$

16. $\dfrac{7}{10} + \dfrac{49}{30}$

17. $\dfrac{4}{7} + 1\dfrac{1}{3}$

18. $\left(-2\dfrac{1}{4}\right) + 1\dfrac{2}{5}$

19. $\dfrac{5}{6} - \dfrac{2}{3}$

20. $\dfrac{3}{4} - \dfrac{3}{8}$

21. $\left(-\dfrac{6}{7}\right) - \dfrac{7}{6}$

22. $\dfrac{19}{8} - \dfrac{9}{20}$

23. $2 - \left(-\dfrac{13}{11}\right)$

24. $4\dfrac{1}{2} - 3\dfrac{4}{9}$

TEXTBOOK LINK

On pages S9–S11, you added and subtracted fractions. You will learn more about these topics in Lessons 6.1 and 6.2 in your textbook.

25. COOKING You are making a batch of rolls and a batch of muffins for a bake sale. You need $4\dfrac{1}{2}$ cups of flour for the rolls and $2\dfrac{1}{4}$ cups of flour for the muffins. How much flour do you need for both foods?

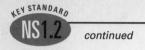
TEXTBOOK REFERENCES

Skills Review, pp. 677, 678

Lessons 6.3, 6.5

KEY WORDS

• product

MULTIPLYING FRACTIONS

To find the product of two fractions, multiply the numerators of the fractions to get the numerator of the product, and multiply the denominators of the fractions to get the denominator of the product.

Example 1

Find the product $\dfrac{3}{4} \cdot \dfrac{8}{9}$.

▶ **Solution**

$$\dfrac{3}{4} \cdot \dfrac{8}{9} = \dfrac{3 \cdot 8}{4 \cdot 9} \qquad \text{Multiply numerators and multiply denominators.}$$

$$= \dfrac{24}{36} \qquad \text{Simplify numerator and denominator.}$$

$$= \dfrac{2}{3} \qquad \text{Simplify fraction.}$$

Example 2

My Notes

Find the product $4\dfrac{2}{3} \cdot \left(-1\dfrac{2}{7}\right)$.

▶ **Solution**

$$4\dfrac{2}{3} \cdot \left(-1\dfrac{2}{7}\right) = \dfrac{14}{3} \cdot \left(-\dfrac{9}{7}\right) \qquad \text{Rewrite as improper fractions.}$$

$$= \dfrac{14 \cdot (-9)}{3 \cdot 7} \qquad \text{Multiply numerators and multiply denominators.}$$

$$= \dfrac{-126}{21} \qquad \text{Simplify numerator and denominator.}$$

$$= -6 \qquad \text{Simplify fraction.}$$

Checkpoint ✓ Multiplying Fractions

Find the product. Write the answer in simplest form.

1. $\dfrac{2}{3} \cdot \dfrac{1}{5}$ 　　　　**2.** $\left(-\dfrac{4}{3}\right) \cdot \dfrac{9}{16}$ 　　　　**3.** $\left(-\dfrac{6}{25}\right) \cdot \left(-3\dfrac{3}{4}\right)$

KEY WORDS
- quotient
- dividend
- divisor
- reciprocal

DIVIDING FRACTIONS

To find the quotient of two fractions, multiply the dividend by the reciprocal of the divisor.

Example 3

Find the quotient $\dfrac{4}{3} \div \dfrac{11}{7}$.

▶ **Solution**

$$\dfrac{4}{3} \div \dfrac{11}{7} = \dfrac{4}{3} \cdot \dfrac{7}{11} \qquad \text{Multiply } \dfrac{4}{3} \text{ by } \dfrac{7}{11} \text{, the reciprocal of } \dfrac{11}{7}.$$

$$= \dfrac{4 \cdot 7}{3 \cdot 11} \qquad \text{Multiply numerators and multiply denominators.}$$

$$= \dfrac{28}{33} \qquad \text{Simplify.}$$

Example 4

Find the quotient $\left(-4\dfrac{3}{4}\right) \div \left(-2\dfrac{1}{5}\right)$.

▶ **Solution**

$$\left(-4\dfrac{3}{4}\right) \div \left(-2\dfrac{1}{5}\right) = \left(-\dfrac{19}{4}\right) \div \left(-\dfrac{11}{5}\right) \quad \text{Rewrite as improper fractions.}$$

$$= \left(-\dfrac{19}{4}\right) \cdot \left(-\dfrac{5}{11}\right) \quad \text{Multiply by the reciprocal of } -\dfrac{11}{5}.$$

$$= \dfrac{(-19) \cdot (-5)}{4 \cdot 11} \quad \begin{array}{l}\text{Multiply numerators and} \\ \text{multiply denominators.}\end{array}$$

$$= \dfrac{95}{44}, \text{ or } 2\dfrac{7}{44} \quad \text{Simplify.}$$

Checkpoint ✓ **Dividing Fractions**

Find the quotient. Write the answer in simplest form.

4. $\dfrac{3}{5} \div \dfrac{2}{5}$

5. $\dfrac{5}{8} \div \left(-\dfrac{11}{12}\right)$

6. $\left(-3\dfrac{1}{9}\right) \div \left(-4\dfrac{2}{3}\right)$

My Notes

Summarizing Key Ideas

To find the product of two fractions, multiply the numerators to get the numerator of the product, and multiply the denominators to get the denominator of the product.

To find the quotient of two fractions, multiply the dividend by the reciprocal of the divisor.

You can use these rules to multiply or divide two fractions:

Multiplying fractions

$$\frac{a}{b} \cdot \frac{c}{d} = \frac{a \cdot c}{b \cdot d}$$

Dividing fractions

$$\frac{a}{b} \div \frac{c}{d} = \frac{a}{b} \cdot \frac{d}{c}$$

Exercises Multiplying and Dividing Fractions

Find the product or quotient. Write the answer in simplest form.

1. $\dfrac{1}{2} \cdot \dfrac{1}{3}$

2. $\dfrac{21}{8} \cdot \dfrac{4}{9}$

3. $\left(-\dfrac{5}{12}\right) \cdot \dfrac{8}{15}$

4. $\dfrac{7}{4} \cdot \left(-\dfrac{16}{7}\right)$

5. $\left(-\dfrac{2}{15}\right) \cdot \left(-\dfrac{25}{6}\right)$

6. $\left(-\dfrac{17}{24}\right) \cdot \dfrac{3}{24}$

7. $1\dfrac{1}{2} \cdot 1\dfrac{1}{5}$

8. $24 \cdot \dfrac{7}{12}$

9. $2\dfrac{2}{3} \cdot 4\dfrac{1}{4}$

10. $\dfrac{2}{5} \div \dfrac{2}{3}$

11. $\dfrac{7}{8} \div \dfrac{3}{4}$

12. $\dfrac{13}{10} \div \dfrac{5}{2}$

13. $\left(-\dfrac{4}{7}\right) \div \dfrac{8}{3}$

14. $\dfrac{5}{18} \div \left(-\dfrac{7}{12}\right)$

15. $\left(-\dfrac{20}{21}\right) \div \dfrac{15}{28}$

16. $\left(-\dfrac{3}{11}\right) \div \left(-\dfrac{9}{22}\right)$

17. $8 \div \dfrac{4}{5}$

18. $\left(-4\dfrac{1}{12}\right) \div 7\dfrac{7}{8}$

AGRICULTURE In Exercises 19–21, use the following information.
You want to use a pasture as grazing land for horses. The pasture is a rectangle $\dfrac{1}{2}$ mile long by $\dfrac{3}{8}$ mile wide. Each horse needs $1\dfrac{1}{2}$ acres of pasture for grazing.

19. What is the area of the pasture in square miles?

20. What is the area of the pasture in acres? (*Hint:* 1 square mile = 640 acres.)

21. How many horses can the pasture support?

22. Show that the value of $\dfrac{5x}{14} \div \dfrac{10x}{21}$ is the same for any nonzero value of x. What is the value of the expression?

Textbook Link

On pages S12–S14, you multiplied and divided fractions. You will learn more about these topics in Lessons 6.3 and 6.5 in your textbook.

Topic Review *Fraction Operations*

These exercises will help you check that you can add, subtract, multiply, and divide fractions. If you have any questions about fraction operations, be sure to get them answered before going on to the next section.

Evaluate. Write the answer in simplest form.

1. $\left(-\dfrac{7}{8}\right) + \dfrac{3}{8}$

2. $\dfrac{19}{24} - \dfrac{11}{24}$

3. $\left(-\dfrac{2}{9}\right) - \dfrac{16}{9}$

4. $1\dfrac{3}{7} + 3\dfrac{2}{7}$

5. $8\dfrac{3}{10} - 6\dfrac{7}{10}$

6. $\left(-\dfrac{3}{4}\right) + \dfrac{5}{6}$

7. $\dfrac{2}{7} \cdot \dfrac{7}{9}$

8. $\dfrac{9}{8} \cdot \dfrac{4}{3}$

9. $\left(-\dfrac{25}{44}\right) \cdot \left(-\dfrac{33}{40}\right)$

10. $\left(-4\dfrac{2}{3}\right) \cdot 5\dfrac{1}{7}$

11. $\dfrac{3}{4} \div \dfrac{1}{3}$

12. $\dfrac{3}{8} \div \dfrac{9}{5}$

13. $\dfrac{3}{20} \cdot \dfrac{30}{7}$

14. $\dfrac{17}{8} - \dfrac{9}{8}$

15. $\left(-3\dfrac{1}{2}\right) \cdot \dfrac{4}{7}$

16. $\left(-\dfrac{1}{18}\right) + \dfrac{19}{24}$

17. $\dfrac{8}{7} \div (-12)$

18. $1\dfrac{1}{27} \, 4 \, 2\dfrac{2}{9}$

19. $3\dfrac{2}{5} + 5\dfrac{13}{15}$

20. $2\dfrac{3}{16} - 1\dfrac{7}{20}$

21. $5\dfrac{5}{12} \cdot \left(-1\dfrac{2}{13}\right)$

22. INSECTS A honeybee colony contains three types of bees: a queen bee, drones, and worker bees. The average lengths of these bees are shown.

Queen: $\dfrac{3}{4}$ inch   **Drone:** $\dfrac{5}{8}$ inch   **Worker:** $\dfrac{1}{2}$ inch

How much longer is a queen than a drone? How much longer is a drone than a worker? How much longer is a queen than a worker?

23. WATER You fill a pitcher with $\dfrac{3}{4}$ gallon of water and pour the water into glasses that each hold $\dfrac{1}{8}$ gallon. How many glasses will the pitcher fill?

My Review Questions

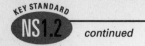
TEXTBOOK REFERENCES
Skills Review, pp. 675, 676
Lesson 4.7

KEY WORDS
• sum
• difference
• decimals

> **STUDY TIP**
> Writing zeros after the
> last digit to the right of
> the decimal point does
> not change the value of
> a number.

Decimal Operations

ADDING AND SUBTRACTING DECIMALS

When you add decimals, you must make sure you're adding tenths to
tenths, hundredths to hundredths, and so on. To do this, make sure to line
up the decimal points. Then add as if you were adding whole numbers.

Use the same plan when subtracting decimals. Line up the decimal points
and then subtract as if you were subtracting whole numbers. Write zeros
to make the columns even, if one number has fewer digits after the
decimal point than the other.

Example 1

Find the sum or difference.

a. $4.75 + 0.666 + 32.46$ **b.** $22.93 - 21.1$

▶ **Solution**

   a.   4.750   ❶ *Line up the decimal points.*

          0.666   ❷ *Write zeros to make the columns even.*

    + 32.460   ❸ *Add.*
         ———

        37.876

    ▶ $4.75 + 0.666 + 32.46 = 37.876$

   b.   22.93   ❶ *Line up the decimal points.*

    − 21.10   ❷ *Write zeros to make the columns even.*
       ———

      1.83   ❸ *Subtract.*

    ▶ $22.93 - 21.1 = 1.83$

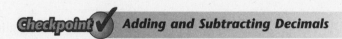

Checkpoint ✓   **Adding and Subtracting Decimals**

Find the sum or difference.

  1. $6.2 + 0.444$ **2.** $4.068 - 1.29$ **3.** $0.8 - 0.126$

KEY WORDS

• product
• quotient
• divisor
• dividend

MULTIPLYING AND DIVIDING DECIMALS

You can multiply a decimal by a decimal using the same method for multiplying a whole number by a decimal. The product of a decimal multiplication problem has the same number of decimal places as the sum of the numbers of decimal places in both factors.

You can divide by a decimal by multiplying the divisor and the dividend by the same power of ten. You choose the power of 10 that turns the divisor into a whole number.

▶ **STUDY TIP**
To multiply a number by 100, move the decimal point two places to the right.

Example 2

Find the product or quotient.

a. 32.6×0.08 **b.** $31.79 \div 1.1$

▶ **Solution**

a.   32.6   Multiply as with whole numbers.

    $\times\ 0.08$

     2.608   32.6 has 1 decimal place and 0.08 has 2 decimal places,
                    so the product has $1 + 2 = 3$ decimal places.

b. Multiply the divisor and the dividend by a power of 10 that will make the divisor a whole number. 1.1 has 1 decimal place, so multiply by 10^1, or 10.

    $1.1 \times 10 = 11$ $31.79 \times 10 = 317.9$

          28.9
    $11\overline{)317.9}$ Place the decimal point in the quotient. Then divide.

When multiplying or dividing decimals, it may help to first estimate the answer. This will help you place the decimal point and decide if your answer is reasonable.

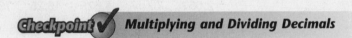

Checkpoint ✓ **Multiplying and Dividing Decimals**

Find the product or quotient.

    4. 4.1×0.0037 **5.** $0.231 \div 0.07$ **6.** $1.22 \div 0.4$

SUMMARIZING KEY IDEAS

The only difference between operations with decimals and operations with whole numbers is that when you are working with decimals, you need to remember to think about where the decimal points are.

Exercises   Decimal Operations

Find the sum.

1. $5.34 + 2.96$ **2.** $0.538 + 0.257$ **3.** $0.56 + 2.489$

4. $8.001 + 0.77$ **5.** $7 + 11.436 + 3.08$ **6.** $4.035 + 8.99$

Find the difference.

7. $3.8 - 2.1$ **8.** $9.1 - 6.05$ **9.** $3.06 - 1.9$

10. $0.93 - 0.256$ **11.** $9.784 - 2.659$ **12.** $7 - 6.52$

Evaluate.

13. $6.25 + 4.794$ **14.** $0.29 + 6.68$ **15.** $9.3 + 3.708$

16. $69.793 - 2.693$ **17.** $8.5 - 3.25$ **18.** $12.5 - 7.4$

19. $67.29 + 19.01$ **20.** $0.155 - 0.09$ **21.** $6.74 - 2.695$

Find the product.

22. 1.9×9 **23.** 35.15×25 **24.** 2.065×1.2

25. 91.4×0.7 **26.** 37.01×0.2 **27.** 40.31×0.4

Find the quotient. Round to 3 decimal places if necessary.

28. $6.48 \div 0.6$ **29.** $1.29 \div 5.5$ **30.** $416.8 \div 0.2$

31. $6.5 \div 3.2$ **32.** $20.83 \div 7.3$ **33.** $3.643 \div 0.67$

Evaluate. Round quotients to 3 decimal places if necessary.

34. $2.4 \div 0.3$ **35.** 0.1×75.4 **36.** 0.65×0.1

37. $9.483 \div 8.7$ **38.** $0.685 \div 2.74$ **39.** 0.001×265.3

40. 13.8×9.5 **41.** $0.8449 \div 0.71$ **42.** 6.07×3.15

In Exercises 43–45, choose numbers from the list.

2.657   26.57   4.625   46.25   79   1.719   17.19   7.9

43. Find three numbers whose sum is about 70.

44. Which two numbers have a sum of exactly 28.289?

45. The difference between which two numbers is exactly 52.43?

TEXTBOOK LINK

On pages S16–S18, you added, subtracted, multiplied, and divided decimals. In Lesson 4.7 in your textbook, you will solve equations involving decimals.

TEXTBOOK REFERENCES
Lessons 1.3, 6.7, 6.8

KEY WORDS

- exponential notation
- power
- base
- exponent
- factor

Powers of Rational Numbers

POSITIVE POWERS OF FRACTIONS

You can represent repeated multiplication of the same number by using exponential notation.

$$a^m = \underbrace{a \cdot a \cdot a \cdot \ldots \cdot a}_{m \text{ factors}}$$

exponent ← base

Example 1

Simplify the expression.

a. $\left(\dfrac{1}{2}\right)^5$

b. $\left(\dfrac{3}{5}\right)^4$

▶ **Solution**

a. $\left(\dfrac{1}{2}\right)^5 = \dfrac{1}{2} \cdot \dfrac{1}{2} \cdot \dfrac{1}{2} \cdot \dfrac{1}{2} \cdot \dfrac{1}{2}$ Use repeated multiplication.

$\qquad = \dfrac{1 \cdot 1 \cdot 1 \cdot 1 \cdot 1}{2 \cdot 2 \cdot 2 \cdot 2 \cdot 2}$ Multiply fractions.

$\qquad = \dfrac{1^5}{2^5}$, or $\dfrac{1}{32}$ Simplify.

b. $\left(\dfrac{3}{5}\right)^4 = \dfrac{3}{5} \cdot \dfrac{3}{5} \cdot \dfrac{3}{5} \cdot \dfrac{3}{5}$ Use repeated multiplication.

$\qquad = \dfrac{3 \cdot 3 \cdot 3 \cdot 3}{5 \cdot 5 \cdot 5 \cdot 5}$ Multiply fractions.

$\qquad = \dfrac{3^4}{5^4}$, or $\dfrac{81}{625}$ Simplify.

Checkpoint ✓ **Positive Exponents**

Simplify the expression.

1. 4^2 **2.** $\left(\dfrac{5}{6}\right)^2$ **3.** $\left(\dfrac{1}{3}\right)^4$ **4.** $\left(\dfrac{4}{7}\right)^3$

TEXTBOOK REFERENCES
Developing Concepts 6.8
Lesson 6.8

NEGATIVE POWERS OF FRACTIONS

For any integer n and any number $a \neq 0$, a^{-n} is the reciprocal of a^n.

That is $a^{-n} = \dfrac{1}{a^n}$ which can also be written as $\left(\dfrac{1}{a}\right)^n$.

▶ **STUDY TIP**
There is an agreement among mathematicians that any nonzero number to the zero power is one.
So, $4^0 = 1$ and $62^0 = 1$.

Example 2

Simplify the expression.

a. 4^{-3}

b. $\left(\dfrac{3}{4}\right)^{-2}$

▶ *Solution*

a. $4^{-3} = \left(\dfrac{1}{4}\right)^3$ Use the definition of negative exponents.

$= \dfrac{1}{4 \cdot 4 \cdot 4}$ Multiply.

$= \dfrac{1}{64}$ Simplify.

b. $\left(\dfrac{3}{4}\right)^{-2} = \left(\dfrac{1}{\frac{3}{4}}\right)^2$ Use the definition of negative exponents.

$= \dfrac{1}{\frac{3}{4} \cdot \frac{3}{4}}$ Multiply.

$= \dfrac{1}{\frac{9}{16}}$ Simplify.

$= 1 \cdot \dfrac{16}{9}$ Multiply by the reciprocal.

$= \dfrac{16}{9}$, or $1\dfrac{7}{9}$ Simplify.

Checkpoint ✓ Negative Exponents

Simplify the expression.

5. 8^{-2} **6.** $\left(\dfrac{1}{3}\right)^{-4}$ **7.** $\left(\dfrac{3}{5}\right)^{-3}$

SUMMARIZING KEY IDEAS
To find powers of fractions, remember what you know about powers of integers and about multiplying fractions.

Exercises   Positive and Negative Exponents

Simplify the expression.

1. 6^2

2. 5^3

3. 10^4

4. $\left(\dfrac{1}{3}\right)^5$

5. $\left(\dfrac{1}{4}\right)^{10}$

6. $\left(\dfrac{3}{7}\right)^5$

Simplify the expression.

7. 7^{-3}

8. 3^{-4}

9. 12^{-2}

10. $\left(\dfrac{1}{3}\right)^{-5}$

11. $\left(\dfrac{2}{5}\right)^{-3}$

12. $\left(\dfrac{4}{9}\right)^{-2}$

Find the number.

13. The number that equals 100 when it is squared.

14. The number that equals 27 when it is cubed.

15. What whole number raised to the fourth power equals 1296?

16. What is the greatest number that can be written with 3 digits?

TEXTBOOK LINK
On pages S19–S21, you evaluated powers of rational numbers. In Lesson 6.7 in your textbook, you will learn how to multiply and divide powers. In Lesson 6.8, you will learn more about negative exponents.

My Review Questions

Topic Review   Decimals and Powers

These exercises will help you check that you can evaluate expressions involving decimals or powers of rational numbers. If you have any questions about these topics, be sure to get them answered before going on to the next section.

1. $1.08 - 0.9$

2. $6.784 + 0.528$

3. 0.77×51

4. $2.198 \div 0.07$

5. $62.4 \div 3.9$

6. $39.7 - 36.03$

7. $1.05 + 12.9$

8. 0.05×0.06

9. 2.07×1.004

10. $0.832 \div 0.52$

11. $9.5 + 12.32 + 6.4$

12. $5.002 - 3.45$

13. $2.3414 \div 0.46$

14. $2.304 - 0.87$

15. 1.48×3.6

16. $\left(\dfrac{2}{9}\right)^3$

17. $\left(\dfrac{1}{5}\right)^4$

18. $\left(-\dfrac{1}{2}\right)^{-4}$

19. $\left(\dfrac{4}{5}\right)^{-3}$

20. $\left(\dfrac{2}{3}\right)^{-4}$

21. $\left(\dfrac{2}{3}\right)^6$

TEXTBOOK REFERENCES
Lesson 9.2

KEY WORDS
• rational number
• irrational number

▶ **VOCABULARY TIP**
A fraction is one way to write the *ratio* of two numbers. A number that can be written as the ratio of two integers is *rational*.

Rational and Irrational Numbers

Numbers that can be written as the ratio of two integers are called **rational numbers**. Rational numbers can also be written as terminating decimals or repeating decimals. Some decimals are not terminating decimals *or* repeating decimals. These decimals are **irrational numbers** because they cannot be written as a ratio of two integers.

Example 1

Explain why the number is rational.

a. $\dfrac{35}{91}$ **b.** 0.13   **c.** $3.\overline{6}$

▶ **Solution**

a. $\dfrac{35}{91}$ is written as a ratio of two integers.

b. 0.13 is a terminating decimal.

c. $3.\overline{6}$ is a repeating decimal.

If you can think of a pattern of numbers that continues forever without repeating itself, you can write an irrational number. For example, you could use the sequence of even numbers as the decimal places to write an irrational number.

$$0.246810121416182022 24\ldots$$

Example 2

Describe the pattern in the digits of the irrational number. Then write the irrational number giving the next 10 decimal places.

$$0.1223334444555556\ldots$$

▶ **Solution**

Starting with 1 in the tenths place, there are one 1, two 2s, three 3s, four 4s, etc. So written to the next 10 decimal places, the irrational number is

$$0.12233344445555566666677777\ldots$$

Many irrational numbers do not have a pattern of digits. One example of this type of irrational number is $\sqrt{2}$. The square root of a whole number is either a whole number or it is irrational. Decimals may have either rational or irrational square roots.

STUDY TIP
If the square root of a terminating decimal is rational, its square root will have fewer decimal places than the original terminating decimal.

Example 3

Tell whether the number is *rational* or *irrational*.

  a. $\sqrt{3}$ **b.** $\sqrt{4}$ **c.** $\sqrt{7.4}$ **d.** $\sqrt{6.25}$

▶ *Solution*

  a. $\sqrt{3} = 1.7320508\ldots$

      Because $\sqrt{3}$ is not a whole number, it is irrational.

  b. $\sqrt{4} = 2$

      Because $\sqrt{4}$ is a whole number, it is rational.

  c. $\sqrt{7.4} = 2.720294\ldots$

      Because $\sqrt{7.4}$ has more decimal places than 7.4, it is irrational.

  d. $\sqrt{6.25} = 2.5$

      Because $\sqrt{6.25}$ is a terminating decimal, it is rational.

SUMMARIZING KEY IDEAS
Numbers that can be written as ratios of integers or as terminating or repeating decimals are rational. Numbers that cannot be written as ratios of integers are irrational.

Checkpoint ✓   *Identifying Rational and Irrational Numbers*

Tell whether the number is *rational* or *irrational*.

1. $\dfrac{41}{37}$ **2.** $0.36912151821\ldots$ **3.** $5.\overline{6547}$ **4.** $\sqrt{81}$

TEXTBOOK LINK
On pages S22 and S23 you learned how to recognize rational numbers and some types of irrational numbers. You will learn more about irrational numbers in Lesson 9.2 in your textbook.

Exercises   *Rational and Irrational Numbers*

Tell whether the number is *rational* or *irrational*.

1. $\dfrac{56}{13}$ **2.** 0.528 **3.** $7.\overline{35}$ **4.** $-3.67\overline{2}$

5. -5.8 **6.** $\sqrt{9}$ **7.** $\sqrt{1.21}$ **8.** 19.494

9. $\sqrt{5}$ **10.** $\sqrt{8.1}$ **11.** $\sqrt{1.44}$ **12.** $\sqrt{\dfrac{1}{4}}$

KEY STANDARD

NS1.5

Know that every rational number is either a terminating or a repeating decimal and be able to convert terminating decimals into reduced fractions.

TEXTBOOK REFERENCES

Lesson 5.5

KEY WORDS

• terminating decimal
• repeating decimal

Rational Numbers and Decimals

WRITING A FRACTION AS A DECIMAL

You can write any fraction as a decimal by dividing the numerator by the denominator. If the division ends with a remainder of zero, the decimal is a **terminating decimal**. If the division produces a repeating pattern of nonzero remainders that does not end, the decimal is a **repeating decimal**.

Example 1

Write the fraction as a decimal.

a. $\dfrac{4}{5}$

b. $\dfrac{26}{11}$

▶ *Solution*

a.
$$5\overline{)4.0}^{\,0.8}$$
Divide the numerator of the fraction by the denominator.

▶ The remainder is zero. The decimal 0.8 is a terminating decimal.

b. Divide the numerator of the fraction by the denominator.

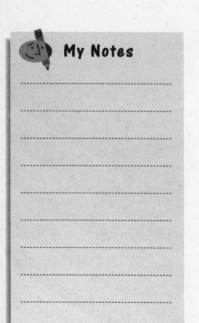

$$
\begin{array}{r}
2.3636\ldots \\
11\overline{)26.0000} \\
22 \\
\hline
40 \\
33 \\
\hline
70 \\
66 \\
\hline
40 \\
33 \\
\hline
70 \\
66 \\
\hline
4
\end{array}
$$

The quotient suggests that 36 repeats without end.

This sequence of numbers will continue to repeat without ever changing.

▶ $\dfrac{26}{11} = 2.3636\ldots$ The decimal 2.3636… is a repeating decimal.

You can use **bar notation** to indicate that the "36" repeats: $2.\overline{36}$.

My Notes

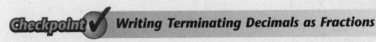

Checkpoint ✓   Writing Fractions as Decimals

Write the fraction or mixed number as a decimal.

1. $\dfrac{7}{12}$ **2.** $-4\dfrac{3}{20}$ **3.** $\dfrac{9}{16}$

TERMINATING DECIMALS

You can write a terminating decimal as a fraction or mixed number.

> **STUDY TIP**
> Try saying the decimal aloud. When you do, you'll see that it sounds like a fraction. For example, you can read 0.24 as "24 hundredths" which is the same way you read $\dfrac{24}{100}$.

Example 2

Write 0.24 as a fraction.

▶ *Solution*

$$0.24 = \frac{24}{100}$$ Write the decimal as a fraction with 100 as the denominator.

$$= \frac{24 \div 4}{100 \div 4}$$ Divide the numerator and denominator by the GCF.

$$= \frac{6}{25}$$ Simplify the fraction.

Example 3

Write 0.4 as a fraction.

▶ *Solution*

$$0.4 = \frac{4}{10}$$ Write the decimal as a fraction with 10 as the denominator.

$$= \frac{4 \div 2}{10 \div 2}$$ Divide the numerator and denominator by the GCF.

$$= \frac{2}{5}$$ Simplify the fraction.

Checkpoint ✓   Writing Terminating Decimals as Fractions

Write the terminating decimal as a fraction in simplest form.

4. 0.8   **5.** -0.74 **6.** 0.135

REPEATING DECIMALS

To write a repeating decimal as a fraction, you can use algebra.

Example 4

Write $0.\overline{45}$ as a fraction.

▶ **Solution**

Let the variable n equal the given decimal.

$$n = 0.\overline{45}$$ Multiply each side by 10^2, or 100, because 2 digits repeat.

$$100n = 45.\overline{45}$$

Subtract to eliminate the repeating part, $0.\overline{45}$.

$$100n = 45.45454545\ldots$$
$$-\quad n = 0.45454545\ldots$$ The subtraction property of equality allows you to subtract equal quantities from each side.

$$99n = 45.00000000\ldots$$

$$99n = 45$$

Now solve the new equation.

$$99n = 45$$

$$\frac{99n}{99} = \frac{45}{99}$$ Divide each side by 99.

$$n = \frac{45}{99}$$ Simplify.

$$n = \frac{45 \div 9}{99 \div 9} = \frac{5}{11}$$ Divide the numerator and denominator by the GCF.

▶ So, $0.\overline{45} = \dfrac{5}{11}$.

▶ STUDY TIP
When you write a repeating decimal as a fraction, the number of digits that repeat tells you what power of 10 to multiply by:

If 1 digit repeats, multiply by 10^1 or 10.

If 2 digits repeat, multiply by 10^2 or 100.

If n digits repeat, multiply by 10^n.

Checkpoint ✓ *Write Repeating Decimals as Fractions*

Write the repeating decimal as a fraction in simplest form.

7. $0.\overline{6}$ **8.** $2.\overline{35}$ **9.** $0.\overline{083}$

Every number that can be written as a fraction can also be written as a decimal. Not all decimals can be written as fractions. You can write terminating decimals and repeating decimals as fractions. Decimals that do not either terminate or repeat cannot be written as fractions.

SUMMARIZING KEY IDEAS

All rational numbers can be written as either terminating or repeating decimals. Decimals that do not terminate or repeat are not rational numbers. You can write a fraction as a decimal, and you can write a repeating or terminating decimal as a fraction.

Exercises *Rational Numbers and Decimals*

Write the fraction or mixed number as a decimal.

1. $\frac{1}{2}$ **2.** $\frac{1}{4}$ **3.** $5\frac{3}{4}$ **4.** $6\frac{1}{3}$

5. $-3\frac{2}{5}$ **6.** $-\frac{3}{5}$ **7.** $\frac{7}{8}$ **8.** $\frac{4}{3}$

9. $\frac{5}{9}$ **10.** $\frac{1}{11}$ **11.** $\frac{5}{8}$ **12.** $-\frac{1}{8}$

13. $\frac{4}{-9}$ **14.** $-5\frac{5}{12}$ **15.** $\frac{11}{16}$ **16.** $8\frac{5}{6}$

Write the terminating decimal as a fraction in simplest form.

17. 0.3 **18.** 1.6 **19.** -0.7 **20.** 2.8

21. 3.25 **22.** 0.75 **23.** 0.45 **24.** -1.55

25. -0.58 **26.** 3.65 **27.** -0.32 **28.** 0.54

29. 0.125 **30.** -0.368 **31.** 4.121 **32.** -0.0125

Write the repeating decimal as a fraction in simplest form.

33. $0.\overline{1}$ **34.** $-0.\overline{3}$ **35.** $-0.\overline{5}$ **36.** $0.\overline{8}$

37. $-0.\overline{16}$ **38.** $5.\overline{81}$ **39.** $0.\overline{36}$ **40.** $-0.7\overline{2}$

41. $0.2\overline{7}$ **42.** $-0.8\overline{3}$ **43.** $1.58\overline{3}$ **44.** $-0.\overline{185}$

45. Give three examples of a denominator of a fraction that will always produce a terminating decimal when the fraction is expressed as a decimal.

46. Give three examples of commonly used fractions that repeat when written as decimals. Write the decimal equivalent of each.

TEXTBOOK LINK

On pages S24–S27, you wrote rational numbers as terminating or repeating decimals. You also converted terminating and repeating decimals into fractions. In Lesson 5.5 of your textbook, you will learn more about these topics.

KEY STANDARD

NS 1.7 Solve problems that involve discounts, markups, commissions, and profit, and compute simple and compound interest.

TEXTBOOK REFERENCES
Skills Review, p. 677
Lesson 7.6

KEY WORDS
• profit
• markup
• retail price

Percent Problems

SOLVING PROBLEMS INVOLVING MARKUP

To make a profit, stores charge more for merchandise than they pay for it. The amount the store's cost is increased is called the **markup**.

$$\boxed{\text{Store's cost}} + \boxed{\text{Markup}} = \boxed{\text{Retail price}}$$

Example 1

A notebook costs a store $.79. The store wants a 65% markup on the notebooks. At what price should the notebooks sell?

▶ **Solution**

First find the markup. Then find the retail price.

65% of $.79 = 0.65 × $.79 ≈ $.51	**Multiply to find the markup.**
$.79 + $.51 = $1.30	**Store's cost + Markup = Retail price**

▶ The notebooks should sell for $1.30.

My Notes

Example 2

A store sells a blazer for $60. The markup is 25%. What is the store's cost for the blazer?

▶ **Solution**

$\boxed{\text{Store's cost}} + \boxed{\text{Markup}} = \boxed{\text{Retail price}}$	
$c + 0.25c = 60$	**Write an equation.**
$1.25c = 60$	**Combine like terms.**
$c = 48$	**Divide each side by 1.25.**

▶ The store's cost for the blazer is $48.

Checkpoint ✔ Problems Involving Markup

1. A store sells televisions. The store's cost for a TV is $89. The store wants a 60% markup. At what price should the store sell the TVs?

KEY WORDS
• discount
• sale price

SOLVING PROBLEMS INVOLVING DISCOUNT

When an item goes on sale, a store reduces its regular price to a sale price. The amount the regular price is reduced is called the discount.

$$\boxed{\text{Regular price}} - \boxed{\text{Discount}} = \boxed{\text{Sale price}}$$

Example 3

A store is having a 20% off sale. What is the price of a printer that regularly costs $159.89?

▶ **Solution** First find the discount. Then find the sale price.

20% of $159.89 = 0.20 × $159.89	**Multiply to find the discount.**
≈ $31.98	**Round up to the nearest cent.**
$159.89 − $31.98 = $127.91	**Regular price − Discount = Sale price**

▶ The sale price of the printer is $127.91.

Example 4

You are going to a 40% off sale. You want to buy a tennis racket at the sale price of $48. What is the regular price of the tennis racket?

▶ **Solution** Let n = regular price. The discount is 40% of the regular price.

$$\boxed{\text{Regular price}} - \boxed{\text{Discount}} = \boxed{\text{Sale price}}$$

$n - 0.40n = 48$	**Write an equation.**
$0.60n = 48$	**Combine like terms.**
$n = 80$	**Divide each side by 0.60.**

▶ The regular price of the tennis racket is $80.

▶**STUDY TIP**
Remember that you round up if the next smaller decimal place is 5 or greater. So, rounded to the nearest cent:

$31.7649 rounds to $31.76

$31.3651 rounds to $31.37

Checkpoint ✓ *Problems Involving Discount*

2. Find the sale price of an item that has a regular price of $180 and is discounted 40%.

3. Find the regular price of an item that has a sale price of $28.95 and is discounted 20%.

PROFIT AND COMMISSION

The profit on an item is the difference between the selling price and the expenses. Profit is often related to the markup on the item.

$$\boxed{\text{Profit}} = \boxed{\text{Selling price}} - \boxed{\text{Expenses}}$$

Many salespeople receive a **commission** as part of their pay. This is often a percent of the total sales that the salesperson makes.

$$\boxed{\text{Commission}} = \boxed{\text{Commission rate}} \cdot \boxed{\text{Total sales}}$$

Example 5

A store sells T-shirts. Each one costs the store $6.70. The store makes a profit of 50% on each T-shirt. What is the selling price of the T-shirts?

▶ **Solution** Let x be the selling price of the T-shirts.

$$\boxed{\text{Profit}} = \boxed{\text{Selling price}} - \boxed{\text{Expenses}}$$

$0.50 \cdot 6.70 = x - 6.70$	**The profit is 50% of the store's cost.**
$3.35 = x - 6.70$	**Simplify the left-hand side of the equation.**
$3.35 + 6.70 = x$	**Add 6.70 to both sides of the equation.**
$10.05 = x$	**Simplify.**

▶ The selling price of the T-shirts is $10.05.

Example 6

Mary receives a 5% commission on all the clothing that she sells during a month. If she sells $1735 worth of clothing, how much is her commission?

▶ **Solution**

Commission = 5% · Total sales	**Commission is a percent of sales.**
= 0.05 · 1735	**Substitute 1735 for Total sales.**
= 86.75	**Simplify.**

▶ Her commission is $86.75.

Checkpoint ✓ Problems Involving Profit and Commission

5. Charles receives a 7% commission on each house that he sells. He sells a house for $210,000. What is his commission?

SUMMARIZING KEY IDEAS

Markup, discount, profit, and commission problems are types of percent problems. Remember that a markup *increases* the price and a discount *decreases* the price.

Exercises   *Percent Problems*

Find the retail price. Round to the nearest cent.

1. store's cost: $60
markup rate: 60%

2. store's cost $115
markup rate: 55%

3. store's cost: $9.50
markup rate: 35%

Find the store's cost. Round to the nearest cent.

4. retail price: $180
markup rate: 40%

5. retail price: $35
markup rate: 25%

6. retail price: $15.50
markup rate: 150%

Find the sale price. Round to the nearest cent.

7. regular price: $55
discount rate: 30%

8. regular price: $76
discount rate: 25%

9. regular price: $43
discount rate: 45%

Find the regular price. Round to the nearest cent.

10. sale price: $80
discount rate: 20%

11. sale price: $12
discount rate: 25%

12. sale price: $28
discount rate: 30%

Find the store's profit. Round to the nearest cent.

13. store's cost: $45
profit rate: 70%

14. store's cost: $176
profit rate: 45%

15. store's cost: $149
profit rate: 20%

Find the salesperson's commission. Round to the nearest cent.

16. sales: $2000
commission: 10%

17. sales: $29
commission: 7%

18. sales: $154.95
commission: 3%

19. If the store's cost is considered 100% of the cost, how can you combine the percents for the store's cost and for the markup to find the retail price? Give examples to explain your reasoning.

20. If the regular price is considered 100% of the cost, how can you combine the percents for the regular price and for the discount to find the sale price?

A store's cost for a pair of sneakers is $25. The store uses a 40% markup for the sneakers, and then sells them at a 15% off sale.

21. What is the price of the sneakers before the sale? What is the sale price of the sneakers?

22. Is the sale price the same as the price would be if the store used a markup of 25% (40% markup − 15% discount)?

TEXTBOOK LINK

On pages S28–S31, you solved problems involving markup, discount, profit, and commission. You will learn more about these topics in Lesson 7.6 in your textbook.

TEXTBOOK REFERENCES
Lessons 7.8, 7.9

KEY WORDS
- interest rate
- principal
- balance
- simple interest

Simple and Compound Interest

FINDING SIMPLE INTEREST

When you deposit money in a savings account, the bank pays you interest at a certain percentage called the **interest rate**. The money you initially deposit is the **principal**. The **balance** in an account is the principal plus interest earned. **Simple interest** is interest earned only on the principal.

> **SIMPLE INTEREST**
>
> $$I = Prt$$
>
> where I is the simple interest, P is the principal, r is the interest rate per year (as a decimal), and t is the time in years.

Example 1

You deposit $200 in a bank account. The interest rate is 6% per year. How much simple interest will the account earn in 5 years?

▶ **Solution**

$I = Prt$	Use the simple interest formula.
$= 200 \cdot 0.06 \cdot 5$	Substitute. Use 0.06 for 6%.
$= 60$	Multiply.

▶ The account earns $60 interest.

Example 2

You borrow $5000 at 7% simple interest for 3 years. What is the total amount you will pay?

▶ **Solution** First find the interest. Then add the principal and interest to find the total amount.

$I = Prt$	Use the simple interest formula.
$= 5000 \cdot 0.07 \cdot 3$	Substitute. Use 0.07 for 7%.
$= 1050$	Multiply.

Account balance $= P + I = 5000 + 1050 = 6050$

▶ The total amount of money you will pay is $6050.

Checkpoint ✓ **Finding Simple Interest**

1. Find the final balance for an account with a principal of $900 at 3% simple interest for 2 years.

KEY WORDS

• principal
• interest
• compound interest
• balance

FINDING COMPOUND INTEREST

When a bank pays interest on both the principal and the interest that an account has already earned, the bank is paying compound interest.

COMPOUND INTEREST

$$A = P(1 + rt)^n$$

where A is the account balance, P is the principal, r is the interest rate per year (as a decimal), t is the time in years between compoundings, and n is the number of compounding periods.

Example 3

You deposit $200 in an account that earns 6% compounded annually. Find the balance after 3 years.

▶ **Solution**

$A = P(1 + rt)^n$ Use the compound interest formula.

$\quad = 200(1 + (0.06)(1))^3$ Substitute 200 for P, 0.06 for r, 1 for t, and 3 for n.

$\quad \approx 238.20$ Round the to the nearest hundredth.

▶ At the end of three years, the balance is $238.20.

Example 4

You invest $575 at 6.25% annual interest compounded quarterly. What will your balance be after 5 years?

▶ **STUDY TIP**
In Example 4, the time is $t = 0.25$ because the compounding occurs quarterly. In 5 years, there are 20 quarterly compoundings.

▶ **Solution**

$A = P(1 + rt)^n$ Use the compound interest formula.

$\quad = 575(1 + (0.0625)(0.25))^{20}$ Substitute 575 for P, 0.0625 for r, 0.25 for t, and 20 for n.

$\quad \approx 783.65$ Round to the nearest hundredth.

▶ After 5 years, your balance will be $783.65.

Checkpoint ✓ *Finding Compound Interest*

Find the final balance for the account.

2. $1700 at 7% compounded annually for 2 years

3. $14,000 at 3.25% compounded annually for 3 years

4. $850 at 5.5% compounded quarterly for 5 years

SUMMARIZING KEY IDEAS

Simple interest is paid only on the principal, not on interest that has already been paid. Unlike simple interest, compound interest is paid on the principal and on interest that has already been paid.

Exercises *Finding Simple and Compound Interest*

Find the final balance for the account. Round to the nearest cent.

1. $2000 at 6% simple interest for 3 years

2. $2500 at 6% compounded annually for 3 years

3. $5000 at 5% simple interest for 10 years

4. $5000 at 5% compounded annually for 10 years

5. $6000 at 5% compounded quarterly for 8 years

6. $1750 at 5% simple interest for 2 years

7. $800 at 4.25% simple interest for 6 years

8. $1250 at $4\frac{1}{2}$% compounded quarterly for 3 years

Answer the question.

9. You invest $500. How much will it grow to in 20 years at 6% simple interest?

10. In Exercise 9, how much more will you have in the account if the interest is compounded annually?

11. Which earns more simple interest, $1000 at 5% for 10 years or $1000 at 10% for 5 years? How much more?

12. Which earns more interest compounded annually, $1000 at 5% for 10 years or $1000 at 10% for 5 years? How much more?

TEXTBOOK LINK

On pages S32–S34 you calculated simple interest and compound interest. You will learn more about these topics in Lessons 7.8 and 7.9 in your textbook.

Topic Review *Percent Problems*

These exercises will help you check that you can solve problems that involve discounts, markups, and profit, and compute simple and compound interest. If you have any questions about these topics, be sure to get them answered before going on to the next section.

Find the missing information. Round to the nearest cent.

1. store's cost: $12.50
   markup rate: 50%
   selling price: ?

2. regular price: $10
   discount: 20%
   sale price: ?

3. store's cost: ?
   markup rate: 10%
   selling price: $64.49

4. regular price: $20.95
   discount rate: 15%
   sale price: ?

5. store's cost: $2000
   markup rate: 95%
   selling price: ?

6. regular price: $4000
   discount rate: 15%
   sale price: ?

7. store's cost: $21.00
   markup rate: 100%
   selling price: ?

8. store's cost: ?
   markup rate: 45%
   selling price: $25.50

9. store's cost: ?
   markup rate: 20%
   selling price: $55

10. store's cost: $40.00
    markup rate: ?
    selling price: $60.00

11. total sales: $312,000
    commission rate: 4%
    commission: ?

12. total sales: $3176
    commission rate: 2.5%
    commission: ?

13. store's cost: $21.90
    profit rate: 45%
    selling price: ?

14. store's cost: $210
    profit rate: 36%
    selling price: ?

Find the balance for each account. Round to the nearest cent.

15. $4500 at 8% compounded annually for 3 years

16. $198 at $5\frac{1}{2}$% simple interest for 3 years

17. $1000 at 4% simple interest for $2\frac{1}{2}$ years

18. $2000 at $3\frac{1}{2}$% compounded quarterly for 2 years

My Review Questions

KEY STANDARD

Number
Sense

NS2.2

Add and subtract fractions by using factoring to find common denominators.

TEXTBOOK REFERENCES
Skills Review, p. 677
Lessons 6.1, 6.2

KEY WORDS
• common denominator
• least common denominator (LCD)

Add and Subtract Fractions

USING A RULE

THE SUM AND DIFFERENCE OF TWO FRACTIONS

$$\frac{a}{b} + \frac{c}{d} = \frac{ad + bc}{bd} \qquad \frac{a}{b} - \frac{c}{d} = \frac{ad - bc}{bd}$$

where b and d are not zero.

Example 1

Find the sum or difference.   **a.** $\frac{2}{3} + \frac{3}{4}$ **b.** $\frac{7}{12} - \frac{5}{4}$

▶ **Solution**

My Notes

a. $\frac{2}{3} + \frac{3}{4} = \frac{2(4) + 3(3)}{3(4)}$ Use the rule for the sum of fractions.

$= \frac{8 + 9}{12} = \frac{17}{12}$, or $1\frac{5}{12}$ Simplify.

b. $\frac{7}{12} - \frac{5}{4} = \frac{7(4) - 12(5)}{12(4)}$ Use the rule for the difference of fractions.

$= \frac{28 - 60}{48} = \frac{-32}{48}$ Simplify. Then subtract.

$= \frac{-1 \cdot 2 \cdot 2 \cdot 2 \cdot 2 \cdot 2}{2 \cdot 2 \cdot 2 \cdot 2 \cdot 3} = \frac{-2}{3}$ Factor the numerator and denominator and simplify.

Checkpoint ✓ Add and Subtract Fractions

Find the sum or the difference.

1. $\frac{1}{2} + \frac{3}{5}$ **2.** $\frac{3}{7} - \frac{1}{5}$ **3.** $\frac{2}{3} + \frac{5}{6}$

USING FACTORING TO FIND THE LCD

You can use factoring to find the least common denominator. Often, this will make the numbers smaller and sometimes it will make the solution easier to simplify.

Example 2

> **STUDY TIP**
> Notice in part (b) of Example 1 that the denominator of $\frac{5}{4}$ is a factor of the denominator of $\frac{7}{12}$.
> So you can write the fractions with a LCD of 12.

Evaluate the expression.

a. $\dfrac{7}{12} - \dfrac{5}{4}$

b. $\dfrac{5}{12} + \dfrac{3}{16}$

▶ **Solution**

a. $\dfrac{7}{12} - \dfrac{5}{4} = \dfrac{7}{12} - \dfrac{5(3)}{4(3)}$ The least common multiple (LCM) of 12 and 4 is 12. So write $\dfrac{5}{4}$ with a denominator of 12.

$= \dfrac{7}{12} - \dfrac{15}{12}$

$= \dfrac{7 - 15}{12}$

$= \dfrac{-8}{12}$

These numbers are easier to work with than the numbers in part (b) of Example 1.

$= \dfrac{-8 \div 4}{12 \div 4} = -\dfrac{2}{3}$

b. Factor the denominators to find the LCD.

$12 = \boxed{2 \cdot 2} \cdot 3$

$16 = \boxed{2 \cdot 2} \cdot 2 \cdot 2$ Use repeated factors only once.

The LCM of 12 and 16 is $\boxed{2 \cdot 2} \cdot 2 \cdot 2 \cdot 3 = 48$.

$\dfrac{5}{12} + \dfrac{3}{16} = \dfrac{5(4)}{12(4)} + \dfrac{3(3)}{16(3)}$ Write the fractions with their LCD.

$= \dfrac{20}{48} + \dfrac{9}{48}$ Simplify.

$= \dfrac{20 + 9}{48}$ Add.

$= \dfrac{29}{48}$ Simplify.

SUMMARIZING KEY IDEAS

To add or subtract fractions, first find a common denominator. Two choices for a common denominator are: (1) the product of the fractions' denominators, and (2) the LCM of the denominators.

Checkpoint ✓ **Factoring to Find the LCD**

Use factoring to find the LCM.

4. 2, 10   **5.** 6, 9   **6.** 30, 42

Evaluate the expression.

7. $\dfrac{1}{2} + \dfrac{7}{10}$ **8.** $\dfrac{7}{9} - \dfrac{1}{6}$ **9.** $\dfrac{1}{30} + \dfrac{5}{42}$

When adding and subtracting fractions, using factoring to find the LCD gives the same result as using the rules.

Exercises Adding and Subtracting Fractions

Use factoring to find the LCM.

1. 6, 7   **2.** 12, 9   **3.** 45, 60   **4.** 56, 96

Use the rules to find the sum or difference. Then use factoring to find the LCD before adding or subtracting.

5. $\dfrac{5}{6} + \dfrac{1}{8}$ **6.** $\dfrac{4}{5} - \dfrac{11}{20}$ **7.** $\dfrac{6}{10} - \dfrac{3}{100}$ **8.** $\dfrac{3}{5} + \dfrac{2}{7}$

Find the sum or difference.

9. $\dfrac{1}{2} + \dfrac{1}{3}$ **10.** $\dfrac{1}{4} + \dfrac{2}{5}$ **11.** $\dfrac{2}{3} - \dfrac{1}{4}$ **12.** $\dfrac{2}{5} - \dfrac{2}{3}$

13. $\dfrac{6}{7} - \dfrac{1}{6}$ **14.** $\dfrac{5}{9} - \dfrac{1}{6}$ **15.** $\dfrac{5}{12} + \dfrac{5}{6}$ **16.** $\dfrac{3}{10} + \dfrac{7}{15}$

17. $\dfrac{5}{3} + \dfrac{7}{21}$ **18.** $\dfrac{13}{14} - \dfrac{4}{21}$ **19.** $\dfrac{7}{24} - \dfrac{3}{10}$ **20.** $\dfrac{5}{8} - \dfrac{3}{7}$

21. Copy and complete.

$$\frac{a}{b} - \frac{c}{d} = \frac{a(?)}{b(?)} - \frac{?}{bd}$$

$$= \frac{a(?) - ?}{?}$$

TEXTBOOK LINK

On pages S36–S38, you used a common denominator to add and subtract fractions. You will learn more about this topic in Lessons 6.1 and 6.2 in your textbook.

Multiply, divide, and simplify rational expressions by using exponent rules.

TEXTBOOK REFERENCES

Lesson 6.7

KEY WORDS

• power
• base
• exponent
• product of powers property

Exponent Rules

MULTIPLYING POWERS

You can use repeated multiplication or the product of powers property to multiply powers with the same base.

> **PRODUCT OF POWERS PROPERTY**
>
> When you multiply powers with the same base, keep the base and add the exponents.
>
> $$a^m \cdot a^n = a^{m+n}$$

Example 1

Simplify the product. **a.** $7^5 \cdot 7^3$ **b.** $-\dfrac{3}{4} \cdot \left(-\dfrac{3}{4}\right)^2$

▶ *Solution*

a. METHOD 1

$$7^5 \cdot 7^3 = \underbrace{(7 \cdot 7 \cdot 7 \cdot 7 \cdot 7)}_{\text{5 factors}} \cdot \underbrace{(7 \cdot 7 \cdot 7)}_{\text{3 factors}} = 7^8 \qquad \text{Use repeated multiplication.}$$

METHOD 2

$$7^5 \cdot 7^3 = 7^{5+3} = 7^8 \qquad \text{Use product of powers property.}$$

b. $-\dfrac{3}{4} \cdot \left(-\dfrac{3}{4}\right)^2 = \left(-\dfrac{3}{4}\right)^{1+2} = \left(-\dfrac{3}{4}\right)^3 \qquad$ Use product of powers property.

Checkpoint ✓ *Multiplying Powers*

Simplify the product. Use repeated multiplication or the product of powers property.

1. $2^3 \cdot 2^2$ **2.** $(-6)^4 \cdot (-6)^5$ **3.** $\left(\dfrac{2}{7}\right)^2 \cdot \left(\dfrac{2}{7}\right)^2$ **4.** $\left(-\dfrac{3}{5}\right)^3 \cdot \left(-\dfrac{3}{5}\right)^4$

My Notes

KEY WORDS

• quotient of powers property

DIVIDING POWERS

You can use repeated multiplication or the quotient of powers property to divide powers with the same base.

> ### QUOTIENT OF POWERS PROPERTY
>
> When you divide powers with the same base, keep the base and subtract the exponents.
>
> $$\frac{a^m}{a^n} = a^{m-n}$$

Example 2

Simplify the quotient.   **a.** $\dfrac{(-3)^4}{-3}$ **b.** $\dfrac{a^5}{a^3}$

▶ **Solution**

a. METHOD 1

$$\frac{(-3)^4}{-3} = \frac{(-3) \cdot (-3) \cdot (-3) \cdot (-3)}{-3} = (-3)^3 \qquad \text{Use repeated multiplication.}$$

METHOD 2

$$\frac{(-3)^4}{-3} = (-3)^{4-1} = (-3)^3 \qquad \text{Use quotient of powers property.}$$

b. METHOD 1

$$\frac{a^5}{a^3} = \frac{a \cdot a \cdot a \cdot a \cdot a}{a \cdot a \cdot a} = a^2 \qquad \text{Use repeated multiplication.}$$

METHOD 2

$$\frac{a^5}{a^3} = a^{5-3} = a^2 \qquad \text{Use quotient of powers property.}$$

Checkpoint ✓ *Dividing Powers*

Simplify the quotient.

5. $\dfrac{7^8}{7^3}$ **6.** $\dfrac{(-10)^6}{(-10)^4}$ **7.** $\dfrac{x^4}{x^2}$ **8.** $\dfrac{(-n)^9}{(-n)^5}$

SUMMARIZING KEY IDEAS

When you multiply powers with the same base, you add the exponents. When you divide powers with the same base, you subtract the exponents.

Exercises Multiplying and Dividing Powers

Simplify the product.

1. $7^3 \cdot 7^2$

2. $9^4 \cdot 9^3$

3. $(-3)^4 \cdot (-3)^6$

4. $(-8)^3 \cdot (-8)^9$

5. $\left(\dfrac{9}{5}\right)^2 \cdot \left(\dfrac{9}{5}\right)^3$

6. $\left(\dfrac{1}{10}\right)^3 \cdot \dfrac{1}{10}$

7. $\left(\dfrac{5}{6}\right)^5 \cdot \left(\dfrac{5}{6}\right)^6$

8. $\left(-\dfrac{7}{3}\right)^8 \cdot \left(-\dfrac{7}{3}\right)^2$

9. $\left(-\dfrac{4}{11}\right)^{15} \cdot \left(-\dfrac{4}{11}\right)^{10}$

Simplify the quotient.

10. $\dfrac{5^6}{5^4}$

11. $\dfrac{2^{10}}{2^7}$

12. $\dfrac{(-7)^5}{(-7)^2}$

13. $\dfrac{(-16)^7}{(-16)^7}$

14. $\dfrac{a^6}{a^2}$

15. $\dfrac{t^9}{t^5}$

16. $\dfrac{(-y)^8}{(-y)^3}$

17. $\dfrac{(-m)^{15}}{(-m)^8}$

Describe and correct the error.

18.

$$2^5 \cdot 2^3 = 4^8$$

19.

$$\dfrac{3^4}{3^3} = 1$$

Simplify the expression.

20. $\dfrac{(-50)^7}{(-50)^5}$

21. $-73 \cdot (-73)^2$

22. $202^4 \cdot 202^8$

23. $\dfrac{123^9}{123^3}$

24. $b^3 \cdot b$

25. $(-s)^6 \cdot (-s)^4$

26. $\dfrac{x^6}{x^5}$

27. $\dfrac{(-n)^{10}}{(-n)^2}$

Write and simplify a numerical expression for the given phrase.

28. The product of five squared and five raised to the fourth power

29. The quotient of seven raised to the ninth power and seven raised to the eighth power

Tell whether the statement is *true* or *false*. If it is false, rewrite the right side of the equation to make it true.

30. $5^4 \cdot 5^3 = 5^{12}$

31. $9^4 \cdot 9^7 \cdot 9^3 = 9^{14}$

32. $\dfrac{8^6}{8^2} = 8^3$

TEXTBOOK LINK

On pages S39–S41, you used repeated multiplication and properties of exponents to simplify powers. You will learn more about these topics in Lesson 6.7 in your textbook.

Understand the meaning of the absolute value of a number; interpret the absolute value as the distance of the number from zero on a number line, and determine the absolute value of real numbers.

TEXTBOOK REFERENCES

Lesson 3.1

KEY WORDS

• absolute value
• opposite

Absolute Value

The **absolute value** of a number is its distance from 0 on a number line. You write "the absolute value of -3" as $|-3|$.

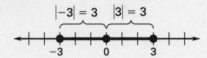

Two numbers that have the same absolute value but opposite signs are called **opposites**. You write the opposite of 3 as -3.

Example 1

Find the absolute value of 6. Then write the opposite of 6.

▶ **Solution**

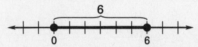

On a number line, 6 is 6 units from 0. So, $|6| = 6$.
On a number line, -6 is also 6 units from 0. So, -6 is the opposite of 6.

My Notes

Example 2

Find the absolute value of -8. Then write the opposite of -8.

▶ **Solution**

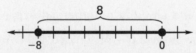

On the number line, -8 is 8 units from 0. So, $|-8|$ is 8.
On a number line, 8 is also 8 units from 0. So, 8 is the opposite of -8.

Checkpoint ✓ *Finding Absolute Values*

Find the absolute value of the given number. Then write the opposite of the given number.

1. 3   **2.** -1 **3.** 0   **4.** -15

The absolute value of a number is its distance from zero on a number line. Absolute value is written with two vertical rules called absolute value bars.

WRITE: **SAY:**

$$\left| -4\frac{1}{2} \right| = 4\frac{1}{2}$$ The absolute value of $-4\frac{1}{2}$ is $4\frac{1}{2}$.

Two numbers that have the same absolute value but have opposite signs are called opposites.

WRITE: **SAY:**

$-(-14.6) = 14.6$ The opposite of -14.6 is 14.6.

SUMMARIZING KEY IDEAS

Absolute value tells the distance a number is from zero, not its direction from zero. Therefore absolute value is never negative. Two numbers are opposites if they have the same absolute value but opposite signs.

Exercises *Finding Absolute Values*

Find the absolute value of the number.

1. $|3|$ **2.** $|-2|$ **3.** $|-1|$ **4.** $|50|$

5. $|-47|$ **6.** $|95|$ **7.** $|-44.33|$ **8.** $|-18.6|$

9. $|10.34|$ **10.** $\left| -2\frac{4}{5} \right|$ **11.** $\left| 4\frac{1}{2} \right|$ **12.** $\left| -8\frac{9}{10} \right|$

Write the opposite of the number.

13. 3 **14.** -2 **15.** -10 **16.** 74

17. -38 **18.** 100 **19.** 2.3 **20.** 6.6

21. -1.75 **22.** $-3\frac{4}{5}$ **23.** $8\frac{8}{9}$ **24.** $-1\frac{1}{4}$

Graph the numbers on a number line.

25. Two numbers that have an absolute value of 5

26. Two numbers that have an absolute value of 7.2

27. Two numbers that have an absolute value of $1\frac{3}{4}$

TEXTBOOK LINK

On pages S42 and S43, you used a number line to find absolute values. You will learn more about this topic in Lesson 3.1 in your textbook.

Answer the question. Give examples to explain your reasoning.

28. How is the absolute value of a negative number related to its opposite?

29. Why is the opposite of a negative number a positive number?

Simplify numerical expressions by applying the properties of rational numbers (e.g., identity, inverse, distributive, associative, commutative) and justify the process used.

TEXTBOOK REFERENCES
Lessons 1.7

KEY WORDS
- terms
- factors
- commutative
- associative
- opposite of a number

Commutative and Associative Properties

ADDITION AND MULTIPLICATION PROPERTIES

Use the commutative property to group opposites, group negative numbers, or to make multiples of 10. Use the associative property to change the grouping of the terms or the factors.

COMMUTATIVE AND ASSOCIATIVE PROPERTIES

COMMUTATIVE PROPERTY OF ADDITION
The order of the terms does not change the sum.

$8 + 12 = 12 + 8$ $a + b = b + a$

COMMUTATIVE PROPERTY OF MULTIPLICATION
The order of the factors does not change the product.

$8 \cdot 12 = 12 \cdot 8$ $ab = ba$

ASSOCIATIVE PROPERTY OF ADDITION
The grouping of the terms does not change the sum.

$(4 + 5) + 7 = 4 + (5 + 7)$ $(a + b) + c = a + (b + c)$

ASSOCIATIVE PROPERTY OF MULTIPLICATION:
The grouping of the factors does not change the product.

$(4 \cdot 5) \cdot 7 = 4 \cdot (5 \cdot 7)$ $(ab)c = a(bc)$

My Notes

Example 1

Find the missing number. (Do not evaluate.)

a. $29 + 46 = 46 + \underline{\ ?\ }$ **b.** $20 + (18 + 7) = (\underline{\ ?\ } + 18) + 7$

c. $18 \cdot 31 = 31 \cdot \underline{\ ?\ }$ **d.** $10 \cdot (28 \cdot 5) = (\underline{\ ?\ } \cdot 28) \cdot 5$

▶ **Solution**

a. Comm. prop. of addition
   $29 + 46 = 46 + \mathbf{29}$

b. Assoc. prop. of addition
   $20 + (18 + 7) = (\mathbf{20} + 18) + 7$

c. Comm. prop. of multiplication
   $18 \cdot 31 = 31 \cdot \mathbf{18}$

d. Assoc. prop. of multiplication
   $10 \cdot (28 \cdot 5) = (\mathbf{10} \cdot 28) \cdot 5$

▶**STUDY TIP**
Parentheses are used to group numbers in an expression. Do the work within the parentheses first.

STUDY TIP
Evaluating numerical expressions can be made simpler by combining the commutative and associative properties with mental math strategies.

Example 2

Evaluate 5 + (−7) + (−5). Justify each step.

▶ *Solution*

Look for numbers that are easy to add. Notice that 5 and −5 are opposites.

$$5 + (-7) + (-5) = 5 + (-5) + (-7) \quad \text{Commutative property of addition}$$
$$= 0 + (-7) \quad \text{Add 5 and −5.}$$
$$= -7 \quad \text{Add 0 and −7.}$$

Example 3

Evaluate 25 · (7 · 4). Justify each step.

▶ *Solution*

Look for numbers that are easy to multiply. Notice that multiplying 25 by 4 is 100, a multiple of 10.

$$25 \cdot (7 \cdot 4) = 25 \cdot (4 \cdot 7) \quad \text{Commutative property of multiplication}$$
$$= (25 \cdot 4) \cdot 7 \quad \text{Associative property of multiplication}$$
$$= 100 \cdot 7 \quad \text{Multiply inside parentheses.}$$
$$= 700 \quad \text{Multiply 100 and 7.}$$

Checkpoint ✔ Addition and Multiplication Properties

Evaluate the expression. Justify each step.

1. $16 + 37 + (-16)$ **2.** $5 \cdot 7 \cdot 8$ **3.** $5 \cdot 31 \cdot (-2)$

SUBTRACTION AND DIVISION EXPRESSIONS

If you reverse the order of the terms in a subtraction or division expression, the value of the expression changes.

$$2 - 8 = -6 \qquad\qquad 8 \div 2 = 4$$

$$8 - 2 = 6 \qquad\qquad 2 \div 8 = \frac{1}{4}$$

Subtraction and division are not commutative.

Example 4

Tell whether the statement is true or false.

a. $6 - (3 - 2) \stackrel{?}{=} (6 - 3) - 2$ **b.** $6 \div (3 \div 2) \stackrel{?}{=} (6 \div 3) \div 2$

▶ *Solution*

a. $6 - (3 - 2) = 6 - 1 = 5$ **b.** $6 \div (3 \div 2) = 6 \div \dfrac{3}{2} = 4$

$(6 - 3) - 2 = 3 - 2 = 1$ $(6 \div 3) \div 2 = 2 \div 2 = 1$

False.   False.

From Example 4 you can see that subtraction and division are not associative. You can rewrite a subtraction problem as an addition problem or a division problem as a multiplication problem if you want to use properties to evaluate these expressions.

Example 5

Rewrite $687 + 419 - 187$ as an addition expression and evaluate using mental math.

▶ *Solution*

$687 + 419 - 187 = 687 + 419 + (-187)$ To subtract 187, add its opposite.

$= 687 + (-187) + 419$ Commutative property of addition

$= 500 + 419$ Add 687 and −187.

$= 919$ Add 500 and 419.

> ▶**STUDY TIP**
> Check the result of a subtraction by using addition. For example, to check that $3 - 6 = -3$, note that $6 + (-3) = 3$.

Checkpoint ✓ *Subtraction and Division Expressions*

Rewrite the expression as an addition expression or as a multiplication expression. Then evaluate the expression using mental math.

4. $-661 - 134 - 39$ **5.** $1046 - 350 + 54$ **6.** $175 + 714 - 25$

7. $500 \cdot 13 \div 5$ **8.** $256 \cdot 5 \div 16$ **9.** $110 \cdot 37 \div 11$

Use the commutative property and the associative property to group opposites, to group negative numbers, or to make multiples of 10.

Group opposites.	Group negatives.	Make multiples of 10.
$(-8) + (-15) + 8$	$-13 + 25 + (-18) + 9$	$6 + (-28) + 54$
$= (-8) + 8 + (-15)$	$= -13 + (-18) + 25 + 9$	$= 6 + 54 + (-28)$
$= 0 + (-15)$	$= -31 + 34$	$= 60 + (-28)$
$= -15$	$= 3$	$= 32$

SUMMARIZING KEY IDEAS

When using mental math to evaluate expressions, look for numbers that are easy to add or multiply. This can be done by grouping opposites, grouping negative numbers, or making multiples of 10.

Exercises Commutative and Associative Properties

Name the property shown by the statement.

1. $g \cdot t = t \cdot g$ **2.** $5 \cdot (6 \cdot 9) = (5 \cdot 6) \cdot 9$

3. $(7 + 3) + 4 = (3 + 7) + 4$ **4.** $(x + y) + z = x + (y + z)$

Use the properties of addition and multiplication to evaluate the numerical expression.

5. $22 + (25 + 18)$ **6.** $2 \cdot (-327 \cdot 5)$ **7.** $(5 \cdot 27) \cdot 2$

8. $30 + (45 + 70)$ **9.** $(75 + 18) + 25$ **10.** $4 \cdot (15 \cdot 5)$

11. $-250 \cdot (7 \cdot 4)$ **12.** $(25 + 32) + 8$ **13.** $17 + (49 + 3)$

14. $(50 \cdot 25) \cdot 2$ **15.** $-4 \cdot 356 \cdot 25$ **16.** $8 + (44 + 12)$

Evaluate each expression using mental math. Explain your method.

17. $-3 + 14 + (-7) + 6$ **18.** $(-55) + (-63) + 55$

19. $4 + (-8) + 19 + (-7)$ **20.** $87 + 32 + 13$

21. $178 + 288 + 22$ **22.** $-5 + 2 + 18 + (-45)$

TEXTBOOK LINK

On pages S44–S47, you used the commutative and associative properties to add and multiply numbers. In Lesson 1.7 in your textbook, you will use the properties to justify an answer.

Rewrite each expression as an addition expression or a multiplication expression. Then evaluate using mental math.

23. $514 - 250 + 86$ **24.** $1021 - 112 - 21$ **25.** $222 \cdot (-17) \div 111$

26. $144 \cdot 7 \div 12$ **27.** $333 - 401 + 167$ **28.** $-482 - 350 + 32$

29. $500 \cdot 19 \div 5$ **30.** $72 \cdot (-11) \div 8$ **31.** $-1567 + 59 - 433$

TEXTBOOK REFERENCES
Lessons 1.8, 2.2

KEY WORDS

• sum
• difference
• variable
• like terms
• expression

The Distributive Property

The distributive property combines multiplication with addition or subtraction.

DISTRIBUTIVE PROPERTY

$a(b + c) = a(b) + a(c)$ $\qquad$ $4(7 + 3) = 4(7) + 4(3)$

$a(b - c) = a(b) - a(c)$ $\qquad$ $4(7 - 3) = 4(7) - 4(3)$

You can use the distributive property to rewrite one factor as the sum or difference of two numbers.

Example 1

Evaluate 25(14).

▶ **Solution**

$25(14) = 25(10 + 4)$ $\qquad$ $14 = 10 + 4$

$\qquad = 25(10) + 25(4)$ $\qquad$ **Use the distributive property.**

$\qquad = 250 + 100$ $\qquad$ **Multiply.**

$\qquad = 350$ $\qquad$ **Add.**

Example 2

Evaluate (7 · 14) + (7 · 26).

▶ **Solution**

$(7 \cdot 14) + (7 \cdot 26) = 7(14 + 26)$ $\qquad$ **Use the distributive property.**

$\qquad = 7(40)$ $\qquad$ **Add inside the parentheses.**

$\qquad = 280$ $\qquad$ **Multiply.**

When evaluating a variable expression, you can use the distributive property to write an equivalent expression. Then substitute the variable before you evaluate. Sometimes the distributive property is written as:

$$(a + b)c = a \cdot c + b \cdot c \quad \text{or} \quad (a - b)c = a \cdot c - b \cdot c$$

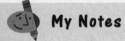
My Notes

Example 3

Use the distributive property to write an equivalent variable expression for the expression $12(n - 4)$. Then evaluate the equivalent expression when $n = 6$.

▶ **Solution**

$$12(n - 4) = 12n - (12 \cdot 4)$$ Use the distributive property.

$$= 12n - 48$$ Simplify.

$$= 12 \cdot 6 - 48$$ Substitute 6 for n.

$$= 72 - 48 = 24$$ Simplify.

Example 4

Simplify $5x + 2(2x + y)$.

▶ **Solution**

$$5x + 2(2x + y) = 5x + 2(2x) + 2(y)$$ Use the distributive property.

$$= 5x + 4x + 2y$$ Multiply.

$$= 9x + 2y$$ Add like terms.

Checkpoint ✓ The Distributive Property

Write an equivalent expression using the distributive property. Then evaluate the equivalent expression.

1. $(x \cdot 76) + (x \cdot 24)$ when $x = 9$ **2.** $23(t + 5)$ when $t = 3$

3. $(a + 5)3$ when $a = 8$ **4.** $12(p - 8)$ when $p = 11$

Simplify the variable expression.

5. $14s - 5(2s + 3t)$ **6.** $10b + 7(5c + 4b)$

7. Here is one way to evaluate $40(99.5)$. Justify each step.

$$40(99.5) = 40(100 - 0.5)$$

$$= 40(100) - 40(0.5)$$

$$= 4000 - 20$$

$$= 3980$$

SUMMARIZING KEY IDEAS
You can use the distributive property to rewrite one factor as the sum or difference of two numbers.

Exercises The Distributive Property

Use the distributive property and mental math to evaluate the expression.

1. $8(3.9)$ **2.** $16(210)$ **3.** $5(250.3)$ **4.** $15(2300)$

5. $(11 \cdot 110) - (11 \cdot 99)$ **6.** $(14 \cdot 32) + (14 \cdot 168)$

7. $(44 \cdot 16) - (40 \cdot 16)$ **8.** $(13 \cdot 50) + (7 \cdot 50)$

9. $(64 \cdot 5) + (24 \cdot 5) + (12 \cdot 5)$ **10.** $(96 \cdot 3) + (14 \cdot 3) - (22 \cdot 3)$

Simplify the expression by adding or subtracting like terms.

11. $15b + 7(2b + 9)$ **12.** $3x + 11(2y + 9x)$ **13.** $6 - t + 9(4t + 5)$

14. $2m + 6(13m + n)$ **15.** $24(2a + 5c) - 7c$ **16.** $5(x + 4y) + x + y$

17. To find the area of the shaded region at the right, subtract the area of the smaller rectangle from the area of the larger rectangle. Write a variable expression for the area of this shaded region. Then simplify this expression.

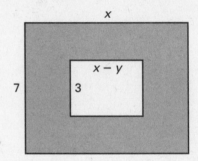

Write an equivalent expression using the distributive property. Then evaluate the equivalent expression.

18. $4(6 + x)$ when $x = 3$ **19.** $(8 + k)6$ when $k = 5$

20. $20(c - 4)$ when $c = 11$ **21.** $(a + 3)5$ when $a = 8$

22. $t(7 - 4)$ when $t = 9$ **23.** $(y - 2)5$ when $y = 15$

24. $n(12 - 4)$ when $n = 7$ **25.** $(4 + p)8$ when $p = 9$

Write an expression to describe the situation. Then use the distributive property to evaluate the expression.

26. A store sold 64 video tapes on Thursday and 36 on Friday. Each tape costs $18. What was the total video tape sales for both days?

27. You run 8 laps at each practice session. You practiced 4 times last week and 5 times this week. How many laps did you run?

TEXTBOOK LINK
On pages S48–S50, you used the distributive property to combine two operations and to simplify expressions. In Lessons 1.8 and 2.2 in your textbook, you will use the distributive property to write equivalent expressions and to solve problems.

TEXTBOOK REFERENCES
Lessons 2.2, 3.3, 6.3

KEY WORDS
- sum
- product
- opposite
- multiplicative inverse

Identity and Inverse Properties

Two additional properties of addition and multiplication that can be used to simplify expressions are the identity property and the inverse property.

IDENTITY AND INVERSE PROPERTIES

IDENTITY PROPERTY OF ADDITION
The sum of a number and 0 is the number.

$$a + 0 = a \qquad\qquad 3 + 0 = 3$$

IDENTITY PROPERTY OF MULTIPLICATION
The product of a number and 1 is the number.

$$a \cdot 1 = a \qquad\qquad 3 \cdot 1 = 3$$

INVERSE PROPERTY OF ADDITION
The sum of an integer and its opposite is 0.

$$a + (-a) = 0 \qquad\qquad 3 + (-3) = 0$$

INVERSE PROPERTY OF MULTIPLICATION
The product of a nonzero rational number and its multiplicative inverse is 1.

$$\frac{a}{b} \cdot \frac{b}{a} = 1 \qquad\qquad \frac{3}{5} \cdot \frac{5}{3} = 1$$

My Notes

Example 1

Identify the property that makes the statement true.

a. $(-111) + 0 = -111$

b. $-21 + 21 = 0$

c. $-14 \cdot \left(-\dfrac{1}{14}\right) = 1$

d. $\dfrac{3}{8} \cdot 1 = \dfrac{3}{8}$

▶ **Solution**

a. Identity property of addition

b. Inverse property of addition

c. Inverse property of multiplication

d. Identity property of multiplication

SUMMARIZING KEY IDEAS
The sum of an integer and its additive inverse is 0, the identity for addition. The product of a nonzero rational number and its multiplicative inverse is 1, the identity for multiplication.

Example 2

Evaluate $49 + 13\left(1 + \dfrac{1}{13}\right) - 49$. Justify each step.

▶ **Solution**

$$49 + 13\left(1 + \frac{1}{13}\right) - 49$$

$= 49 + 13(1) + 13\left(\dfrac{1}{13}\right) - 49$	Use the distributive property.
$= 49 + 13 + 13\left(\dfrac{1}{13}\right) - 49$	Identity property of multiplication
$= 49 + 13 + 1 - 49$	Inverse property of multiplication
$= 49 + 14 + (-49)$	Add 13 and 1. Rewrite as an addition expression.
$= 49 + (-49) + 14$	Commutative property of addition
$= 0 + 14$	Inverse property of addition
$= 14$	Identity property of addition

Checkpoint ✓ *Identity and Inverse Properties*

Evaluate the expression. Justify each step.

1. $-274 + 1513 + 274$

2. $318\left(\dfrac{1}{318} + 1\right) - 318$

Exercises *Identity and Inverse Properties*

Name the property shown by each statement.

1. $(1)\left(\dfrac{1}{428}\right) = \dfrac{1}{428}$

2. $-395 + 395 = 0$

3. $0 + (-d) = -d$

Evaluate the expression. Justify each step.

4. $2315 + 68 - 2315 - 68$

5. $441 \cdot \dfrac{1}{441} + 0$

6. $\left(\dfrac{13}{61} \cdot \dfrac{61}{13}\right) \cdot 118$

7. $(-357 + 357) + (-601)$

TEXTBOOK LINK
On pages S51 and S52, you used the identity and inverse properties when simplifying expressions. In your textbook, Lessons 2.2, 3.3, and 6.3, pp. 57–60, 116–120, and 278–282, you will use these properties to justify an answer.

Topic Review *Properties of Operations*

These exercises will help you check that you can apply properties of addition and multiplication when evaluating and simplifying expressions. If you have any questions about these properties, be sure to get them answered before going on to the next section.

Name the property shown by each statement.

1. $(17 \cdot 22) \cdot 6 = 17 \cdot (22 \cdot 6)$ **2.** $x(y + z) = xy + xz$

3. $(b + c) + d = (c + b) + d$ **4.** $-921 + 921 = 0$

Evaluate the numerical expression.

5. $8(31) + 8(19)$ **6.** $12 \cdot (-32) \cdot 5$ **7.** $1250 \cdot 1 \cdot \dfrac{1}{250}$

8. $(-64 + 64) - 213$ **9.** $7(3004)$ **10.** $5.5 + 2.4 + 7.5$

11. $-13 \cdot 55 \cdot \dfrac{1}{13}$ **12.** $169 \cdot 3 \div 169$ **13.** $129 + 0 + 71$

14. $-555 - 226 - 45$ **15.** $273 + 140 - 273$ **16.** $60 \cdot 250 \div (-15)$

17. $3(421)$ **18.** $(411 + 346) - 11$ **19.** $20 \cdot (78 \cdot 5)$

20. $4.4 + (1.9 + 3.6)$ **21.** $36(14) - 16(14)$ **22.** $(0.5 \cdot 3.7) \cdot 2$

Simplify the variable expression. Justify each step.

23. $2(n + 12) + 40n$ **24.** $31(1) + 9(10 + a)$ **25.** $6(8x - y) - 17x$

26. $11(s - 3t) + 34t$ **27.** $70m - 5(m - 9)$ **28.** $(p + 25q)8 - 15p$

29. $\left(11a + \dfrac{1}{3} - 4a\right)3$ **30.** $7(1 + 30c) - 90c$ **31.** $5(3m - n) - 5m$

Write an expression to describe the situation. Then use the distributive property to write an equivalent variable expression.

32. A music store sold 170 compact discs yesterday and n today. Each compact disc costs $15. What was the total compact disc sales for the two days?

33. In your last two basketball games, you made only 2 point field goals. You made y field goals last week and 14 this week. How many total points did you score in the two games?

My Review Questions

Graph linear functions, noting that the vertical change (change in *y*-value) per unit of horizontal change (change in *x*-value) is always the same and know the ratio ("rise over run") is called the slope of a graph.

TEXTBOOK REFERENCES

Developing Concepts, p. 582
Lesson 11.5

KEY WORDS

• slope
• x-coordinate
• y-coordinate

> **STUDY TIP**
> By looking at the graph of a line, you can tell if its slope is positive or negative. A line with a positive slope rises as the value of *x* increases. A line with a negative slope falls as the value of *x* increases.

My Notes

Slope of a Line

UNDERSTANDING SLOPE

One characteristic of a line is its slope. Slope is a measure of a line's slant. To describe the way a line slants, you need to observe how the coordinates on the line change as you move right.

$$\text{slope} = \frac{\text{vertical change}}{\text{horizontal change}} = \frac{\text{rise}}{\text{run}}$$

Example 1

Find the slope of the line in the graph shown.

▶ **Solution**

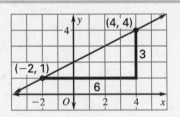

Choose two points along the line: $(-2, 1)$ and $(4, 4)$. Count the units of horizontal change and vertical change between the points.

$$\text{slope of a line} = \frac{\text{vertical change}}{\text{horizontal change}} = \frac{4 - 1}{4 - (-2)} = \frac{3}{6} = \frac{1}{2}$$

Example 2

Use the graph shown at the right to determine how air temperature changes in relation to altitude.

▶ **Solution**

Find the slope of the line in the graph.

$$\text{slope} = \frac{\text{rise}}{\text{run}} = \frac{-7 \text{ degrees}}{2000 \text{ feet}}$$

▶ Air temperature decreases 7 degrees for every 2000 feet.

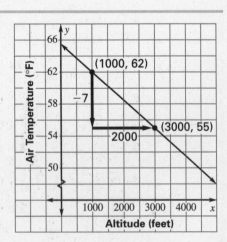

Checkpoint ✓ **Understanding Slope**

Find the slope of the line that contains the given points.

1. $(-2, 7)$ and $(4, 1)$ **2.** $(-1, -2)$ and $(3, 4)$

FINDING SLOPE

Points lie on a line if and only if the vertical change per unit of horizontal change for any pair of points is always the same.

Example 3

Determine whether the data shown in the table represent a linear function. If so, graph the function.

Input, x	Output, y
0	7
2	4
4	1
6	-2

▶ **Solution**

Check that the change in y-coordinates per unit of change in the x-coordinates is always the same.

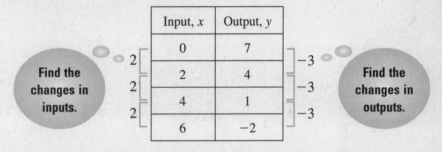

Find the changes in inputs.

Input, x	Output, y
0	7
2	4
4	1
6	-2

Find the changes in outputs.

For every 2 units of horizontal change, there is always -3 units of vertical change. So the data represent a linear function. To graph the linear function, plot the y-intercept $(0, 7)$.

Since the slope is $-\dfrac{3}{2}$, plot a second point by moving to the right 2 units and down 3 units. Draw a line through the two points.

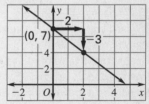

▶ **STUDY TIP**

The slope $-\dfrac{3}{2}$ is equal to $\dfrac{-3}{2}$ and $\dfrac{3}{-2}$. In Example 3, it is possible to plot a second point by moving to the left 2 units and up 3 units.

Checkpoint ✓ **Finding Slope**

3. Determine whether the data in the table represent a linear function. If so, graph the function.

Input, x	−1	0	1	2	3
Output, y	2	0	−2	−4	−6

SUMMARIZING KEY IDEAS

Slope is a number indicating the steepness of a line. It is the ratio of vertical rise to horizontal run. For linear functions, the vertical change per unit of horizontal change is always the same.

Exercises *Slope of a Line*

Find the slope of the line.

1.

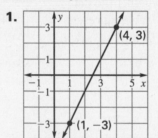

2.

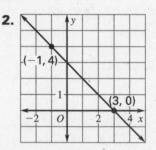

Determine how y changes in relation to x.

3.

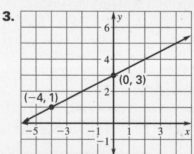

4.

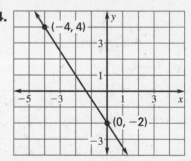

Determine whether the data in the table represent a linear function. If so, graph the function.

TEXTBOOK LINK

📖 On pages S54–S56, you used a graph to find slope. Then you graphed a linear function from a table of values. In your textbook, Lesson 11.5, you will use a formula to find slope.

5.

Input, x	Output, y
0	−3
1	−1
2	1
3	3

6.

Input, x	Output, y
−6	−4
−3	−2
0	0
3	2

TEXTBOOK REFERENCES
Developing Concepts, p. 588
Lesson 11.6

KEY WORDS
• *y*-intercept
• slope-intercept form

Slope-Intercept Form

EQUATIONS IN SLOPE-INTERCEPT FORM

The *y*-intercept of a line is where the line crosses, or intercepts, the *y*-axis. To find the slope and *y*-intercept of a linear equation, it can be helpful to write the equation in slope-intercept form.

> ### SLOPE-INTERCEPT FORM
>
> An equation of the form $y = mx + b$ is in slope-intercept form. The graph is a line with slope *m* and *y*-intercept *b*.

Example 1

Identify the slope and *y*-intercept of each equation.

a. $y = \dfrac{1}{2}x$ **b.** $y = x - 4$

▶ **Solution**

a. $y = \dfrac{1}{2}x + 0$; The slope is $\dfrac{1}{2}$ and the *y*-intercept is 0.

b. $y = 1x - 4$; The slope is 1 and the *y*-intercept is -4.

Example 2

Graph the equation $y = -\dfrac{3}{5}x + 4$.

▶ **Solution**

Plot the *y*-intercept (0, 4). Since the slope is $-\dfrac{3}{5}$, plot a second point by moving right 5 units and down 3 units. Draw a line through the points.

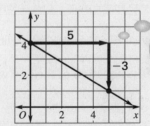

5 is the horizontal run and −3 is the vertical rise.

My Notes

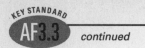
Checkpoint ✓ **Equations in Slope-Intercept Form**

Identify the slope and *y*-intercept. Then graph the equation.

1. $y = -3x + 4$ **2.** $y = \frac{3}{4}x + 2$ **3.** $y = \frac{1}{2}x - 3$

USING A GRAPH TO WRITE LINEAR EQUATIONS

You can use the graph of a line to write an equation in slope-intercept form. To find an equation of a line when you are given two points that the line contains, first find the slope and then find the *y*-intercept.

Example 3

Write an equation in slope-intercept form for the line shown in the graph.

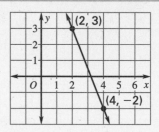

▶**STUDY TIP**
When using the slope formula to find the slope of a line, you can use any two points that lie on the line.

▶ **Solution**

Find the slope of the line. Let $(x_1, y_1) = (4, -2)$ and $(x_2, y_2) = (2, 3)$.

$$m = \frac{\text{rise}}{\text{run}} = \frac{y_2 - y_1}{x_2 - x_1} = \frac{3 - (-2)}{2 - 4} = \frac{5}{-2} = -\frac{5}{2}$$

Find the *y*-intercept.

$y = mx + b$ Write the slope-intercept form.

$3 = -\dfrac{5}{2}(2) + b$ Substitute $-\dfrac{5}{2}$ for *m*, 2 for *x*, and 3 for *y*.

$3 = -5 + b$ Simplify.

$b = 8$ Solve for *b*.

Finally, write an equation of the line.

$y = mx + b$ Write the slope-intercept form.

$y = -\dfrac{5}{2}x + 8$ Substitute $-\dfrac{5}{2}$ for *m* and 8 for *b*.

▶ The equation of the line written in slope-intercept form is

$y = -\dfrac{5}{2}x + 8.$

SUMMARIZING KEY IDEAS

An equation of a line can be written in the slope-intercept form $y = mx + b$. The slope of the line is m and the y-intercept is b. The y-intercept is the y-coordinate of the point where the line crosses the y-axis.

Checkpoint ✓ Using a Graph to Write Linear Equations

Write an equation in slope-intercept form for the line shown.

4.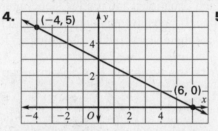

5.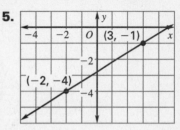

Exercises Slope-Intercept Form

Identify the slope and y-intercept of the equation.

1. $y = 3x - 2$
2. $y = \dfrac{4}{7}x + 5$
3. $y = -2x - 8$

Graph the linear equation.

4. $y = -\dfrac{1}{3}x + 5$
5. $y = 4x + 3$
6. $y = \dfrac{1}{4}x + \dfrac{1}{2}$

7. $y = -2x - 1$
8. $y = \dfrac{2}{3}x - 6$
9. $y = -3x - 4$

Write the equation in slope-intercept form for the line shown.

10.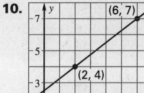

11.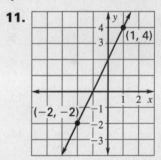

TEXTBOOK LINK

On pages S57–S59, you used the slope-intercept form to graph a linear equation and to write an equation of a line when you knew the coordinates of two points. In Lesson 11.6, you will find the slope and y-intercept of a graph and write equations in slope-intercept form. Then you will use the slope-intercept form to sketch a quick graph.

12. MATHEMATICAL REASONING The table of values below does not represent a linear function. Explain why not.

Input, x	1	2	3	4	5
Output, y	1	4	9	16	25

Topic Review   *Graphing Linear Functions*

These exercises will help you check that you can find the slope of a line, graph equations, and use the slope-intercept form to write an equation of a line. If you have any questions about graphing linear functions, be sure to get them answered before going on to the next section.

Write the equation in slope-intercept form for the line shown.

1.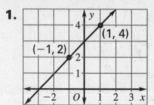

2.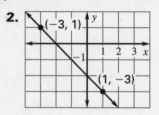

Determine whether the data in the table represent a linear function. If so, graph the function.

3.

Input, x	Output, y
-2	0
-1	0.5
0	1
1	1.5
2	2

4.

Input, x	Output, y
-1	7
0	3
1	-1
2	-5
3	-9

Graph the linear equation.

5. $y = 2x + 3$

6. $y = -5x - 2$

7. $y = -3x + 2$

8. $y = x - 3$

9. $y = 0.5x - 4$

10. $y = 5x$

11. $y = \frac{3}{4}x - 3$

12. $y = -\frac{2}{5}x + 2$

13. $y = -\frac{4}{3}x + 4$

14. You are selling singles and couples tickets for a school dance. The capacity of the hall where the dance will be held is 500. The number of singles tickets you can sell is a function of the number of couples tickets you sell, as shown in the graph. Determine how the number of singles tickets you sell changes in relation to the number of couples tickets you sell.

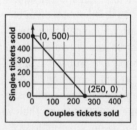

My Review Questions

Plot the values of quantities whose ratios are always the same (e.g., cost to the number of an item, feet to inches, circumference to diameter of a circle). Fit a line to the plot and understand that the slope of the line equals the quantities.

TEXTBOOK REFERENCES

Lessons 3.8, 11.5, 11.6

KEY WORDS

• linear function
• ratio
• slope-intercept form

Graphing Linear Functions

The slope of a nonvertical line is the ratio of the change in y to the change in x. For some linear functions, the ratio of output to input is constant.

Example 1

You earn $9 an hour at a part-time job. Make an input-output table to represent pay as a function of hours worked. Then graph the ordered pairs (hours worked, pay) and draw a line through the points. What do you notice about the ratio $\dfrac{\text{pay}}{\text{hours}}$ and the slope of the line?

▶ **Solution**

Input, x (hours worked)	Output, y (pay)	$\dfrac{\text{pay}}{\text{hours}}$
1	9	$\dfrac{9}{1} = 9$
2	18	$\dfrac{18}{2} = 9$
4	36	$\dfrac{36}{4} = 9$
7	63	$\dfrac{63}{7} = 9$

The ratio $\dfrac{\text{pay}}{\text{hours}}$ is always 9.

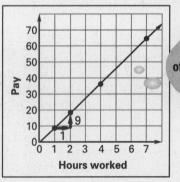

The slope of the line through the points is $\dfrac{9}{1}$ or 9.

▶ The ratio $\dfrac{\text{pay}}{\text{hours}}$ is equal to the slope of the line through the points.

My Notes

When the ratio $\dfrac{\text{output}}{\text{input}}$ is constant for a function, the function is linear

and the ratio $\dfrac{\text{output}}{\text{input}}$ is the slope of the graph of the function.

Example 2

The input-output table at the right gives the relationship between miles and kilometers. Does the table represent a linear function? Write a function that relates the number of kilometers to the number of miles.

Input, x (miles)	Output, y (kilometers)
1	1.609
2	3.218
3	4.827
5	8.045

▶ **Solution**

To determine whether the table of values represents a linear function, find the ratio of the number of kilometers to the number of miles.

Input, x (miles)	Output, y (kilometers)	$\dfrac{\text{kilometers}}{\text{miles}}$
1	1.609	$\dfrac{1.609}{1} = 1.609$
2	3.218	$\dfrac{3.218}{2} = 1.609$
3	4.827	$\dfrac{4.827}{3} = 1.609$
5	8.045	$\dfrac{8.045}{5} = 1.609$

Since the ratio $\dfrac{\text{kilometers}}{\text{miles}}$ always equals 1.609, the function is linear and the slope of the line is 1.609. The y-intercept is the point $(0, 0)$. You can use these to write the equation for the line in slope-intercept form.

$y = mx + b$ **Write slope-intercept form.**

$y = 1.609x$ **Substitute 1.609 for m and 0 for b.**

▶ A function that relates the number of kilometers to the number of miles is $y = 1.609x$.

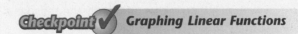 **Graphing Linear Functions**

1. It takes you 8.7 minutes to run one mile. A function that models the relationship between the number n of miles and the total time T is $T = 8.7n$. Find the ratio $\dfrac{\text{time}}{\text{miles}}$ and compare it to the slope.

2. Complete the table by finding the ratio of output to input. Then graph the ordered pairs and write an equation to represent the linear function.

Input, x	−5	−2	2	3	6	7
Output, y	−10.5	−4.2	4.2	6.3	12.6	14.7
Ratio	?	?	?	?	?	?

SUMMARIZING KEY IDEAS

For a linear function, if the ratio of output to input is constant, then it is also the slope of the graph of the line.

Exercises   **Graphing Linear Functions**

1. The table gives the relationship between the radius r and the circumference C of a circle. Determine whether the table represents a linear function. If so, graph the function.

r	1	2	3	4	5
C	6.28	12.56	18.84	25.12	31.40

2. A kilogram is approximately 2.205 pounds. Complete the table. Then write a function that relates pounds to kilograms.

Input, x (kilograms)	1	2	4	7	10
Output, y (pounds)	?	?	?	?	?
Ratio	?	?	?	?	?

TEXTBOOK LINK

On pages S61–S63, you investigated the relationship between the ratio $\dfrac{\text{output}}{\text{input}}$ for some linear functions and the slopes of their graphs. In Lessons 11.6 and 11.7 in your textbook, you will write, evaluate, and graph linear functions.

3. The Fahrenheit scale and Celsius scale are related by $F = \frac{9}{5}C + 32$.

   a. Make an input-output table to represent this function. Then find the ratio of Fahrenheit to Celsius for each ordered pair in the table.

   b. Graph the ordered pairs and draw a line through the plotted points.

   c. Explain the relationship between the ratio $\dfrac{\text{Fahrenheit}}{\text{Celsius}}$ and the slope of the line graphed in part (b).

Algebra and Functions

AF4.1

Solve two-step linear equations and inequalities in one variable over the rational numbers, interpret the solution or solutions in the context from which they arose, and verify the reasonableness of the results.

TEXTBOOK REFERENCES

Lesson 4.1

KEY WORDS

• equation
• variable
• inverse operation
• equivalent equations

Solving Two-Step Equations

USING INVERSE OPERATIONS

When solving a two-step equation, you can use two inverse operations to write an equivalent equation. To do this, first isolate the term that contains the variable. Then isolate the variable.

Example 1

Solve $2x - 3 = 11$.

▶ **Solution**

$2x - 3 = 11$	Write original equation.
$2x - 3 + 3 = 11 + 3$	Add 3 to each side.
$2x = 14$	Simplify.
$\dfrac{2x}{2} = \dfrac{14}{2}$	Divide each side by 2.
$x = 7$	Simplify. *x* is by itself.

▶ The solution is 7.

Check ✓ $2x - 3 = 11$	Write original equation.
$2(7) - 3 \stackrel{?}{=} 11$	Substitute 7 for *x*.
$11 = 11$ ✓	The solution checks.

Checkpoint ✓ *Using Inverse Operations*

Solve the equation. Then check your solution.

1. $4x + 7 = 27$ **2.** $\dfrac{y}{5} - 2 = 8$ **3.** $2n + 11 = 3$

4. $\dfrac{t}{2} + 1 = 15$ **5.** $6s - 5 = 19$ **6.** $\dfrac{p}{3} - 8 = 12$

My Notes

WRITING TWO-STEP EQUATIONS

You can use two-step equations to solve everyday problems.

Example 2

Three friends shared equally the cost of renting a boat. Each person paid a total of $20, which included a life preserver for $4. What was the cost of renting the boat?

▶ *Solution*

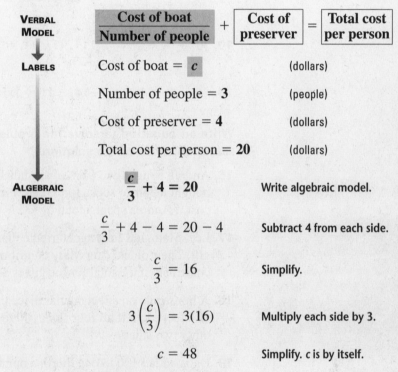

VERBAL MODEL

$$\frac{\text{Cost of boat}}{\text{Number of people}} + \boxed{\begin{array}{c}\text{Cost of} \\ \text{preserver}\end{array}} = \boxed{\begin{array}{c}\text{Total cost} \\ \text{per person}\end{array}}$$

LABELS

Cost of boat = c (dollars)

Number of people = **3**   (people)

Cost of preserver = **4**   (dollars)

Total cost per person = **20**   (dollars)

ALGEBRAIC MODEL

$\dfrac{c}{3} + 4 = 20$	Write algebraic model.
$\dfrac{c}{3} + 4 - 4 = 20 - 4$	Subtract 4 from each side.
$\dfrac{c}{3} = 16$	Simplify.
$3\left(\dfrac{c}{3}\right) = 3(16)$	Multiply each side by 3.
$c = 48$	Simplify. c is by itself.

▶ The cost of renting the boat was $48.

Checkpoint ✓ *Writing Two-Step Equations*

Write an equation to solve each problem. Check the solution to see if your answer is reasonable.

7. Your track coach recommends that you run 5 days a week and a total of 35 miles each week. If you plan to run 10 miles twice a week, how many miles should you average on the other 3 days you run?

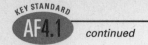
SUMMARIZING KEY IDEAS

When solving a two-step equation, undo addition and subtraction first, then undo multiplication and division.

Exercises Solving Two-Step Equations

Solve the equation. Then check your solution.

1. $3s - 4 = 8$

2. $\dfrac{k}{5} + 1 = 6$

3. $-7 = 9 + 2g$

4. $-5 = \dfrac{x}{2} - 5$

5. $\dfrac{n}{-8} + 2 = -3$

6. $-5 + 10b = -75$

7. $4m - 12 = 0$

8. $\dfrac{1}{2} = 9y + 4\dfrac{1}{2}$

9. $5 + \dfrac{k}{9} = -31$

10. $30 = 18 + 2b$

11. $11z - 6 = 335$

12. $\dfrac{x}{-8} - 7 = -9$

13. $4m + 8 = 4$

14. $-11 = 1 + 3n$

15. $3 + \dfrac{m}{-10} = 6$

Write an equation to solve the problem. Then check the reasonableness of the solution.

16. Andrea bought two pairs of sandals for the same price. She also bought a pair of socks for $3. How much did one pair of sandals cost if Andrea spent a total of $31?

17. Lee, Matt, and Jessica contribute the same amount to their father's gift. Their older sister Mary contributes $12. How much does Matt contribute if the total for the gift is $30?

18. A house sits on a rectangular piece of land. Two of the sides measure 104 feet each. If all four sides add to 576 feet, how long is each of the other two sides?

19. Dana added 120 to one fourth a number for a result of 200. What is the number?

20. If you subtract 9.4 from one-third of a number, the result is 8.7. What is the number?

21. The gas tank in your car currently contains 3 gallons of gas. If you add one-half of the tank's total capacity to the 3 gallons, the tank will have a total of 11 gallons. What is the total capacity of the gas tank?

22. The cost of a long-distance phone call is $.56 for the first minute and $.32 for each additional minute. What was the total length of a call for $9.20?

TEXTBOOK LINK

On pages S64 and S65, you used inverse operations to write and solve a two-step equation. In your textbook, Lesson 4.1, you will solve two-step linear equations in one variable, interpret the solution of an equation, and verify the reasonableness of the result.

TEXTBOOK REFERENCES
Lesson 4.5

KEY WORDS
• like terms
• variable
• distributive property
• commutative property
• associative property

Solving Equations with Variables on Both Sides

COMBINING LIKE TERMS

To solve an equation, you want to isolate the variable on one side of the equation. An equation may have variables on one or both sides of the equal sign. In order to combine like terms and isolate the variable, you may have to use properties of addition and multiplication.

Example 1

Solve $12(n - 3) = 6n + 24$.

▶ **Solution**

$12(n - 3) = 6n + 24$	Write original equation.
$12n - 36 = 6n + 24$	Distributive property
$12n - 36 - 6n = 6n + 24 - 6n$	Subtract 6n from each side.
$12n - 6n - 36 = 6n - 6n + 24$	Commutative property of addition
$6n - 36 = 24$	Combine like terms.
$6n - 36 + 36 = 24 + 36$	Add 36 to each side.
$6n = 60$	Combine like terms.
$\dfrac{6n}{6} = \dfrac{60}{6}$	Divide each side by 6.
$n = 10$	Simplify. *n* is by itself.

▶ The solution is 10.

Check ✓ $12(n - 3) = 6n + 24$	Write original equation.
$12(10 - 3) \stackrel{?}{=} 6(10) + 24$	Substitute 10 for *n*.
$12(7) \stackrel{?}{=} 60 + 24$	Simplify.
$84 = 84$ ✓	The solution checks.

> **STUDY TIP**
> To avoid a negative coefficient, collect variables on the side with the greater variable coefficient.

✏ **My Notes**

Checkpoint ✓ *Combining Like Terms*

Solve the equation. Then check your solution.

1. $12z - 8 = z + 3$ **2.** $29 + 2d = 5(d - 2)$ **3.** $2(z - 1) + z = 16$

SHORTCUT METHODS FOR SOLVING EQUATIONS

Sometimes there are many ways to solve an equation. You should reach the same conclusion with each method, but you may spend less time when you use a shortcut. Solving equations with decimal coefficients can be simplified by multiplying each side of the equation by a power of 10.

Example 2

Solve $0.11y = 1.5 + 0.1y$.

▶ **Solution**

$0.11y = 1.5 + 0.1y$	Write original equation.
$(100)(0.11y) = 100(1.5 + 0.1y)$	Multiply each side by 100.
$11y = 100(1.5) + 100(0.1y)$	Distributive property
$11y = 150 + 10y$	Simplify.
$11y - 10y = 150 + 10y - 10y$	Subtract 10y from each side.
$y = 150$	Combine like terms.

▶ The solution is 150. Check this in the original equation.

....

When each term of an equation has a common factor, you can simplify by dividing both sides of the equation by that common factor.

Example 3

Solve $9a = 3(a - 2)$.

▶**STUDY TIP**
The equation
$9a = 3(a - 2)$ can be simplified by distributing the 3, but note that both $9a$ and $3(a - 2)$ are divisible by 3.

▶ **Solution**

$9a = 3(a - 2)$	Write original equation.
$\dfrac{9a}{3} = \dfrac{3(a - 2)}{3}$	Divide each side by 3.
$3a = a - 2$	Simplify.
$3a - a = a - 2 - a$	Subtract a from each side
$2a = -2$	Simplify.
$\dfrac{2a}{2} = \dfrac{-2}{2}$	Divide each side by 2.
$a = -1$	Simplify. a is by itself.

▶ The solution is -1. Check this in the original equation.

Checkpoint ✓ *Shortcut Methods for Solving Equations*

Solve and check. Use shortcuts where possible.

4. $0.2y - 0.4 = 1.6$ **5.** $0.01x + 0.2 = 0.3$ **6.** $12p = 6(1752 - p)$

SUMMARIZING KEY IDEAS

When solving an equation with variables on both sides, you will need to combine like terms and isolate the variable. You can sometimes use shortcuts to solve equations.

Exercises *Solving Equations with Variables on Both Sides*

Solve the equation. Then check your solution.

1. $1 - 6y = 1 + 4y$ **2.** $7x + 4 = 15x + 36$

3. $-13x = -2x - x - 10$ **4.** $2(n - 3) = 12 - 8n$

5. $-2(3 - m) = 15 - m$ **6.** $3s - 10 = -6 - 3s + s + 1$

7. $3(b + 4) = 24(2 - b)$ **8.** $-5(3 - d) = 25 + d$

9. $(c + 2) + (c + 4) = 27 - c$ **10.** $4(2 + p) = 32 - 3(p + 1)$

11. $8y + 20 = y + 2y - 5y$ **12.** $-22 - 3d = -2d + d - 3d$

13. $-42 + 4c = -c + 3c - c$ **14.** $-7f + 2f = -36 + 4f$

Solve and check. Use shortcuts where possible.

15. $0.2q + 0.07(q + 4) = -0.01q$ **16.** $0.1a + 0.05(2 - a) = 0.08$

17. $-36(7 - 3t) = -6(2 + 2t)$ **18.** $-8(4y - 6) = 16(2y - 5)$

19. $-0.5n + 0.2n = 8.4 - 4.5n$ **20.** $0.001b = 0.02 - 0.001b$

21. $32t - 16 = 4t + 24$ **22.** $100 + 50c = 75(3 - c)$

23. ERROR ANALYSIS Describe and correct the error.

$$3x = -14 - 4x$$
$$3x - 4x = -14 - 4x + 4x$$
$$-7x = -14$$
$$\frac{-7x}{-7} = \frac{-14}{-7}$$
$$x = 2$$

TEXTBOOK LINK

On pages S67–S69, you solved equations by combining like terms. You also solved equations with variables on both sides of the equation. Finally, you used a shortcut to solve equations with decimals. In Lesson 4.5 in your textbook, you will solve equations with variables on both sides by collecting like terms and using the distributive property.

TEXTBOOK REFERENCES

Lesson 9.8

KEY WORDS

• inequality
• variable
• inverse operations

Solving Two-Step Inequalities

USING INVERSE OPERATIONS

Solving a two-step inequality is similar to solving a two-step equation. You can use inverse operations to write equivalent inequalities and to isolate the variable on one side of the inequality.

Example 1

Solve $9 - \dfrac{2}{3}x < 1$ and graph the solution.

▶ **Solution**

> **STUDY TIP**
> When you multiply or divide by a negative number to solve an inequality, remember that you have to reverse the order of the inequality.

$$9 - \frac{2}{3}x < 1$$ Write original inequality.

$$9 - \frac{2}{3}x - 9 < 1 - 9$$ Subtract 9 from each side.

$$-\frac{2}{3}x < -8$$ Simplify.

$$-\frac{3}{2}\left(-\frac{2}{3}x\right) > -\frac{3}{2}(-8)$$ Multiply each side by $-\frac{3}{2}$ and reverse the inequality.

$$x > 12$$ Simplify. x is by itself.

▶ The solution is all real numbers greater than 12. Check 15, for example, in the original inequality.

🖍 **My Notes**

_____

_____

_____

_____

_____

_____

_____

_____

_____

_____

_____

```
        12
+---+---+-o-+---+---+---+
0   5   10  15  20  25  30
```

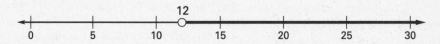

Checkpoint ✔ Using Inverse Operations

Solve the inequality.

1. $5 + \dfrac{1}{3}x > 4$ **2.** $5 + \dfrac{2}{3}d < 11$ **3.** $y + 2 - 5y \geq 22$

WRITING TWO-STEP INEQUALITIES

In many real-life situations, a two-step inequality can be written to solve the problem.

Example 2

Rates at a car rental agency are $160 a week plus $.10 per mile. If you rent a car for a week, how far can you drive if you want to spend no more than $250?

▶ **Solution**

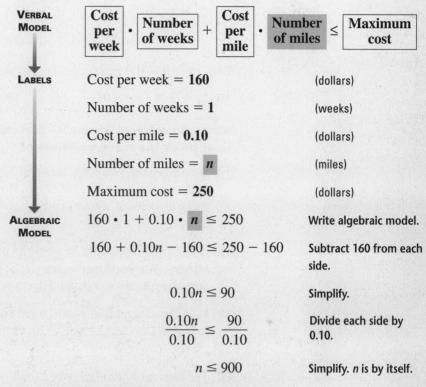

VERBAL MODEL

$$\boxed{\begin{array}{c}\text{Cost} \\ \text{per} \\ \text{week}\end{array}} \cdot \boxed{\begin{array}{c}\text{Number} \\ \text{of weeks}\end{array}} + \boxed{\begin{array}{c}\text{Cost} \\ \text{per} \\ \text{mile}\end{array}} \cdot \boxed{\begin{array}{c}\text{Number} \\ \text{of miles}\end{array}} \le \boxed{\begin{array}{c}\text{Maximum} \\ \text{cost}\end{array}}$$

LABELS

Cost per week = **160**   (dollars)

Number of weeks = **1**   (weeks)

Cost per mile = **0.10**   (dollars)

Number of miles = **n**   (miles)

Maximum cost = **250**   (dollars)

ALGEBRAIC MODEL

$160 \cdot 1 + 0.10 \cdot n \le 250$ Write algebraic model.

$160 + 0.10n - 160 \le 250 - 160$ Subtract 160 from each side.

$0.10n \le 90$ Simplify.

$\dfrac{0.10n}{0.10} \le \dfrac{90}{0.10}$ Divide each side by 0.10.

$n \le 900$ Simplify. *n* is by itself.

▶ You can drive less than or equal to 900 miles.

Checkpoint ✓ *Writing Two-Step Inequalities*

4. A freight elevator can safely hold no more than 2000 pounds. It currently holds 500 pounds of boxes. What is the greatest number of additional 60-pound boxes the elevator can safely hold?

SUMMARIZING KEY IDEAS

Solving an inequality is much like solving an equation: apply inverse operations and combine like terms to write a chain of equivalent inequalities. Remember to reverse the order of an equality when multiplying or dividing by a negative number.

Exercises Solving Two-Step Inequalities

Solve the inequality and graph the solution on a number line. Then check your solution by substituting at least one solution in the original inequality.

1. $2x - 3 < 12$ **2.** $2x - 1 > 5$

3. $1 + a < 3 - 2a$ **4.** $6a - 5 > 11 - 2a$

5. $-3y - 6 \geq 12$ **6.** $1 + 4x < 5 + 6x$

7. $5x + 3x - 4 > 4$ **8.** $3 - 4d \leq 17$

9. $3x + 4 > 10x$ **10.** $6x + 2 - 8x < 14$

11. $n + 5 - 7n \geq 13$ **12.** $-9d - 4 \geq 12 - 5d$

13. $11n - 9 > 160 - 2n$ **14.** $7y - 4 < 6 + 2y$

15. $5y + 3 \geq 13 + 10y$ **16.** $0.4p - 4 > 3.6$

Write and solve an inequality that represents the given situation. Then check the reasonableness of the solution.

17. Freddie works two jobs. He earns $6 per hour doing one job and $100 a week doing the other job. How many hours must he work per week on the first job so that his combined weekly income is no less than $244?

18. A company's policy is to spend no more than $350,000 a year for salaries. The president's salary is $110,000. The salaries of the eight other employees are equal. How much can be spent on each salary?

19. Lisa's grades on four exams were 80, 92, 86, and 78. What is the lowest grade she can receive on the next exam to have an average greater than 85?

20. The amount of rainfall over a three-year period was 65 inches, 72 inches, and 59 inches. How many inches of rain must fall during the fourth year for the average rainfall to be at least 68 inches for the four years?

21. The length of a rectangle is 4 meters more than twice its width. Find the greatest possible value for the width of the rectangle if the perimeter is at most 38 meters.

TEXTBOOK LINK

On pages S70 and S71, you solved two-step inequalities. You also used two-step inequalities to write and solve real problems. You will solve two-step inequalities in Lesson 9.8 of your textbook.

Topic Review Solving Two-Step Linear
Equations and Inequalities

These exercises will help you check that you can solve two-step linear
equations and inequalities. If you have any questions, be sure to get them
answered before going on to the next section.

Solve and check.

1. $-9t - 17 = -26$

2. $\dfrac{m}{4} + 6 = 3$

3. $4r + 6 \geq 14$

4. $3 - \dfrac{x}{2} < -9$

5. $\dfrac{n}{-8} + 7 = 18$

6. $84 \leq 79 + \dfrac{1}{12}p$

7. $0.5d - 0.7d = 0.8$

8. $9y + 11 > 6y - 7$

9. $14.9 \leq 8.6 - 0.9m$

10. $6 - 9r = 4(r + 3)$

11. $-2d + 18 = 11(3 - d)$

12. $3t + 27 = -8$

13. $5b - 6 > 11(b - 6)$

14. $-7v + 4 = 19 + 3v$

**My Review
Questions**

15. $4.6y + 8.42 = 2 + 3.6y$

16. $\dfrac{k}{-9} + 6 < -4$

17. $4n - 7(n - 9) \leq 42$

18. $4(2k - 7) = 46 - 3(k - 1)$

19. $4b + 28 = 48 + 16b$

20. $-0.2n + 7.9 \geq 8.4 - 0.3n$

**Write an equation or inequality and solve. Then check the
reasonableness of the solution.**

21. A student has 13 coins, all nickels and dimes, worth $.95. The
number of dimes is 1 less than the number of nickels. How many
nickels are there?

22. José has $3 more than twice as many dollars as Jonathan. If José has
$15, then how much does Jonathan have?

23. Amy and Jeff want to pay at most $10,000 for a car. They pay an
initial deposit of $2000 and plan to pay the remaining balance off in
20 months. How much will they pay each month in order to pay for
the car?

KEY STANDARD

Algebra and
Functions

AF4.2

Solve multistep problems involving rate, average speed, distance and
time or a direct variation.

TEXTBOOK REFERENCES

Lesson 11.7

KEY WORDS

• direct variation
• constant of variation

Direct Variation

Sometimes two variables x and y can vary directly with each other.

DIRECT VARIATION

Two variables x and y vary directly if they are related by a
linear function of the form $y = kx$, where k is a nonzero
constant called the constant of variation. It represents the
rate at which the function is changing.

Example 1

Use the table of values to determine
if the amount of tip Maria leaves at
a restaurant varies directly with the
cost of her meal. If so, state the
constant of variation.

Cost of Meal	Amount of Tip
$10	$1.50
$20	$3.00
$30	$4.50
$40	$6.00

My Notes

▶ **Solution**

Cost of Meal	Amount of Tip	Amount of Tip / Cost of Meal
$10	$1.50	$\dfrac{1.50}{10} = 0.15$
$20	$3.00	$\dfrac{3.00}{20} = 0.15$
$30	$4.50	$\dfrac{4.50}{30} = 0.15$
$40	$6.00	$\dfrac{6.00}{40} = 0.15$

The amount of tip
and the cost of the
meal are related
by $y = 0.15x$.

The ratio of the amount of tip to the cost of the meal is always the same.
So this is a direct variation and the constant of variation is 0.15. This
suggests that Maria always leaves a 15% tip when she eats in a restaurant.

Example 2

A variable y varies directly with x, and $y = 40$ when $x = 5$. Find the constant of variation. Then find the value of y when $x = 7$.

▶ Solution

It is given that y varies directly with x, so x and y are related by the equation $y = kx$, where k is a nonzero constant.

$y = kx$	**Write model for direct variation.**
$40 = k(5)$	**Substitute 40 for y and 5 for x.**
$8 = k$	**Divide each side by 5.**

The constant of variation is 8. So the equation that relates x and y is $y = 8x$. You can use this equation to find the value of y when $x = 7$.

$y = 8x$	**Write equation relating x and y.**
$y = 8(7) = 56$	**Substitute 7 for x and simplify.**

▶ When $x = 7$, $y = 56$.

> **STUDY TIP**
> The direct variation model $y = kx$ can also be written as $\frac{y}{x} = k$. In Example 2, $\frac{y}{x} = 8$, which means the ratio of y to x is always equal to 8.

Example 3

You come to a stop while driving, then accelerate at a constant rate, reaching 24 miles per hour after 4 seconds. At the same rate of acceleration, how long will it take you to reach a speed of 52 miles per hour?

▶ Solution

At a constant rate of acceleration, the speed s varies directly with time t.

$s = kt$	**Write model for direct variation.**
$24 = k \cdot 4$	**Substitute 24 for s and 4 for t.**
$k = 6$	**Solve for k.**

The equation relating speed to time is $s = 6t$. Use the direct variation equation to find the time it takes to reach a speed of 52 miles per hour.

$s = 6t$	**Write direct variation equation relating speed and time.**
$52 = 6t$	**Substitute 6 for k and 52 for s.**
$t = 8\frac{2}{3}$	**Solve for t.**

▶ It will take you $8\frac{2}{3}$ seconds to reach a speed of 52 miles per hour.

SUMMARIZING KEY IDEAS

The variables x and y vary directly if there is a nonzero constant k such that $y = kx$. You can also use the equivalent equation $k = \dfrac{y}{x}$ to determine if y varies directly with x. The ratio of y to x is always equal to the constant k if x and y vary directly.

Checkpoint ✓ **Direct Variation**

In Exercises 1–3, determine whether x and y vary directly. If they do, state the constant of variation.

1. $y = 3x$

2. $y = \dfrac{1}{2}x$

3. $y = 5x + 1$

4. Suppose the number of lines of type on a book's page varies directly with the number of pages. A book has 144 lines of type on 3 pages. Find the constant of variation and use it to find the number of pages filled by 312 lines of type.

Exercises **Direct Variation**

Determine whether x and y vary directly. If they do, state the constant of variation.

1. $y = 2x^2$

2. $y = 0.6x - 2$

3. $y = \dfrac{3}{4}x$

In Exercises 4–9, the variables x and y vary directly. Find the constant of variation. Then write an equation that relates the two variables.

4. $y = 9$ when $x = 3$

5. $y = 210$ when $x = 30$

6. $y = 5.6$ when $x = 0.7$

7. $y = 1\dfrac{3}{4}$ when $x = \dfrac{1}{2}$

8. The variables x and y vary directly, and $y = 5$ when $x = 25$. Find the value of y when $x = 55$.

9. The variables A and B vary directly, and $B = 4$ when $A = 150$. Find the value of B when $A = 200$.

10. The variables M and N vary directly, and $N = 84$ when $M = 12$. Find the value of N when $M = 14$.

11. The amount of simple interest earned on a savings account varies directly with the amount of money in the account. If $5000 earns $350 interest, how much interest is earned on $8000?

12. A train travels 240 miles in 4 hours at a constant speed. Find the distance the train will travel in 7 hours using a direct variation model.

TEXTBOOK LINK

📖 On pages S74–S76, you solved problems involving direct variation. You will solve multistep problems involving rate, average speed, distance and time or a direct variation in Lesson 11.7 of your textbook.

Measurement and Geometry

KEY STANDARD

MG1.3

Use measures expressed as rates (e.g., speed, density) and measures expressed as products (e.g., person-days) to solve problems; check the units of the solutions; and use dimensional analysis to check the reasonableness of the answer.

TEXTBOOK REFERENCES
Skills Review, p. 671
Lessons 1.5, 2.7, 4.6, and 6.5

KEY WORDS
• dimensional analysis (or unit analysis)

Dimensional Analysis

CHECKING REASONABLENESS OF A SOLUTION

When you are simplifying an expression or solving an equation, you can use **dimensional analysis** (called *unit analysis* in your textbook) to make sure that the units used in your answer are correct.

Example 1

A car is traveling on a highway at a constant speed of 55 miles per hour. How long will it take for the car to travel 198 miles?

▶ *Solution*

$d = r \cdot t$	Write formula.
$198 = 55t$	Substitute 198 for d and 55 for r.
$\dfrac{198}{55} = \dfrac{55t}{55}$	Divide each side by 55.
$3.6 = t$	Simplify.

It will take 3.6 hours for the car to travel 198 miles. Use dimensional analysis to check that the units used in the solution are correct.

$$\text{Distance} = \text{rate} \cdot \text{time}$$

$$\text{miles} = \frac{\text{miles}}{\text{hour}} \cdot \text{hours}$$

$$\text{miles} = \text{miles} \checkmark$$

My Notes

Checkpoint ✓ *Checking Reasonableness of a Solution*

Use dimensional analysis to give the correct units of measure for the solution.

1. $\dfrac{5 \text{ people}}{\text{table}} \cdot 15 \text{ tables} = 75 \ \underline{\ ?\ }$

2. $40 \text{ dollars} + \dfrac{5 \text{ dollars}}{\text{hour}} \cdot 6 \text{ hours} = 70 \ \underline{\ ?\ }$

Key Standards S77

TEXTBOOK REFERENCES
Skills Review, p. 681
Lesson 7.1

CONVERTING UNITS OF MEASUREMENT

Example 2

Write a *conversion fraction* a (fraction equal to 1) for 1 hour = 60 minutes. Then use it to convert 7 hours to minutes.

▶ **Solution**

1 hour = 60 minutes	Write original equation.
$\dfrac{1 \text{ hour}}{1 \text{ hour}} = \dfrac{60 \text{ minutes}}{1 \text{ hour}}$	Divide each side by 1 hour.
$1 = \dfrac{60 \text{ minutes}}{1 \text{ hour}}$	Fraction equal to 1

Because the fraction $\frac{60 \text{ minutes}}{1 \text{ hour}}$ is equal to 1, you can multiply by this fraction without changing the given measurement.

$$7 \text{ hours} \cdot \frac{60 \text{ minutes}}{1 \text{ hour}} = 7 \cdot 60 \text{ minutes} = 420 \text{ minutes}$$

▶ So, 7 hours is equal to 420 minutes.

Checkpoint ✓ *Converting Units of Measurement*

3. Which conversion fraction, $\dfrac{100 \text{ cm}}{1 \text{ m}}$ or $\dfrac{1 \text{ m}}{100 \text{ cm}}$ would you use to convert 120 centimeters to meters?

SUMMARIZING KEY IDEAS

In a conversion fraction, the units being converted *to* should be in the numerator and the units being converted *from* should be in the denominator.

Exercises *Dimensional Analysis*

Solve the problem. Check the reasonableness of the solution.

1. A car gets a gas mileage of 32 miles per gallon when driving in the city. How many gallons of gas would it take to drive 400 city miles?

2. A long distance phone call costs $1.95 for the first minute plus $.80 for each additional minute. Find the cost of a 5-minute call.

Use a conversion fraction to convert the measurement.

3. 4 m = __?__ cm   **4.** 360 in. = __?__ yd   **5.** 9 mm = __?__ cm

6. 17 yd = __?__ ft   **7.** 2.5 ft = __?__ in.   **8.** 35 m = __?__ km

TEXTBOOK LINK

On pages S77 and S78, you used dimensional analysis to check the reasonableness of a solution and to convert between units of measurement. You'll learn more about these topics in Lessons 1.5, 4.6, and 6.5 in your textbook. You'll use measures expressed as rates and products to solve problems in Lessons 2.7 and 7.1.

Know and understand the Pythagorean theorem and its converse and use it to find the length of the missing side of a right triangle and the lengths of the other line segments and, in some situations, empirically verify the Pythagorean theorem by direct measurement.

The Pythagorean Theorem

The Pythagorean theorem describes a relationship that is true of all **right triangles**.

THE PYTHAGOREAN THEOREM

For any right triangle, the sum of the squares of the lengths of the legs, a and b, equals the square of the length of the hypotenuse, c.

$$a^2 + b^2 = c^2$$

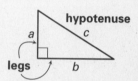

Example 1

Each diagram below shows a large square that has an area of $(a + b)^2$. Use the diagrams to show that $a^2 + b^2 = c^2$.

DIAGRAM 1

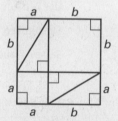

DIAGRAM 2

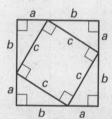

▶ *Solution*

First express the area of each large square as the sum of the areas of the triangles and smaller squares.

DIAGRAM 1: $(a + b)^2 = a^2 + b^2 + 4(\text{area of triangle})$

DIAGRAM 2: $(a + b)^2 = c^2 + 4(\text{area of triangle})$

By the subtraction property of equality, you can subtract *4(area of triangle)* from each side of each equation.

DIAGRAM 1: $(a + b)^2 - 4(\text{area of triangle}) = a^2 + b^2$

DIAGRAM 2: $(a + b)^2 - 4(\text{area of triangle}) = c^2$

By the transitive property, $a^2 + b^2 = c^2$.

My Notes

Example 2

Use the Pythagorean theorem to find the
length of the hypotenuse of the right triangle.

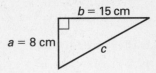

▶ **Solution**

$a^2 + b^2 = c^2$	Use Pythagorean theorem.
$8^2 + 15^2 = c^2$	Substitute 8 for a and 15 for b.
$64 + 225 = c^2$	Square 8 and 15.
$289 = c^2$	Add.
$\sqrt{289} = c$	Take positive square root of each side.
$17 = c$	Simplify.

▶ The length of the hypotenuse is 17 cm.

Example 3

Find the value of b. Leave your answer in
simplest radical form.

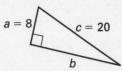

▶ **Solution**

$a^2 + b^2 = c^2$	Use Pythagorean theorem.
$8^2 + b^2 = 20^2$	Substitute 8 for a and 20 for c.
$64 + b^2 = 400$	Square 8 and 20.
$b^2 = 336$	Subtract 64 from each side.
$b = \sqrt{336}$	Take positive square root of each side.
$b = \sqrt{16(21)}$	Write 336 as a product involving a perfect square factor.
$= 4\sqrt{21}$	Simplify.

▶**STUDY TIP**

A radical expression is
in simplest form when
the following are true:

• The number under the
radical sign has no
perfect square factors
other than 1.

• The number under the
radical sign does not
contain a fraction.

• The denominator does
not contain a radical
expression.

Checkpoint ✓ *The Pythagorean Theorem*

**Let a and b be the lengths of the legs of a right triangle. Let c be
the length of the hypotenuse. Use the Pythagorean theorem to
find the missing length.**

1. $a = 6, b = 8$ **2.** $a = 10, b = 24$ **3.** $a = 5, b = 12$

4. $b = 24, c = 26$ **5.** $a = 4, c = 12$ **6.** $b = 15, c = 39$

Example 4

The right triangle is drawn on centimeter
graph paper. Measure the missing length
and check it using the Pythagorean theorem.

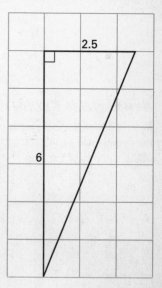

▶ **Solution**

Using a ruler, the hypotenuse seems to be
6.5 cm long. Check this as follows.

$a^2 + b^2 = c^2$	Use Pythagorean theorem.
$2.5^2 + 6^2 \stackrel{?}{=} 6.5^2$	Substitute.
$6.25 + 36 \stackrel{?}{=} 42.25$	Square 2.5, 6, and 6.5.
$42.25 = 42.25$ ✓	Add.

▶ So, the length of the hypotenuse is 6.5 cm.

Checkpoint ✓ **The Pythagorean Theorem**

7. The lengths of the legs of a right triangle are 9 and 12. Draw the legs
on centimeter graph paper, then draw and measure the hypotenuse.
Use the Pythagorean theorem to check your measurement.

▶ **STUDY TIP**
In a right triangle, the
sum of the lengths of
the legs must be
greater than the length
of the hypotenuse.
You can use this
relationship to check
the reasonableness of
your answer.

Example 5

The map at the right shows that Danvers
is 10 miles from Carver and 15 miles
from Melville. How far is Melville
from Carver?

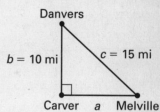

▶ **Solution**

$a^2 + b^2 = c^2$	Use Pythagorean theorem.
$a^2 + 10^2 = 15^2$	Substitute 10 for b and 15 for c.
$a^2 + 100 = 225$	Square 10 and 15.
$a^2 = 125$	Subtract 100 from each side.
$a = \sqrt{125}$	Take positive square root of each side.
$a = 5\sqrt{5}$	Simplify.

▶ You can use a calculator to find that $5\sqrt{5} \approx 11.2$. So, Melville is about
11.2 miles from Carver.

Checkpoint ✓ **The Pythagorean Theorem**

8. A 10-foot ladder leans against a wall. The bottom of the ladder is 7 feet from the wall. How high up the wall is the ladder?

SUMMARIZING KEY IDEAS

In a right triangle, the square of the hypotenuse equals the sum of the squares of the legs.

Exercises **The Pythagorean Theorem**

Use the Pythagorean theorem to find the missing length.

1.

2.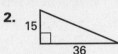

3.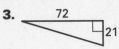

4.

5.

6.

Let *a* and *b* be the lengths of the legs of a right triangle. Draw the legs on centimeter graph paper, then draw and measure the hypotenuse. Use the Pythagorean theorem to check your measurement.

7. $a = 8, b = 15$ **8.** $a = 4, b = 7.5$ **9.** $a = 3.5, b = 12$

Let *a* and *b* be the lengths of the legs of a right triangle. Let *c* be the length of the hypotenuse. Use the Pythagorean theorem to find the missing length. Round your answer to the nearest tenth.

10. $a = 5, b = 7$ **11.** $b = 11, c = 12$ **12.** $a = 1, b = 1$

13. $a = 9, c = 21$ **14.** $a = 3, b = 7$ **15.** $a = 1.2, c = 3.5$

TEXTBOOK LINK

On pages S79–S82, you used the Pythagorean theorem to find a missing side length of a right triangle. In Lesson 9.3 in your textbook, you'll use the Pythagorean theorem to solve an isosceles right triangle.

16. A ferry travels from Snug Harbor across the bay to Liberty Island, as shown at the right. Find the distance *x* that the ferry travels.

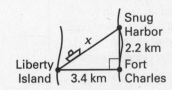

17. A 15-foot-long rope is attached to the top of a tent wall that is 10 feet high. Find the distance *x* from the bottom of the tent wall to where the rope should be attached to the ground.

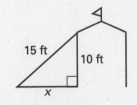

TEXTBOOK REFERENCES

Lesson 9.4

KEY WORDS

• converse of the Pythagorean theorem

Converse of the Pythagorean Theorem

CONVERSE OF THE PYTHAGOREAN THEOREM

Let a, b, and c be the lengths of the sides of a triangle with c the length of the longest side. If $a^2 + b^2 = c^2$, then the triangle is a right triangle.

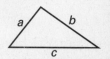

Example 1

You are given $\triangle ABC$, for which $a^2 + b^2 = c^2$. Let $\triangle FED$ be a right triangle with leg lengths a and b. Prove that $\triangle ABC$ is a right triangle.

▶ **Solution**

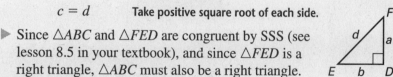

$a^2 + b^2 = c^2$	Given
$a^2 + b^2 = d^2$	Pythagorean theorem
$c^2 = d^2$	Transitive property
$c = d$	Take positive square root of each side.

▶ Since $\triangle ABC$ and $\triangle FED$ are congruent by SSS (see lesson 8.5 in your textbook), and since $\triangle FED$ is a right triangle, $\triangle ABC$ must also be a right triangle.

Example 2

A triangle has side lengths of 7 m, 25 m, and 24 m. Is it a right triangle?

▶ **Solution**

$a^2 + b^2 \stackrel{?}{=} c^2$	Write equation to be tested.
$7^2 + 24^2 \stackrel{?}{=} 25^2$	Substitute 7 for a, 24 for b, and 25 for c.
$49 + 576 \stackrel{?}{=} 625$	Square 7, 24, and 25.
$625 = 625$ ✓	Add.

▶ The triangle is a right triangle.

Checkpoint ✓ **Converse of the Pythagorean Theorem**

1. $\triangle ABC$ has side lengths of 8 cm, 10 cm, and 12 cm. Is it a right triangle?

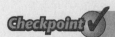

The converse of the Pythagorean theorem leads to the following theorems.

IDENTIFYING ACUTE AND OBTUSE TRIANGLES

In $\triangle ABC$ let c be the length of the longest side and a and b be the lengths of the other sides.

If $a^2 + b^2 > c^2$, then $\triangle ABC$ is acute.

If $a^2 + b^2 < c^2$, then $\triangle ABC$ is obtuse.

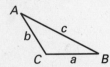

Example 3

Determine whether each triangle is an *acute triangle*, an *obtuse triangle*, or a *right triangle*.

a.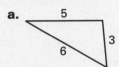

b.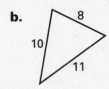

▶ **Solution**

a.

$a^2 + b^2$ **?** c^2 — Write expressions to be compared.

$3^2 + 5^2$ **?** 6^2 — Substitute for a, b, and c.

$9 + 25$ **?** 36 — Square 3, 5, and 6.

34 **?** 36 — Add.

$34 < 36$ — Compare.

▶ Since $a^2 + b^2 < c^2$, the triangle is an obtuse triangle.

b.

$a^2 + b^2$ **?** c^2 — Write expressions to be compared.

$8^2 + 10^2$ **?** 11^2 — Substitute for a, b, and c.

$64 + 100$ **?** 121 — Square 8, 10, and 11.

164 **?** 121 — Add.

$164 > 121$ — Compare.

▶ Since $a^2 + b^2 > c^2$, the triangle is an acute triangle.

Example 4

A triangle has side lengths of 16, 30, and 34. Determine whether the triangle is an *acute triangle*, an *obtuse triangle*, or a *right triangle*.

▶ **Solution**

$a^2 + b^2 \; \boxed{?} \; c^2$	Write expressions to be compared.
$16^2 + 30^2 \; \boxed{?} \; 34^2$	Substitute for *a*, *b*, and *c*.
$256 + 900 \; \boxed{?} \; 1156$	Square 16, 30, and 34.
$1156 \; \boxed{?} \; 1156$	Add.
$1156 = 1156$	Compare.

▶ Since $a^2 + b^2 = c^2$, the triangle is a right triangle.

Checkpoint ✓ *Converse of the Pythagorean Theorem*

2. A triangle has side lengths of 7, 8, and 9. Is the triangle an *acute triangle*, an *obtuse triangle*, or a *right triangle*?

SUMMARIZING KEY IDEAS

If you know the side lengths of a triangle, you can use the converse of the Pythagorean theorem to determine if it is an acute triangle, an obtuse triangle, or a right triangle:

$a^2 + b^2 > c^2$	acute
$a^2 + b^2 < c^2$	obtuse
$a^2 + b^2 = c^2$	right

TEXTBOOK LINK

On pages S83–S85 you used the converse of the Pythagorean theorem to determine if a triangle is an acute triangle, an obtuse triangle, or a right triangle. You will learn more about the converse of the Pythagorean theorem in Lesson 9.4 in your textbook.

Exercises *Converse of the Pythagorean Theorem*

Determine whether the triangle with the given side lengths is a right triangle.

1. 8 cm, 12 cm, 15 cm

2. 9 in., 12 in., 15 in.

3. 10 m, 20 m, 25 m

4. 7 mm, 24 mm, 25 mm

5. 9 yd, 40 yd, 41 yd

6. 10 cm, 25 cm, 26 cm

Determine whether the triangle is an *acute triangle*, an *obtuse triangle*, or a *right triangle*.

7.

8.

9.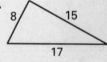

Determine whether the triangle with the given side lengths is an *acute triangle*, an *obtuse triangle*, or a *right triangle*.

10. 15, 8, 21

11. 12, 16, 20

12. 2, 2.5, 3

13. 30, 34, 16

14. 0.3, 0.4, 0.6

15. 11, 12, 15

Topic Review **The Pythagorean Theorem and its Converse**

These exercises will help you check that you can use the Pythagorean theorem and its converse. If you have any questions, be sure to get them answered before going on to the next section.

Tell whether the statement is *true* or *false*.

1. The length of the hypotenuse of a right triangle is equal to the sum of the lengths of the legs.

2. The sum of the lengths of the legs of a right triangle is always greater than the length of the hypotenuse.

3. If you know the lengths of two sides of a triangle, you can use the converse of the Pythagorean theorem to determine if it is a right triangle.

Use the Pythagorean theorem to find the missing length.

4.
5.
6.

My Review Questions

Let *a* and *b* be the lengths of the legs of a right triangle. Let *c* be the length of the hypotenuse. Use the Pythagorean theorem to find the missing length. Round your answer to the nearest tenth.

7. $a = 10$, $b = 17$
8. $b = 5$, $c = 12$
9. $a = 14$, $b = 9$

10. $a = 8$, $c = 20$
11. $a = 3$, $b = 7$
12. $b = 13$, $c = 35$

Determine whether the triangle with the given side lengths is an *acute triangle*, an *obtuse triangle*, or a *right triangle*.

13. 8, 12, 15
14. 11, 60, 61
15. 17, 21, 26

16. 9, 40, 41
17. 10, 20, 25
18. 10, 16, 18

19. 11, 14, 20
20. 9, 13, 16
21. 24, 45, 51

22. Two hikers left camp and walked 1.5 km due east. They then turned due north and walked 1.7 km to a pond. Find the distance *x* between the pond and the camp. Round your answer to the nearest tenth of a kilometer.

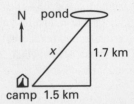

Demonstrate an understanding of conditions that indicate two geometrical figures are congruent and what congruence means about the relationships between the sides and angles of two figures.

TEXTBOOK REFERENCES
Lessons 8.5, 8.7, and 8.8

KEY WORDS
- congruent
- corresponding sides
- corresponding angles
- reflection
- transformation
- rotation
- translation

Congruent Figures

Two figures are **congruent** if their **corresponding sides** and their **corresponding angles** are congruent. Sides are congruent if they are the same length. Angles are congruent if they have the same number of degrees. Congruent figures are the same shape and the same size.

CONGRUENT   **NOT CONGRUENT**

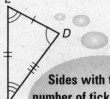

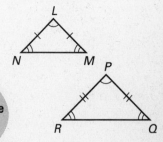

Angles with the same number of arcs, like ∠*A* and ∠*D*, are congruent.

Sides with the same number of tick marks, like $\overline{AB}$ and $\overline{DE}$, are congruent.

If you folded this page vertically between △*ABC* and △*DEF*, △*ABC* would coincide with △*DEF*. This relationship is called a **reflection**.

A reflection is a type of **transformation**. Another type of transformation is a **rotation**. A rotation turns a figure around a fixed point.

A third kind of transformation is a **translation**, or slide. A translation moves every point of a figure the same distance in a plane.

If two figures are congruent, then one figure can be moved so that it coincides with the other figure by using one or more transformations.

My Notes

Example 1

Tell whether the white figure is a *reflection*, a *rotation*, or a *translation* of the gray figure.

a.
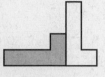

b.

c.

▶ *Solution*

a. rotation   **b.** reflection   **c.** translation

Checkpoint ✓ *Congruent Figures*

1. Sketch an example of a reflection, a rotation, and a translation, using a lowercase letter h.

On the previous page, all three sides and all three angles of △*ABC* are congruent to the corresponding sides and angles of △*DEF*, so △*ABC* is congruent to △*DEF*. This is written △*ABC* ≅ △*DEF*. Note that the corresponding vertices of the triangles are written in the same order to indicate which angles and which sides are corresponding.

Example 2

The two trapezoids at the right are congruent. List the corresponding angles and the corresponding sides. Then write a congruence statement.

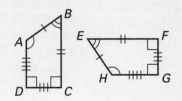

▶ *Solution*

Corresponding angles: ∠*A* ≅ ∠*H*, ∠*B* ≅ ∠*E*, ∠*C* ≅ ∠*F*, ∠*D* ≅ ∠*G*

Corresponding sides: $\overline{AB} ≅ \overline{HE}$, $\overline{BC} ≅ \overline{EF}$, $\overline{CD} ≅ \overline{FG}$, $\overline{DA} ≅ \overline{GH}$

Congruence statement: *ABCD* ≅ *HEFG*

Example 3

Determine whether the quadrilaterals are congruent. If they are, write a congruence statement. If they are not congruent, explain why not.

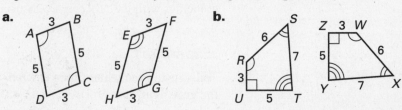

▶ *Solution*

a. Quadrilateral *ABCD* is not congruent to quadrilateral *EFGH* because they do not have corresponding angles that are congruent.

b. All four angles and all four sides of quadrilateral *RSTU* are congruent to the corresponding angles and sides of quadrilateral *WXYZ*. So, *RSTU* ≅ *WXYZ*.

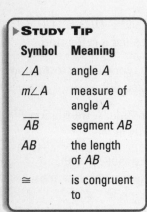

▶ STUDY TIP

Symbol	Meaning
∠*A*	angle *A*
m∠*A*	measure of angle *A*
$\overline{AB}$	segment *AB*
AB	the length of *AB*
≅	is congruent to

Checkpoint ✓ **Congruent Figures**

2. If quadrilateral *LMNO* is congruent to quadrilateral *QRST*, list the corresponding angles and corresponding sides.

Example 4

Pentagon *ABCDE* is congruent to pentagon *FGHJK*. Find the indicated angle measures.

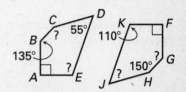

▶ **Solution**

Since *ABCDE* ≅ *FGHJK*, you can use the corresponding angles to find the unknown angle measures.

∠*C* ≅ ∠*H*, so *m*∠*C* = *m*∠*H* = 150°.

∠*E* ≅ ∠*K*, so *m*∠*E* = *m*∠*K* = 110°.

∠*G* ≅ ∠*B*, so *m*∠*G* = *m*∠*B* = 135°.

∠*J* ≅ ∠*D*, so *m*∠*J* = *m*∠*D* = 55°.

SUMMARIZING KEY IDEAS

Two figures are congruent if their corresponding sides and corresponding angles are congruent. If quadrilateral *ABCD* ≅ *EFGH*, then:

∠*A* ≅ ∠*E* $\overline{AB}$ ≅ $\overline{EF}$

∠*B* ≅ ∠*F* $\overline{BC}$ ≅ $\overline{FG}$

∠*C* ≅ ∠*G* $\overline{CD}$ ≅ $\overline{GH}$

∠*D* ≅ ∠*H* $\overline{DA}$ ≅ $\overline{HE}$

Exercises Congruent Figures

Determine whether the figures are congruent. If they are, write a congruence statement. If they are not congruent, explain why not.

1.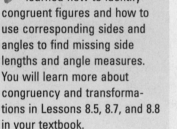

2.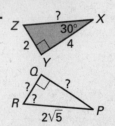

TEXTBOOK LINK

📖 On pages S87–S89, you learned how to identify congruent figures and how to use corresponding sides and angles to find missing side lengths and angle measures. You will learn more about congruency and transformations in Lessons 8.5, 8.7, and 8.8 in your textbook.

The pair of polygons is congruent. Tell whether the white figure is a *reflection*, a *rotation*, or a *translation* of the gray figure. Then find the indicated side lengths and angle measures.

3.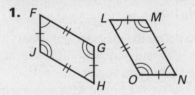

4.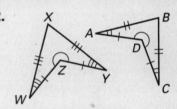

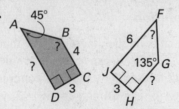

TEXTBOOK REFERENCES
Lesson 8.5

KEY WORDS
- Side-angle-side congruence postulate
- Side-side-side congruence postulate
- Angle-side-angle congruence postulate

Congruent Triangles

You do not need to know that all the corresponding angles and corresponding sides are congruent to show that two triangles are congruent.

CONGRUENT TRIANGLES

SIDE-ANGLE-SIDE (SAS) CONGRUENCE POSTULATE
Two triangles are congruent if two sides and the angle included between the sides of one triangle are congruent to two sides and the angle included between the sides of the second triangle.

SIDE-SIDE-SIDE (SSS) CONGRUENCE POSTULATE
Two triangles are congruent if all three sides of one triangle are congruent to all three sides of the other.

ANGLE-SIDE-ANGLE (ASA) CONGRUENCE POSTULATE
Two triangles are congruent if two angles and the included side of one triangle are congruent to two angles and the included side of a second triangle.

My Notes

Example 1

Explain why $\triangle ABC \cong \triangle CDA$.

▶ **Solution**

The marks on the diagram show that $\overline{AB} \cong \overline{CD}$ and that $\angle B \cong \angle D$. Because they are both right angles, $\angle A \cong \angle C$. $\triangle ABC \cong \triangle CDA$ by the ASA congruence postulate.

Example 2

Explain why $\triangle GHJ \cong \triangle JKG$.

▶ **Solution**

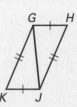

The marks on the diagram show that $\overline{GH} \cong \overline{JK}$ and that $\overline{KG} \cong \overline{HJ}$. Since the third side $\overline{GJ}$ is shared, $\triangle GHJ \cong \triangle JKG$ by the SSS congruence postulate.

Example 3

Explain why △TQS ≅ △RQS.

▶ **Solution**

The marks on the diagram show that
$\overline{QT} \cong \overline{QR}$ and that $\angle TQS \cong \angle RQS$. Since
$\overline{QS}$ is a shared side, $\triangle TQS \cong \triangle RQS$ by the
SAS congruence postulate.

Checkpoint ✓ **Congruent Triangles**

1. Given the markings on the two
   triangles at the right, can you
   conclude that they are congruent?
   Explain why or why not.

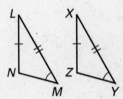

SUMMARIZING KEY IDEAS

You have learned three
congruence postulates:
Side-angle-side (SAS)
Side-side-side (SSS)
Angle-side-angle (ASA)

Exercises Congruent Triangles

If possible determine which triangle is congruent to the given triangle. Justify your answer.

1.

A.

B.

2.

A.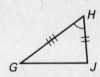

B.

TEXTBOOK LINK

On pages S90 and S91,
you learned how to use
congruence postulates to prove
that two triangles are
congruent. You will learn more
about congruence postulates in
Lesson 8.5 in your textbook.

If possible, determine whether the triangles are congruent. Justify your answer.

3.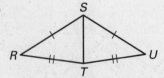

4.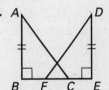

Topic Review Congruency

These exercises will help you check that you can identify congruent figures. If you have any questions, be sure to get them answered before going on to the next section.

Tell whether the white figure is a *reflection*, a *rotation*, or a *translation* of the gray figure.

1.    **2.** 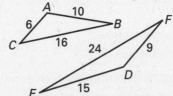   **3.**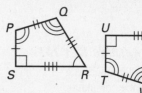

Determine whether the polygons are congruent. If they are, write a congruence statement. If they are not congruent, explain why not.

4.    **5.**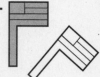

Quadrilateral *ABCD* is congruent to quadrilateral *EFGH*. Find the indicated side lengths or angle measures.

6.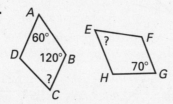

7.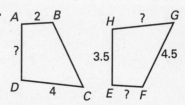

If possible, determine whether the triangles are congruent. Justify your answer.

8. △*STP* and △*RQP*   **9.** △*JKL* and △*MLK*

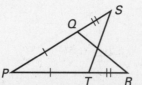   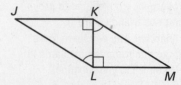

My Review Questions

Identify elements of three-dimensional objects and describe how two or more objects are related in space.

TEXTBOOK REFERENCES

Lesson 10.2

KEY WORDS

• coplanar
• skew lines

Classifying Lines in Space

Points and lines that lie in the same plane are **coplanar**. Lines that do not intersect and are not parallel are **skew lines**. In the figure below, lines m and p are coplanar and lines m and q are skew.

Arrows pointing in the same direction indicate that line m is parallel to line n.

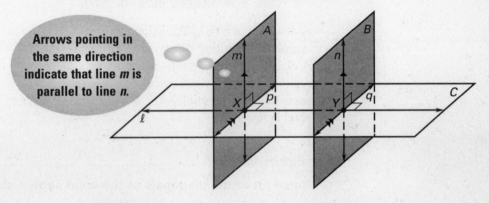

Example 1

Use the figure above.

  a. Name three pairs of coplanar lines.

  b. Other than lines m and q, name a pair of skew lines.

▶ **Solution**

  a. Three pairs of coplanar lines are: q and ℓ, p and ℓ, and q and n.

  b. Lines n and p are skew.

Planes that do not intersect are parallel. Planes that do intersect can intersect in different ways. Some are shown below.

Planes *D, E*, and *F* intersect in a single point.

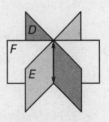

Planes *D, E*, and *F* intersect in a line.

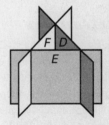

Planes *D, E*, and *F* intersect pairwise.

My Notes

Checkpoint ✓ *Classifying Lines in Space*

Use the diagram of the solid.

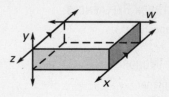

1. Name a pair of parallel lines.

2. Name a pair of coplanar lines.

3. Name a pair of skew lines.

A diagonal of a two-dimensional polygon is a segment connecting two nonconsecutive vertices. A diagonal of a three-dimensional solid is a segment between two vertices that do not lie on the same face. For example, $\overline{AG}$ is a diagonal of the solid at the right.

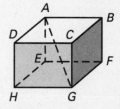

Example 2

Name all of the diagonals of the solid shown above.

▶ **Solution**

There are four diagonals: $\overline{AG}$, $\overline{BH}$, $\overline{DF}$, and $\overline{CE}$.

Exercises *Classifying Lines in Space*

SUMMARIZING KEY IDEAS

Points and lines that lie in the same plane are coplanar. Lines that do not intersect and are not parallel are skew lines.

In Exercises 1–4, use the figure shown. Tell whether the lines are *coplanar* or *skew*.

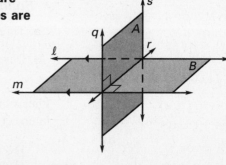

1. Line ℓ and line r

2. Line ℓ and line q

3. Line m and line s

4. Line q and line s

TEXTBOOK LINK

On pages S93 and S94, you classified lines as coplanar or skew and identified diagonals of a solid. You will learn more about coplanar and skew lines in Lesson 10.2 in your textbook.

Use the diagram of the solid at the right.

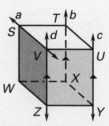

5. Name a pair of parallel lines.

6. Name two pairs of coplanar lines.

7. Name two pairs of skew lines.

8. Name the four diagonals of the solid.

TEXTBOOK REFERENCES
Lessons 10.2, 10.6, and 10.7

KEY WORDS
- polyhedron
- face
- edge
- vertex
- prism
- pyramid
- base
- oblique

▶**STUDY TIP**
A prism is named for the shape of its bases. Since this prism has triangular bases it is a triangular prism.

Exploring Solids

POLYHEDRONS

A **polyhedron** is a closed solid that is bounded by polygons, called **faces** of the polyhedron. Adjacent faces of a polyhedron meet at segments called **edges**. The point where three or more faces of a polyhedron meet is called a **vertex**.

A **prism** is a type of polyhedron. A prism has two congruent and parallel **bases**. All other faces of a prism are parallelograms. A right prism has sides perpendicular to the bases. An **oblique** prism has sides that are not perpendicular to the bases.

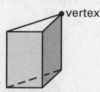 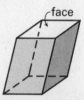

Triangular prism   **Right rectangular prism**   **Oblique rectangular prism**   **Other polyhedrons**

Example 1

Tell how many faces, vertices, and edges the prism has.

a. 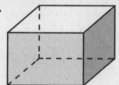   **b.**   **c.**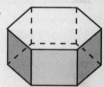

▶ **Solution**

	Type of prism	Number of faces	Number of vertices	Number of edges
a.	rectangular	6	8	12
b.	pentagonal	7	10	15
c.	hexagonal	8	12	18

A **pyramid** is another type of polyhedron. The base of a pyramid is a polygon and all other faces are triangles. A pyramid is named for the shape of its base.

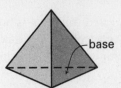

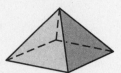

Triangular pyramid   **Square pyramid**

> ▶ **VOCABULARY TIP**
> A triangular pyramid is sometimes called a *tetrahedron*.

Example 2

Tell how many faces, vertices, and edges the pyramid has.

a. 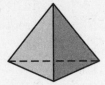   **b.**   **c.**

▶ *Solution*

	Type of pyramid	Number of faces	Number of vertices	Number of edges
a.	triangular	4	4	6
b.	square	5	5	8
c.	pentagonal	6	6	10

Checkpoint ✓ *Exploring Solids*

Name each solid. Then tell how many faces, vertices, and edges the solid has.

1.   **2.**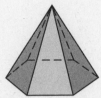

TEXTBOOK REFERENCES
Lesson 10.2

KEY WORDS
- sphere
- cylinder
- cone

> **STUDY TIP**
> In this workbook and in your textbook, all cylinders are circular cylinders and all cones are circular cones.

SPHERES, CYLINDERS, AND CONES

The **sphere**, **cylinder**, and **cone** shown below are solids, but are not polyhedrons because they are not bounded by polygons.

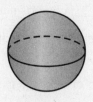
Sphere

Cylinder

Cone

A sphere is the set of all points in space that are a given distance from a point.

A *circular cylinder* is a solid with congruent circular bases that lie in parallel planes. In a *right cylinder*, the segment joining the centers of the bases is perpendicular to the bases. In an *oblique cylinder*, the segment joining the centers of the bases is not perpendicular to the bases.

A *circular cone* has a circular base and a vertex that is not in the same plane as the base.

Example 3

Name the solid.

a.
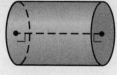

b.

c.

▶ *Solution*

a. right cylinder   **b.** sphere   **c.** cone

Checkpoint ✓ *Spheres, Cylinders, and Cones*

Match the solid with its name.

A. sphere   B. oblique cylinder   C. cone

3.
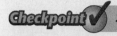

4.

5.

SUMMARIZING KEY IDEAS

Most solids are named for the shape of their base or bases.

Exercises **Exploring Solids**

Complete the sentence.

1. The two __?__ of a prism are congruent and parallel.

2. The segments at which adjacent faces of a polyhedron meet are called __?__.

3. If the sides of a prism are not perpendicular to its bases then the prism is __?__.

Name the solid that best describes the shape of the object.

4. VCR   **5.** basketball   **6.** can of soup

Name the polyhedron. Then tell how many faces, vertices, and edges it has.

7.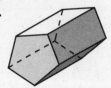
8.
9.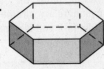

10.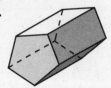
11.
12.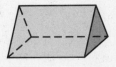

If possible, name the solid. Then tell if it is a polyhedron.

13.
14.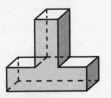
15.

16.
17.
18.

TEXTBOOK LINK

On pages S95–S97, you classified solids. In Lesson 10.2 in your textbook, you will sketch nets for solids. In Lessons 10.3–10.7 you will find the surface area and the volume of solids.

Topic Review *Classifying Lines and Solids*

These exercises will help you check that you can classify lines and solids in space. If you have any questions, be sure to get them answered before going on to the next section.

Use the diagram below. Tell whether the lines are *coplanar* or *skew*.

1. Line *d* and line *e*

2. Line *g* and line *i*

3. Line *j* and line *f*

4. Line *h* and line *j*

5. Line *k* and line *f*

6. Line *h* and line *d*

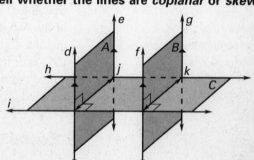

Use the triangular prism at the right.

7. Does the prism have any diagonals? If so, name them. If not, explain why not.

8. Name a pair of coplanar lines and a pair of skew lines.

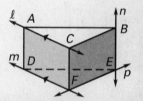

Tell whether the solid is a *prism*, a *pyramid*, or *neither*.

9.
10.
11.

12.
13.
14.

Name the polyhedron. Then tell how many faces, vertices, and edges it has.

15.
16.
17.

KEY STANDARD

Statistics,
Data Analysis,
and Probability

SDP 1.3 Understand the meaning of and be able to compute the minimum, the lower quartile, the median, the upper quartile, and the maximum of a data set.

TEXTBOOK REFERENCES

Lesson 9.9

KEY WORDS

• median
• lower quartile
• upper quartile
• box-and-whisker plot
• range
• interquartile range

Box-and-Whisker Plots

DRAWING BOX-AND-WHISKER PLOTS

Recall that the **median** of a set of data is the middle data value, or mean of the two middle values, when the data values are listed in order. The median divides the data into a lower half and an upper half. The median of the lower half is called the **lower quartile**. The median of the upper half is called the **upper quartile**. A data set that is broken into four parts using the median and quartiles can be displayed in a **box-and-whisker plot**.

Example 1

A survey of 12 students recorded the number of people in each student's family: 6, 4, 3, 5, 7, 4, 6, 8, 5, 9, 3, and 3.

  a. Find the median, the lower quartile, and the upper quartile of the data.

  b. Draw a box-and-whisker plot of the data.

▶ **Solution**

My Notes

$$\text{Median} = \frac{5 + 5}{2} = 5$$

  a. Write the data in increasing order: 3, 3, 3, 4, 4, 5, 5, 6, 6, 7, 8, 9

$$\frac{\text{Lower}}{\text{quartile}} = \frac{3 + 4}{2} = 3.5 \qquad \frac{\text{Upper}}{\text{quartile}} = \frac{6 + 7}{2} = 6.5$$

  b. First draw a number line that includes the minimum data value, 3, and the maximum data value, 9. Plot each of the following five numbers below the number line: the minimum, the lower quartile, the median, the upper quartile, and the maximum. Draw a box from the lower quartile to the upper quartile, Draw a vertical line through the median. Finally, draw "whiskers" from the quartiles to the minimum and the maximum.

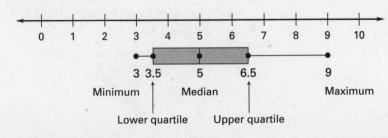

A box-and-whisker plot helps to show how much a set of data varies. One measure of variation is the *range*. The **range** of a set of data is the difference between the maximum and minimum values. The **interquartile range** is the difference between the upper quartile and lower quartile.

Example 2

Below are the reentry cabin temperatures (in degrees Fahrenheit) for Apollo missions. Draw a box-and-whisker plot of the data. Then find the range and the interquartile range.

$$65, 61, 67, 58, 55, 60, 75, 59, 59, 57, 62$$

▶ **Solution**

Write the data in increasing order:

$$55, 57, 58, 59, 59, 60, 61, 62, 65, 67, 75$$

Minimum = 55   Median = 60   Maximum = 75

Lower quartile = 58   Upper quartile = 65

Draw the box-and-whisker plot below a number line that includes the minimum data value, 55, and the maximum data value, 75.

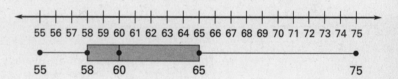

Range = maximum − minimum = 75 − 55 = 20

Interquartile range = upper quartile − lower quartile = 65 − 58 = 7

Checkpoint ✓ *Drawing Box-and-Whisker Plots*

Draw a box-and-whisker plot of the data. Then find the range and the interquartile range.

1. Number of students in each of 10 classes: 15, 13, 18, 24, 30, 12, 15, 22, 28, and 31.

2. Cost (in dollars) of each of 13 books: 10, 12, 13, 8, 15, 15, 25, 20, 12.50, 16, 24, 13, and 10.

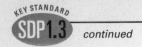
INTERPRETING BOX-AND-WHISKER PLOTS

Box-and-whisker plots can be used to compare two or more sets of data.

Example 3

The box-and-whisker plots below represent the yearly number of satellite and space vehicle launches for the United States and the Soviet Union from 1957–1977. Use the plots to compare the data.

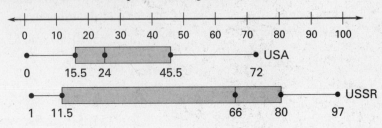

> **STUDY TIP**
> The five plotted points in a box-and-whisker plot divide the data into four parts: the left whisker, the left half of the box, the right half of the box, and the right whisker. Each part represents about 25% of the data.

▶ **Solution**

In general, the Soviet Union launched more satellites and space vehicles per year than the United States did. For example in approximately half of the years, the United States launched between 24 and 72 satellites and space vehicles, while the Soviet Union launched between 66 and 97.

Example 4

The plots below represent the average daily temperatures for Boston and Miami in January of 2000. Which plot more likely represents the average daily temperatures for Miami?

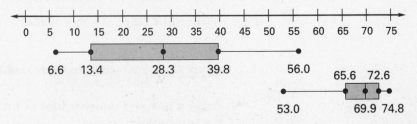

▶ **Solution**

Since Miami is closer to the equator, the temperature in Miami is generally warmer than in Boston. The bottom plot has higher temperatures, so it more likely represents the daily temperatures in Miami.

 **Interpreting Box-and-Whisker Plots**

In Exercises 3 and 4, use the top plot shown in Example 4, which shows the average daily temperature for Boston in January of 2000.

3. About what percent of the days had an average temperature below 13.4°F?

4. About what percent of the days had an average temperature above 28.3°F?

SUMMARIZING KEY IDEAS

A box-and-whisker plot is a way of displaying the minimum, lower quartile, median, upper quartile, and maximum of a data set. The "box" represents about 50% of the data. Each "whisker" represents about 25% of the data.

Exercises **Box-and-Whisker Plots**

In Exercise 1–6, use the box-and-whisker plot, which shows the hours per week one student spent on homework during the school year. Find each number.

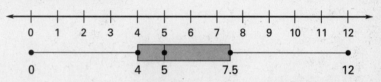

1. Median   **2.** Maximum   **3.** Minimum

4. Lower quartile   **5.** Upper quartile   **6.** Interquartile range

In Exercises 7 and 8, draw a box-and-whisker plot of the data.

7. Number of hits made in one season by players on a baseball team:
25, 24, 2, 0, 5, 30, 12, 18, 13, 13, 18, 17, 16, 9, 11, 20

8. Cost of long distance calls on a phone bill: $.05, $2, $2.25, $.10, $3.80, $2.50, $6.15, $.90, $2.25

9. The box-and-whisker plots below show the ages of the national all-around gymnastics champions for men and women from 1986–1996. What does this tell you about the age differences between the men and women?

TEXTBOOK LINK

On pages S100–S103, you drew and interpreted box-and-whisker plots. You'll learn more about box-and-whisker plots in Lesson 9.9 in your textbook.

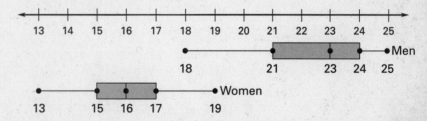

Part 3 Special Topics

TEXTBOOK REFERENCES
Lesson 1.3

KEY WORDS
• binary search

CA STANDARDS
NS 1.2, MR 1.0

ACTIVITY GUESS MY NUMBER

Work with a partner.

❶ Choose an integer from 1 to 128. Have your partner try to guess it by asking only questions that can be answered with "yes" or "no." For example, your partner can ask "Is the number odd?" but not "What is the number's first digit?" Record how many questions your partner needs to guess your number.

❷ Switch roles with your partner, so that you now try to guess an integer from 1 to 128 that your partner chooses. Record how many questions you need to guess your partner's number.

❸ Repeat Steps 1 and 2 several more times. Each time, try to reduce the number of questions you need to ask.

❹ Describe the strategies that you and your partner used to narrow down the list of possible numbers to the correct one. Which strategy do you think is the most efficient? Explain.

In the activity, you can quickly determine your partner's number by using a **binary search**. This procedure is illustrated in the next example.

> **READING TIP**
> In Example 1, the word *inclusive* in Tonya's phrase "between 1 and 8, inclusive" means that 1 and 8 are included in the set of numbers Tonya is describing.

Example 1 Performing a Binary Search

Kim and Tonya are playing a simpler version of the "Guess My Number" game above. Kim picks an integer from 1 to 16, and Tonya tries to guess it by asking only questions with "yes" or "no" answers. Tonya uses a binary search to determine Kim's number after asking only 4 questions.

1. Tonya: Is your number between 1 and 8, inclusive?
Kim: No.
(Now Tonya knows that Kim's number is between 9 and 16, inclusive.)

2. Tonya: Is your number between 9 and 12, inclusive?
Kim: Yes.

3. Tonya: Is your number 9 or 10?
Kim: No.
(Now Tonya knows that Kim's number is either 11 or 12.)

4. Tonya: Is your number 11?
Kim: No.
(Now Tonya knows that Kim's number must be 12.)

Tonya: Your number is 12.

▶ **VOCABULARY TIP**
The word *binary* means "related to 2." It is used to describe the search in Example 1 because at each step, the remaining possibilities are divided into 2 groups: one that contains Kim's number and one that does not.

Each of Tonya's questions reduces the number of integers that could be Kim's number by half. This is shown below. The repeated halving of possibilities is the defining characteristic of a binary search.

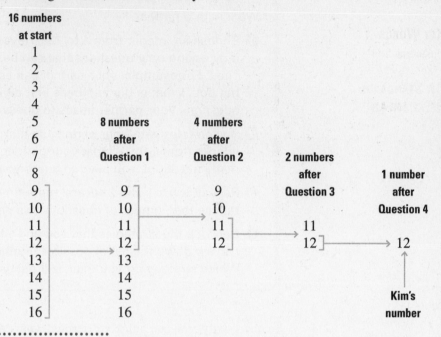

In Example 1, Tonya needs 4 questions to determine Kim's number because it takes 4 halvings to reduce the original $16 = 2^4$ possibilities to 1. In general, determining a number chosen from the integers 1 to 2^n requires n questions using a binary search.

Exercises

1. In the activity on page T1, how many questions do you need to ask if you use a binary search to determine your partner's number? Explain.

2. Your friend chooses an integer from 1 to 32 that you try to guess by asking only questions with "yes" or "no" answers. You use a binary search. If your friend's number is 19, what questions will you end up asking to determine the number? How many questions will you need?

3. When you use a binary search in the game "Guess My Number," how does the number of questions you need to ask change if the number of integers your partner can choose from is doubled? Explain.

4. If you use a *linear search* to guess an integer chosen from 1 to 2^n, you ask "Is the number 1?," "Is the number 2?," "Is the number 3?," and so on until the correct number is reached. At most how many questions are needed? Which is more efficient, a linear search or a binary search? Explain.

TEXTBOOK REFERENCES
Lesson 5.1

KEY WORDS
• divisible
• factor

CA STANDARDS
NS 1.2

A whole number is **divisible** by a nonzero whole number if the second number is a factor of the first. For example,

$$10 = 2 \times 5,$$

factors

so 10 is divisible by 2 and 5. You can use the following properties to derive tests for divisibility by 2, 5, and other whole numbers.

DIVISIBILITY PROPERTIES

Let n and d be whole numbers with $d \neq 0$.

❶ If n is divisible by d, then any multiple of n is divisible by d. So, $6 \times 10 = 60$ is divisible by 5 since 10 is divisible by 5.

❷ If you can write n as sums or differences of whole numbers that are each divisible by d, then n is divisible by d. For example, $39 = 18 + 12 + 9$ and each of 18, 12, and 9 is divisible by 3. So, 39 is divisible by 3.

❸ If you can write n as sums or differences of whole numbers such that exactly one of the numbers is not divisible by d, then n is not divisible by d. For example, $26 = 16 - 8 + 20 - 2$, and although the numbers 16, 8, and 20 are all divisible by 4, the number 2 is not. So, 26 is not divisible by 4.

DIVISIBILITY BY 2 AND 5

Since 10 is divisible by 2 and 5, property (1) above says that all powers of 10 are as well. This lets you tell whether *any* whole number is divisible by 2 or 5.

Example 1 *Determining Divisibility by 2*

Determine whether **(a)** 76 and **(b)** 259 are divisible by 2.

▶ *Solution*

a. Write 76 as $(7 \times 10) + 6$. Note the following.

- By property (1), the first term, 7×10, is divisible by 2 because 10 is divisible by 2.

- $6 \div 2 = 3$, so 6 is divisible by 2.

▶ *Answer* Since both terms of 76 are divisible by 2, property (2) implies that 76 is divisible by 2.

▶ **Solution** continued

b. Write 259 as $(2 \times 100) + (5 \times 10) + 9$. Note the following.

- By property (1), the terms 2×100 and 5×10 are divisible by 2 because 100 and 10 are divisible by 2.

- $9 \div 2 = 4\ \text{R}1$, so 9 is not divisible by 2.

▶ **Answer** Since exactly one term of 259 is not divisible by 2, property (3) implies that 259 is not divisible by 2.

Example 2 **Determining Divisibility by 5**

Determine whether **(a)** 48 and **(b)** 485 are divisible by 5.

▶ **Solution**

a. Write 48 as $(4 \times 10) + 8$. The term 4×10 is divisible by 5 because 10 is divisible by 5. The term 8 is not divisible by 5 since $8 \div 5 = 1\ \text{R}3$.

▶ **Answer** Since exactly one term of 48 is not divisible by 5, you can conclude that 48 is not divisible by 5.

b. Write 485 as $(4 \times 100) + (8 \times 10) + 5$. The terms 4×100 and 8×10 are divisible by 5 because 100 and 10 are divisible by 5. The term 5 is also divisible by 5 since $5 \div 5 = 1$.

▶ **Answer** Since all the terms of 485 are divisible by 5, you can conclude that 485 is divisible by 5.

....

Because any power of 10—and therefore any multiple of a power of 10—is divisible by 2 and 5, you need to look only at the units digit of a number to determine whether the number is divisible by 2 or 5.

Numbers whose units digit is even (0, 2, 4, 6, or 8) are divisible by 2. Numbers whose units digit is 0 or 5 are divisible by 5.

Checkpoint ✔ **Divisibility by 2 and 5**

Determine whether the number is divisible by 2 or 5.

1. 94   **2.** 65   **3.** 603   **4.** 170   **5.** 5558

DIVISIBILITY BY 3

To determine if a number is divisible by 3, write it as the sum of multiples of 9, 99, 999, and so on, plus a "remainder." A whole number whose digits are all 9's is divisible by 3. For example, $9 \div 3 = 3$, $99 \div 3 = 33$, and $999 \div 3 = 333$. If the remainder is also divisible by 3, then so is the original number.

Example 3 *Determining Divisibility by 3*

Determine whether **(a)** 752 and **(b)** 4362 are divisible by 3.

▶ **Solution**

a. Write 752 as follows:

$$752 = (7 \times 100) + (5 \times 10) + 2$$
$$= 7 \times (99 + 1) + 5 \times (9 + 1) + 2$$
$$= (7 \times 99) + (7 \times 1) + (5 \times 9) + (5 \times 1) + 2$$
$$= (7 \times 99) + (5 \times 9) + 7 + 5 + 2$$
$$= (7 \times 99) + (5 \times 9) + 14$$

▶ **Answer** The terms 7×99 and 5×9 are divisible by 3 because 99 and 9 are divisible by 3. The last term, 14, is not divisible by 3 since $14 \div 3 = 4$ R2. So, 752 is not divisible by 3.

b. Write 4362 as follows:

$$4362 = (4 \times 1000) + (3 \times 100) + (6 \times 10) + 2$$
$$= 4 \times (999 + 1) + 3 \times (99 + 1) + 6 \times (9 + 1) + 2$$
$$= (4 \times 999) + (4 \times 1) + (3 \times 99) + (3 \times 1) + (6 \times 9) +$$
$$(6 \times 1) + 2$$
$$= (4 \times 999) + (3 \times 99) + (6 \times 9) + 4 + 3 + 6 + 2$$
$$= (4 \times 999) + (3 \times 99) + (6 \times 9) + 15$$

▶ **Answer** The terms 4×999, 3×99, and 6×9 are divisible by 3 because 999, 99, and 9 are divisible by 3. The last term, 15, is also divisible by 3 since $15 \div 3 = 5$. So, 4362 is divisible by 3.

....

In Example 3, note that the last term in the expanded form of each number is the sum of the number's digits, and that the original number is divisible by 3 if and only if the sum of its digits is divisible by 3. This is true in general. For instance, 549 is divisible by 3 because $5 + 4 + 9 = 18$ is divisible by 3.

DIVISIBILITY BY 11

To determine whether a number is divisible by 11, use the fact that odd powers of 10 are 1 less than a multiple of 11, while even powers of 10 are 1 more than a multiple of 11. This is illustrated below.

$$10^1 = 10 = \mathbf{11} - 1 \qquad\qquad 10^2 = 100 = 9 \times \mathbf{11} + 1$$

$$10^3 = 1000 = 91 \times \mathbf{11} - 1 \qquad 10^4 = 10{,}000 = 909 \times \mathbf{11} + 1$$

$$10^5 = 100{,}000 = 9091 \times \mathbf{11} - 1 \qquad 10^6 = 1{,}000{,}000 = 90{,}909 \times \mathbf{11} + 1$$

Example 4 *Determining Divisibility by 11*

Determine whether **(a)** 539 and **(b)** 2471 are divisible by 11.

▶ *Solution*

a. Write 539 as follows:

$$539 = (5 \times 100) + (3 \times 10) + 9$$
$$= 5 \times (9 \times 11 + 1) + 3 \times (11 - 1) + 9$$
$$= (45 \times 11) + 5 + (3 \times 11) - 3 + 9$$
$$= (45 + 3) \times 11 + (9 - 3 + 5)$$
$$= (48 \times 11) + 11$$

▶ *Answer* The first term, 48×11, is divisible by 11. The second term, 11, is also divisible by 11. So, 539 is divisible by 11.

b. Write 2471 as follows:

$$2471 = (2 \times 1000) + (4 \times 100) + (7 \times 10) + 1$$
$$= 2 \times (91 \times 11 - 1) + 4 \times (9 \times 11 + 1) + 7 \times (11 - 1) + 1$$
$$= (182 \times 11) - 2 + (36 \times 11) + 4 + (7 \times 11) - 7 + 1$$
$$= (182 + 36 + 7) \times 11 + (1 - 7 + 4 - 2)$$
$$= (225 \times 11) - 4$$

▶ *Answer* The first term, 225×11, is divisible by 11. However, the number 4 being subtracted from the first term is not divisible by 11. So, 2471 is not divisible by 11.

....

In Example 4, look at the right sides of the equations $539 = (48 \times 11) + 11$ and $2471 = (225 \times 11) - 4$. The second term equals the expression formed by alternately adding and subtracting the digits of 539 or 2471 from right to left:

For 539: $9 - 3 + 5 = 11$

For 2471: $1 - 7 + 4 - 2 = -4$

The number 539 is divisible by 11 because $9 - 3 + 5 = 11$ is divisible by 11, while 2471 is not divisible by 11 because $|1 - 7 + 4 - 2| = |-4| = 4$ is not divisible by 11. You can use this method of adding and subtracting digits to determine whether any whole number is divisible by 11.

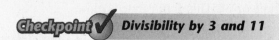 **Checkpoint ✓** *Divisibility by 3 and 11*

Determine whether the number is divisible by 3 or 11.

6. 77   **7.** 57   **8.** 429   **9.** 3805   **10.** 59,191

The divisibility tests for 2, 3, 5, and 11, as well as tests for other divisors, are summarized below.

DIVISIBILITY TESTS

A whole number is divisible by:

- 2 if its last digit is even.
- 3 if the sum of its digits is divisible by 3.
- 4 if the number formed by its last two digits is divisible by 4.
- 5 if its last digit is 0 or 5.
- 6 if it is even and divisible by 3.
- 9 if the sum of its digits is divisible by 9.
- 10 if its last digit is 0.
- 11 if the absolute value of the expression formed by alternately adding and subtracting its digits from right to left is divisible by 11.

Exercises

1. WRITING For each divisibility property given in the box on page T3, write a convincing argument explaining why the property is true.

In Exercises 2–16, determine whether the number is divisible by 2, 3, 5, or 11.

2. 63	**3.** 44	**4.** 90	**5.** 85	**6.** 312
7. 605	**8.** 847	**9.** 728	**10.** 6930	**11.** 1815
12. 4389	**13.** 5600	**14.** 23,625	**15.** 70,818	**16.** 412,610

17. MATHEMATICAL REASONING Explain why the test for divisibility by 4 given in the box above is valid. (*Hint:* 4 divides $10^2 = 100$ and therefore 10^n for any whole number n greater than 2.)

18. MATHEMATICAL REASONING Explain why the test for divisibility by 9 given in the box above is valid. (*Hint:* 9 divides any whole number whose digits are all 9's.)

Determine whether the number is divisible by 4, 6, 9, or 10.

19. 81	**20.** 78	**21.** 96	**22.** 738	**23.** 210
24. 180	**25.** 3276	**26.** 9990	**27.** 41,354	**28.** 246,820

TEXTBOOK REFERENCES
Lesson 5.2

KEY WORDS
• greatest common factor
• prime number
• Euclidean algorithm
• dividend
• divisor
• quotient
• remainder

CA STANDARDS
NS 1.2, AF 2.1

One way to find the greatest common factor (GCF) of two nonzero whole numbers is to factor each number into primes and find the product of the common prime factors. For 60 and 168, the prime factorizations are:

$$60 = 2 \cdot 2 \cdot 3 \cdot 5$$
$$168 = 2 \cdot 2 \cdot 2 \cdot 3 \cdot 7$$

The common prime factors are 2, 2, and 3. So, the GCF of 60 and 168 is $2 \cdot 2 \cdot 3 = 12$. This can be written as GCF(60, 168) = 12.

You can also find the GCF of two numbers using a procedure called the **Euclidean algorithm**. The next example explains this procedure.

Example 1 *Understanding the Euclidean Algorithm*

Use the Euclidean algorithm to find the GCF of 60 and 168.

▶ **Solution**

First divide 168 by 60 using long division. Use the result to write an equation of the form "dividend = divisor × quotient + remainder."

$$\begin{array}{r} 2 \\ 60 \overline{)168} \\ -120 \\ \hline 48 \end{array}$$

dividend quotient

$$168 = 60 \times 2 + 48$$

divisor remainder

> **▶ VOCABULARY TIP**
> The Euclidean algorithm is named after the famous Greek mathematician Euclid, who lived from about 365 B.C. to about 300 B.C.

The equation above implies that the following statements are true. (You will prove these statements in Checkpoint Exercises 1 and 2.)

• If a number d divides 168 and 60, then d must divide 48.

• If a number d divides 60 and 48, then d must divide 168.

Taken together, these results say that a number d divides 168 and 60 if and only if d divides 60 and 48, or equivalently, that 168 and 60 have the same common factors as 60 and 48. This means that:

$$\text{GCF}(168, 60) = \text{GCF}(60, 48)$$

Comparing the equation above with the long-division problem at the beginning of the solution suggests the following more general result:

$$\text{GCF}(\text{dividend, divisor}) = \text{GCF}(\text{divisor, remainder})$$

This equation is the key to the Euclidean algorithm. It reduces the problem of finding the GCF of two numbers to the simpler problem of finding the GCF of two *smaller* numbers.

Now use the equation GCF(dividend, divisor) = GCF(divisor, remainder) to reduce the original problem further.

$$\begin{array}{r} 1 \\ 48\overline{)60} \\ -48 \\ \hline 12 \end{array} \qquad\qquad \begin{array}{r} 4 \\ 12\overline{)48} \\ -48 \\ \hline 0 \end{array}$$

GCF(60, 48) = GCF(48, 12)   GCF(48, 12) = GCF(12, 0) = 12

Combining the equation GCF(168, 60) = GCF(60, 48) from the previous page with the equations above gives:

GCF(168, 60) = GCF(60, 48) = GCF(48, 12) = GCF(12, 0) = 12

▶ **Answer** The GCF of 60 and 168 is 12.

Checkpoint ✓ **Understanding the Euclidean Algorithm**

1. Use the equation $168 = 60 \times 2 + 48$ from Example 1 to show that if a number d divides 168 and 60, then d must divide 48. (*Hint:* Divide each side by d to get $\frac{168}{d} = \frac{60 \times 2}{d} + \frac{48}{d}$. If d divides 168 and 60, what is true about $\frac{168}{d}$ and $\frac{60 \times 2}{d}$? about $\frac{48}{d} = \frac{168}{d} - \frac{60 \times 2}{d}$?)

2. Use the equation $168 = 60 \times 2 + 48$ to show that if a number d divides 60 and 48, then d must divide 168.

3. Use the procedure given in Example 1 to find the GCF of 42 and 138.

The steps of the Euclidean algorithm presented in Example 1 can be summarized as follows.

THE EUCLIDEAN ALGORITHM

To find the GCF of two nonzero whole numbers *a* and *b* where *a* < *b*, let the divisor be *a* and the dividend be *b*. Follow these steps:

❶ Divide. Ignore the quotient, but note the remainder.

❷ **If the remainder is not 0:** Repeat Step 1 using the divisor from the previous division as the new dividend and the remainder from the previous division as the new divisor.

If the remainder is 0: Stop. The last divisor is the GCF of *a* and *b*.

The Euclidean algorithm is especially useful for finding the GCF of large numbers that are difficult to factor into primes.

Example 2   Using the Euclidean Algorithm

Use the Euclidean algorithm to find the GCF of 1258 and 1411.

▶ **Solution**

Let the first divisor be 1258 and the first dividend be 1411. Follow Steps 1 and 2 in the box on page T9.

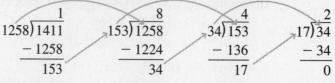

$$
\begin{array}{r} 1 \\ 1258\overline{)1411} \\ -1258 \\ \hline 153 \end{array}
\qquad
\begin{array}{r} 8 \\ 153\overline{)1258} \\ -1224 \\ \hline 34 \end{array}
\qquad
\begin{array}{r} 4 \\ 34\overline{)153} \\ -136 \\ \hline 17 \end{array}
\qquad
\begin{array}{r} 2 \\ 17\overline{)34} \\ -34 \\ \hline 0 \end{array}
$$

Remainder ≠ 0, so continue.   Remainder ≠ 0, so continue.   Remainder ≠ 0, so continue.   Remainder = 0, so stop.

▶ **Answer** The GCF is 17, the last of the divisors.

Checkpoint ✓   Using the Euclidean Algorithm

Use the Euclidean algorithm to find the GCF of the numbers.

4. 42 and 112   **5.** 510 and 900   **6.** 1757 and 2316

Exercises

In Exercises 1–12, use the Euclidean algorithm to find the GCF of the numbers.

1. 15 and 25   **2.** 28 and 133   **3.** 48 and 156

4. 56 and 235   **5.** 37 and 148   **6.** 132 and 256

7. 240 and 560   **8.** 462 and 1326   **9.** 374 and 2662

10. 1274 and 1813   **11.** 5842 and 7239   **12.** 8177 and 26,455

13. Find a 2-digit number and a 3-digit number whose GCF is 6.

14. Find two 4-digit numbers whose GCF is 45.

15. FOOD You buy two giant submarine sandwiches. One is 30 inches long and the other is 72 inches long. If you cut the sandwiches into equal-sized pieces as long as possible, what will the length of each piece be?

16. FENCES You want to put a fence around a rectangular field that is 322 feet long and 294 feet wide. If the fence posts are to be evenly spaced, at most how far apart can the posts be placed?

17. CHALLENGE Let a, b, and c be nonzero whole numbers. Then there are integers x and y that satisfy $ax + by = c$ if and only if GCF(a, b) divides c. Tell whether there are integers x and y that satisfy each equation in parts (a)–(c). If so, find integer solutions x and y.

a. $6x + 8y = 20$ **b.** $63x + 35y = 49$ **c.** $99x + 315y = 871$

The *least common multiple* of two nonzero whole numbers a and b, written LCM(a, b), is the smallest positive number that is a multiple of both a and b. In Exercises 18–23, find the LCM of the numbers.

Example   *Finding the LCM of Two Numbers*

Find the LCM of 48 and 180.

▶ **Solution**

❶ Write the prime factorization of each number. Circle the greatest power of each prime that appears in the factorization of *either* number.

$$48 = 2 \cdot 2 \cdot 2 \cdot 2 \cdot 3 = \boxed{2^4} \cdot 3$$
$$180 = 2 \cdot 2 \cdot 3 \cdot 3 \cdot 5 = 2^2 \cdot \boxed{3^2} \cdot \boxed{5}$$

❷ Find the product of the powers circled in Step 1. This is the LCM.

$$\text{LCM}(48, 180) = 2^4 \cdot 3^2 \cdot 5 = 720$$

▶ **Answer** The LCM of 48 and 180 is 720.

....

18. 4 and 6   **19.** 9 and 18   **20.** 45 and 75

21. 39 and 130   **22.** 56 and 196   **23.** 242 and 255

Exercises 24–27 should be done together.

24. Copy and complete the equations.

a. $540 = 2^? \cdot 3^? \cdot 5^?$ **b.** $1200 = 2^? \cdot 3^? \cdot 5^?$

25. Copy and complete the equations.

a. $\text{GCF}(540, 1200) = 2^? \cdot 3^? \cdot 5^?$

b. $\text{LCM}(540, 1200) = 2^? \cdot 3^? \cdot 5^?$

26. Copy and complete the equations.

a. $540 \cdot 1200 = 2^? \cdot 3^? \cdot 5^?$

b. $\text{GCF}(540, 1200) \cdot \text{LCM}(540, 1200) = 2^? \cdot 3^? \cdot 5^?$

27. MATHEMATICAL REASONING How are the expressions in parts (a) and (b) of Exercise 26 related? Find $a \cdot b$ and $\text{GCF}(a, b) \cdot \text{LCM}(a, b)$ for three other pairs of numbers a and b. Then make a conjecture about the relationship between $a \cdot b$ and $\text{GCF}(a, b) \cdot \text{LCM}(a, b)$.

TEXTBOOK REFERENCES
Lessons 5.4, 6.1–6.3

KEY WORDS
• number line

CA STANDARDS
NS 1.2

If a and b are two numbers such that $a < b$, then the distance on a number line between a and b is $b - a$. This is illustrated below.

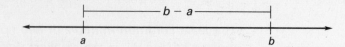

Example 1   *Comparing Distances on a Number Line*

Which is closer to 1 on a number line, $\dfrac{8}{7}$ or $\dfrac{8}{9}$?

▶ **Solution**

To find the distance between $\dfrac{8}{7}$ and 1, note that $1 = \dfrac{7}{7} < \dfrac{8}{7}$. So, the distance between $\dfrac{8}{7}$ and 1 is:

$$\frac{8}{7} - 1 = \frac{8}{7} - \frac{7}{7} = \frac{1}{7}$$

To find the distance between $\dfrac{8}{9}$ and 1, note that $\dfrac{8}{9} < \dfrac{9}{9} = 1$. So, the distance between $\dfrac{8}{9}$ and 1 is:

$$1 - \frac{8}{9} = \frac{9}{9} - \frac{8}{9} = \frac{1}{9}$$

▶ **Answer** Since $\dfrac{1}{9} < \dfrac{1}{7}$, it follows that $\dfrac{8}{9}$ is closer to 1 than $\dfrac{8}{7}$ is.

Checkpoint ✓ *Distances on a Number Line*

Tell which of *a* or *b* is closer to *c* on a number line.

1. $a = \dfrac{97}{96}, b = \dfrac{97}{98}, c = 1$ **2.** $a = \dfrac{44}{21}, b = \dfrac{15}{7}, c = 2$

Suppose you want to find the number x that is halfway between two numbers a and b on a number line, where $a < b$. Since $a < x < b$, the distance between x and a is $x - a$, and the distance between x and b is $b - x$.

The distances
$x - a$ and $b - x$
are equal.

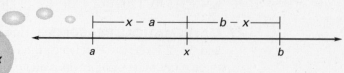

To find x in terms of a and b, solve the equation $x - a = b - x$ for x.

$x - a = b - x$ Distance from x to a = Distance from x to b

$2x - a = b$ Add x to each side.

$2x = a + b$ Add a to each side.

$x = \dfrac{a + b}{2}$ Divide each side by 2.

Example 2   **The Number Halfway Between Two Numbers**

Find the number x halfway between $\dfrac{8}{9}$ and $\dfrac{8}{7}$ on a number line.

► **Solution**

$$x = \dfrac{\dfrac{8}{9} + \dfrac{8}{7}}{2} = \dfrac{1}{2}\left(\dfrac{8}{9} + \dfrac{8}{7}\right) = \dfrac{1}{2}\left(\dfrac{56}{63} + \dfrac{72}{63}\right) = \dfrac{1}{2} \cdot \dfrac{128}{63} = \dfrac{64}{63}$$

Checkpoint ✔   **Numbers Between Pairs of Numbers**

Find the number halfway between the given numbers on a number line.

3. $\dfrac{1}{4}$ and $\dfrac{1}{3}$

4. $\dfrac{2}{7}$ and $\dfrac{3}{8}$

5. $\dfrac{16}{35}$ and $\dfrac{17}{37}$

Exercises

Tell which of a or b is closer to c on a number line.

1. $a = \dfrac{9}{10}, b = \dfrac{10}{9}, c = 1$

2. $a = \dfrac{49}{15}, b = \dfrac{14}{5}, c = 3$

Find the number halfway between the given numbers on a number line.

3. $\dfrac{1}{7}$ and $\dfrac{1}{5}$

4. $\dfrac{2}{9}$ and $\dfrac{4}{11}$

5. $\dfrac{19}{21}$ and $\dfrac{21}{19}$

6. PARKS A straight sidewalk joins the west and east entrances of a park. A bench, a fountain, and a picnic table are located along the sidewalk and are $\dfrac{1}{10}$ mile, $\dfrac{1}{3}$ mile, and $\dfrac{7}{12}$ mile, respectively, from the park's west entrance. Which is closer to the fountain—the bench or the picnic table? If a second bench is placed along the sidewalk halfway between the fountain and the picnic table, how far will this bench be from the park's west entrance?

TEXTBOOK REFERENCES
Lessons 7.1, 7.2

KEY WORDS
• ratio
• proportion

CA STANDARDS
AF 1.1, AF 4.0, MR 2.5

MODELING RATIOS WITH DIAGRAMS

Recall that a ratio of a number a to a nonzero number b is the quotient you get when a is divided by b. The ratio of a to b can be written as $\dfrac{a}{b}$, as $a : b$, or as "a to b." You can use a diagram to model a ratio.

Example 1 *Modeling a Ratio with a Diagram*

TRANSPORTATION An automobile dealership sells 32 cars and 24 trucks during one month. Draw a diagram that models the ratio of the number of cars sold to the number of trucks sold.

▶ **Solution**

First write the ratio of cars to trucks in simplest form.

$$\frac{\text{Number of cars}}{\text{Number of trucks}} = \frac{32}{24} = \frac{\overset{1}{\cancel{8}} \cdot 4}{\underset{1}{\cancel{8}} \cdot 3} = \frac{4}{3}, \text{ or } 4 : 3$$

You can model this ratio using a "bar diagram." Because the ratio of cars to trucks is 4 : 3, use 4 bars to represent the number of cars and 3 bars to represent the number of trucks. All bars should have the same dimensions.

Cars: [ ][ ][ ][ ]

Trucks: [ ][ ][ ]

Checkpoint ✓ *Using Diagrams to Model Ratios*

1. In Example 1, how many vehicles does each bar in the diagram represent? Explain.

2. Draw a bar diagram that models the ratio of the number of cars sold to the total number of vehicles sold by the dealership in Example 1.

3. **CONSUMER ELECTRONICS** During one week, an electronics store sells 35 TVs and 49 VCRs. Draw a bar diagram that models the ratio of the number of TVs sold to the number of VCRs sold.

4. **BIOLOGY** A wildlife biologist catches, tags, and releases 60 bass and 20 trout from a lake. Draw a bar diagram that models the ratio of the number of bass tagged to the number of trout tagged.

USING DIAGRAMS TO SOLVE PROBLEMS

Many problems that you can solve with equations can also be solved using bar diagrams. For example, you can use a bar diagram instead of a proportion to solve a problem in which the ratio of two quantities is constant.

Example 2 Using a Diagram to Solve a Proportion Problem

SUMMER CAMP The director of a summer camp wants to hire 2 counselors for every 5 campers. The director expects to have 80 campers. How many counselors should be hired?

▶ **Solution**

Let x be the number of counselors that should be hired.

METHOD 1 Use a bar diagram to find x.

The ratio of counselors to campers is 2 : 5. A bar diagram of this ratio is shown below. Since the 80 campers are represented by **5** bars, each bar represents $\frac{80}{5} = 16$ people.

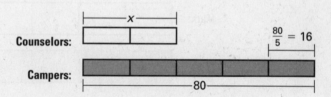

Because the counselors are represented by **2** bars, the number of counselors that should be hired is:

$$x = \mathbf{2} \cdot 16$$
$$= 32$$

▶ **Answer** The camp director should hire 32 counselors.

METHOD 2 Write and solve a proportion to find x.

$\dfrac{\text{Number of counselors}}{\text{Number of campers}} = \dfrac{2}{5}$	Write a proportion.
$\dfrac{x}{80} = \dfrac{2}{5}$	Substitute.
$x \cdot 5 = 80 \cdot 2$	Use cross products property.
$\dfrac{x \cdot 5}{5} = \dfrac{80 \cdot 2}{5}$	Divide each side by 5.
$x = 32$	Simplify. x is by itself.

▶ **Answer** The camp director should hire 32 counselors.

> **▶STUDY TIP**
> Recall that the cross products of a proportion $\frac{a}{b} = \frac{c}{d}$ are $a \cdot d$ and $b \cdot c$. The cross products property says that the cross products of a proportion are equal.

Example 3 *Solving a Problem Involving a Change in a Ratio*

BASEBALL CARDS Mark and Paulo collect baseball cards. The ratio of the number of Mark's cards to the number of Paulo's cards used to be 2 : 3. After Mark buys a new pack of 30 cards, the ratio of the number of Mark's cards to the number of Paulo's cards is 5 : 6. How many cards does Mark have after he buys the new pack? How many cards does Paulo have?

▶ **Solution**

METHOD 1 Use bar diagrams.

The diagram below models the situation *before* Mark buys the new cards.

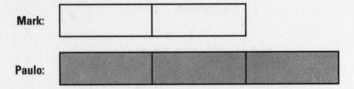

After Mark buys the new cards, the diagram is as follows.

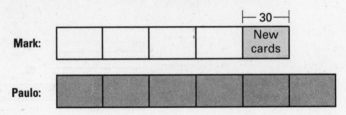

▶ **Answer** The second diagram shows that Mark has 5 • 30 = 150 cards after he buys the new pack. Paulo has 6 • 30 = 180 cards.

METHOD 2 Write and solve an equation.

Let x be the number of Paulo's cards.

Mark's cards without new pack	$+ 30 =$	Mark's cards with new pack	Write verbal model.

$$\frac{2}{3}x + 30 = \frac{5}{6}x \qquad \text{Substitute.}$$

$$6\left(\frac{2}{3}x + 30\right) = 6\left(\frac{5}{6}x\right) \qquad \text{Multiply each side by the LCD, 6.}$$

$$4x + 180 = 5x \qquad \text{Simplify.}$$

$$180 = x \qquad \text{Subtract } 4x \text{ from each side.}$$

▶ **Answer** Paulo has 180 cards. Mark has $\frac{5}{6}$ • 180 = 150 cards after he buys the new pack.

In Exercises 5 and 6, solve the problem in two ways: by using one or more bar diagrams and by writing and solving an equation.

5. PAINTING To make a dark green paint, a painter mixes blue and yellow paint so that the ratio of blue paint to yellow paint is 5 : 3. How many gallons of blue paint should be mixed with 27 gallons of yellow paint to produce the dark green paint?

6. GARDENS The ratio of red roses to yellow roses in Teri's flower garden increased from 3 : 4 to 11 : 12 after Teri planted an additional 18 red roses. How many roses of each color are now in the garden?

Exercises

In Exercises 1–4, draw a bar diagram that models the ratio of the first quantity to the second quantity.

1. 2 pizzas, 8 people

2. 16 cats, 20 dogs

3. 72 wins, 27 losses

4. 630 pine trees, 490 oak trees

5. SPORTS At a pro shop for a professional football team, you buy a T-shirt for $12 and a sweatshirt for $40. Draw a bar diagram that models the ratio of the T-shirt's cost to the sweatshirt's cost.

In Exercises 6–9, solve the problem in two ways: by using one or more bar diagrams and by writing and solving an equation.

6. ASTRONOMY You are making a poster of the planets in the solar system. In your poster, the diameter of Earth is 32 millimeters. The ratio of Earth's diameter to Mercury's diameter is about 8 : 3. What should the diameter of Mercury be in your poster?

7. POLITICS A town is electing a mayor. A poll of 200 of the town's registered voters finds that 120 plan to vote for Candidate A and 80 plan to vote for Candidate B. If 7000 people vote in the election, how many people would you expect to vote for Candidate A? for Candidate B?

8. COMPUTERS A school increases its ratio of computers to students from 1 : 6 to 1 : 4 by buying 20 more computers. How many computers does the school now have? How many students does it have?

9. MUSIC The ratio of Ann's number of CDs to her number of cassettes used to be 4 : 3, but she gave away 6 cassettes that she no longer listened to. Now her ratio of CDs to cassettes is 8 : 5. How many cassettes does Ann currently have? How many CDs does she have?

TEXTBOOK REFERENCES

Lesson 7.1

KEY WORDS

• unit of measure
• rate

CA STANDARDS

AF 4.2, MG 1.0

To convert from one unit of measure to another, you multiply the given unit by an appropriate fraction equal to 1. For example, you can convert 5 feet to inches as follows:

$$5 \text{ ft} = 5 \text{ ft} \cdot \frac{12 \text{ in.}}{1 \text{ ft}} = \frac{5 \cdot 12}{1} \text{ in.} = 60 \text{ in.}$$

Example 1 *Converting Between Two Currencies*

BOOKS Jill's family is vacationing in Canada. Jill buys a paperback book for 6.99 Canadian dollars to read in the car. The spine of the book lists the price in the United States as 5.99 U.S. dollars. The current exchange rate for U.S. and Canadian money is 1 U.S. dollar = 1.48 Canadian dollars. In which country is the book less expensive?

▶ *Solution*

Use the given exchange rate to convert the book's price in Canadian dollars to U.S. dollars.

$$6.99 \text{ Canadian dollars} = 6.99 \text{ Canadian dollars} \cdot \frac{1 \text{ U.S. dollar}}{1.48 \text{ Canadian dollars}}$$

$$= \frac{6.99 \cdot 1}{1.48} \text{ U.S. dollars}$$

$$\approx 4.72 \text{ U.S. dollars}$$

▶ *Answer* The book's price in Canada is equivalent to 4.72 U.S. dollars, which is less than the price of 5.99 U.S. dollars that the book sells for in the United States. So, the book is less expensive in Canada.

Checkpoint ✓ *Converting Units*

1. Solve Example 1 by converting the book's price in the United States to Canadian dollars and comparing the result to the price in Canada.

2. **COMPUTERS** A computer costs 1999 Canadian dollars in Canada and 1299 U.S. dollars in the United States. In which country is the computer less expensive? (Use the exchange rate from Example 1.)

3. **DISTANCES** The family from Example 1 is leaving Toronto, Ontario, and driving to Montreal, Quebec. A sign on the road says that Montreal is 531 kilometers from Toronto. How many miles is Montreal from Toronto? (*Note:* 1 kilometer ≈ 0.621 miles.)

CONVERTING A RATE TO DIFFERENT UNITS

To convert a rate from one set of units (such as miles per hour) to a different set of units (such as meters per second), you may need to multiply the original units by *two* fractions that are equal to 1.

Example 2 Converting a Rate

GAS PRICES The family from Example 1 buys gasoline in Montreal, Quebec, for 0.66 Canadian dollars per liter. In the family's home city of San Diego, California, gasoline costs 1.57 U.S. dollars per gallon. Use the exchange rate given in Example 1 and the fact that 1 gallon ≈ 3.79 liters to determine in which city gasoline is less expensive.

▶ **Solution**

Convert the price of gasoline in Montreal to U.S. dollars per gallon.

0.66 Canadian dollars per liter

$$\approx \frac{0.66 \text{ Canadian dollars}}{1 \text{ liter}} \cdot \frac{1 \text{ U.S. dollar}}{1.48 \text{ Canadian dollars}} \cdot \frac{3.79 \text{ liters}}{1 \text{ gallon}}$$

$$= \frac{(0.66 \cdot 1 \cdot 3.79) \text{ U.S. dollars}}{(1 \cdot 1.48 \cdot 1) \text{ gallons}}$$

$$\approx \frac{2.50 \text{ U.S. dollars}}{1.48 \text{ gallons}}$$

$$\approx 1.69 \text{ U.S. dollars per gallon}$$

▶ **Answer** The price of gasoline in Montreal is equivalent to 1.69 U.S. dollars per gallon, which is more than the price of 1.57 U.S. dollars per gallon in San Diego. So, gasoline is less expensive in San Diego.

Checkpoint ✔ Converting Rates

4. Solve Example 2 by converting the price of gasoline in San Diego to Canadian dollars per liter and comparing the result to the price of gasoline in Montreal.

5. **MILK PRICES** A store in Montreal sells a 2 liter carton of milk for 3.49 Canadian dollars. A store in San Diego sells a $\frac{1}{2}$ gallon carton of milk for 1.85 U.S. dollars. Which carton of milk is a better buy? (Use the exchange rate for U.S. and Canadian money given in Example 1.)

6. **SPACE EXPLORATION** The space shuttle travels at a maximum speed of about 17,000 miles per hour. How fast can the space shuttle travel in feet per second? (*Note:* 1 mile = 5280 feet.)

CONVERTING BETWEEN TEMPERATURE SCALES

Most countries outside the United States measure temperature using the Celsius scale. You can use the following formulas to convert between Celsius temperatures (C) and Fahrenheit temperatures (F).

Celsius to Fahrenheit: $F = \dfrac{9}{5}C + 32$

Fahrenheit to Celsius: $C = \dfrac{5}{9}(F - 32)$

Example 3   Converting Celsius to Fahrenheit

HEALTH While Jill's family is vacationing in Canada, Jill begins to feel sick. Her parents buy a fever thermometer to take her temperature, but it has only a Celsius scale. Jill's temperature is 38.2°C. Her parents know that normal body temperature is 98.6°F. Does Jill have a fever?

▶ **Solution**

Convert Jill's temperature to degrees Fahrenheit.

$F = \dfrac{9}{5}C + 32$ **Use the Celsius-to-Fahrenheit formula.**

$= \dfrac{9}{5}(\mathbf{38.2}) + 32$ **Substitute 38.2 for C.**

≈ 100.8 **Simplify.**

▶ **Answer** Jill's temperature of 38.2°C is equivalent to 100.8°F, which is higher than the normal body temperature of 98.6°F. So, Jill has a fever.

Example 4   Converting Fahrenheit to Celsius

WEATHER In July, the average temperature is 71°F in Los Angeles, California, and 28°C in Monterrey, Mexico. Which city is warmer in July?

▶ **Solution**

Convert the temperature for Los Angeles to degrees Celsius.

$C = \dfrac{5}{9}(F - 32)$ **Use the Fahrenheit-to-Celsius formula.**

$= \dfrac{5}{9}(\mathbf{71} - 32)$ **Substitute 71 for F.**

≈ 22 **Simplify.**

▶ **Answer** The temperature for Los Angeles is 22°C, which is lower than Monterrey's temperature of 28°C. So, Monterrey is warmer in July.

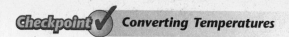

7. What is the normal body temperature for humans in degrees Celsius?

8. Solve Example 4 by converting the average July temperature for Monterrey to degrees Fahrenheit and comparing the result to the temperature for Los Angeles.

► **STUDY TIP**
Equations to help you convert between units (such as 1 mi = 5280 ft) are given in the examples and Checkpoint exercises of this Special Topic as well as in the Table of Measures on page 717 of your text.

Exercises

In Exercises 1–6, perform the conversion.

1. 84 inches to feet

2. 3 quarts to cups

3. 10°C to degrees Fahrenheit

4. −22°F to degrees Celsius

5. $64 per pound to dollars per ounce

6. 90 kilometers per hour to meters per second

7. WAVES In 1933, the tallest wind-generated wave ever reliably measured was sighted by the *U.S.S. Ramapo* in the Pacific Ocean. The wave was 34 meters tall. What was its height in feet? (*Note:* 1 meter ≈ 3.28 feet.)

8. FOOD The table shows the cost of a hamburger at a global fast-food chain in several countries as of April, 2000. Rank the countries from least expensive to most expensive based on the hamburger's cost.

Country	Cost of hamburger	Value of 1 U.S. dollar
Japan	294 yen	107 yen
Mexico	19.9 pesos	9.33 pesos
Russia	33.5 rubles	28.5 rubles
United States	2.43 dollars	————

9. WATER USE In the United States, each person uses an average of 90 gallons of water per day at home. On average, how many liters of water per year does each person use? (Assume 1 year = 365 days.)

10. ANIMALS The Komodo dragon, a giant lizard that lives in Indonesia, can run up to 18 feet per second. Express this speed in miles per hour.

11. WEATHER The hottest temperature ever recorded, 58°C, was measured in Libya in 1922. The coldest temperature, −89°C, was measured in Antarctica in 1983. What are these temperatures in degrees Fahrenheit?

12. SCIENCE At sea level, water freezes at 32°F and boils at 212°F. What are the freezing and boiling points of water in degrees Celsius?